Living your Leadership®

Grow Intentionally, Thrive with Integrity, and Serve Humbly

2nd Edition

CHRIS EWING, PHD

LIVING YOUR LEADERSHIP®

Copyright © 2022 Christopher J. Ewing

All rights reserved.

ISBN: 979-8-40-514815-1

Contents

List of Figures	iv
Foreword	v
Preface	1
Leading Yourself	**16**
Grow Intentionally	18
Temet Nosce (Know Thyself)	32
Integrity and Mentorship	52
Critical Reflection	64
Optimism and Gratitude	92
Leading with Humility	101
Application of Self-Leadership	123
Leading Others	**133**
Management vs Leadership	135
Respect and Human Dignity	151
Leading with Empathy	164
Live Authentically	179
Control and Autonomy	190
Leading Teams	207
Servant Leadership	222
Denouement	**243**
Pitfalls	245
Wrap-up: Living your Leadership	254
Acknowledgments	260
About the Author	262
Abbreviations	263
References	265
Additional References & Recommended Reading	284

List of Figures

Figure 1. Moving leadership competency to the right   12

Figure 2. The Theoretical Framework   14

Figure 3. Self-Talk Loop   37

Figure 4. Emotional Intelligence   42

Figure 5. Triadic Reciprocal Determinism   43

Figure 6. Modified Maslow's Hierarchy of Needs   46

Figure 7. Dunning-Kruger Effect   49

Figure 8. Take a moment to reflect before responding   73

Figure 9. Collins' Level 5 Hierarchy   115

Figure 10. The humorless boss   120

Figure 11. A Taxonomy of Human Motivation   127

Figure 12. The Eisenhower Box   142

Figure 13. Pareto Graph   148

Figure 14. Authority crushes autonomy   157

Figure 15. The Circle of Dialogical Pedagogy   181

Figure 16. Locus of Control Continuum   194

Figure 17. Tuckman's stages of group formation   210

Figure 18. Yerkes-Dodson interpretation   216

Figure 19. Progress during *Living your Leadership*   257

Foreword

by
Colonel Marné Deranger, USAF, Retired

Perhaps you've heard the cliché: "You manage resources, but lead people." It comes up often in leadership training as a reminder: Do Not Treat People as Resources. People aren't interchangeable cogs in the wheel, and as a leader, you will get better performance from them if you appreciate that fact (and them, for that matter. Appreciate them.). Your followers are people - complete with messy emotions, backstories, families, friends, hobbies - who also live outside of the workplace. Sometimes, that spills over into the workplace, thus affecting their performance. Most of the time, it doesn't.

As a leader, there will be situations when you have to get your people to compartmentalize and push through...but you can't do that all the time. That must only be left for special occasions. The rest of the time, you need to remember that they are people. You don't have to hug them or hold hands and sing each morning. It isn't a daycare. You just need to be aware. Always aware. In addition, you have to extend that awareness to yourself as a leader. You need to remember you are a person too and balance accordingly. Train accordingly. Give proper time, study, and effort into improving your leadership as a person. Not selflessly. Not selfishly. Just in a manner that portrays you as self-aware.

Chris Ewing always struck me as incredibly self-aware. He is a thoughtful person. Not thoughtful as in cards and flowers (though I'm sure that's true, too), but in how he thinks about everything. While many might see how Action A produces Result B, and simply be content with repeating Action A next time, Chris always wants to know why. Chris wants to know if Action A only produced Result B given one situation, one individual, and one moment in time. Or can it be repeated? Chris wants to pick apart Action A to see if it could produce even better results, given a tweak or two.

Chris is a leader who refuses to be satisfied by success. He dissects, he studies, and he thoughtfully ponders. He devotes significant time and energy to his continuous improvement. Chris turned that drive for continuous improvement onto the question of leadership and found that even that wasn't sufficient. Leadership is easy to talk about, harder to perform, and even more difficult to write about. Luckily, Chris doesn't shy away from a challenge. It wasn't enough for him to study leadership…he wanted to share what he learned, like the true Servant Leader he is. Thus, *Living your Leadership* was born.

You might wonder if this book is for you, though. So, I ask this question: Are you satisfied with your leadership performance? If you say, "Yes!" Stop reading now. (Of course, you are terribly wrong, but we won't talk about that here.) However, if you feel you could improve, if you want to do better, if you strive to be a good example of leadership, if you seek greater leadership challenges, then read on. In the following pages, Dr. Ewing will lead you through his theory-to-practice approach, demonstrating how to use the most credible, scientific research to your best advantage.

Chris starts, as one should, with self-leadership. As you will read later in this book, "Authentic Servant Leadership relies on the understanding that a leader is not primarily concerned with herself, but with others." An effective leader cannot only be outwardly focused. Just as you should affix your oxygen mask before assisting others, leaders must look inward before attempting to lead others. We must understand our authentic selves, develop self-regulatory behaviors, and learn about integrity, self-reflection, and humility before we can apply the other leadership lessons.

The second section of the book moves the focus outward. Dr. Ewing discusses the importance of empathy, authenticity, autonomy, and servant leadership, using positive and negative examples from his career. More importantly, he addresses a point that many overlook: Leadership is essentially a relationship, and relationships require trust. From the chapter on team leadership: "Transparency and integrity are key components of establishing trust in an organization because they are fundamental aspects of relationship building." If your team trusts you as a leader, you can overcome any obstacle. However, as a leader, you must trust yourself first. The critical self-reflection in the following pages will help you do that.

In his self-reflection, Chris saw the chance I took when I hired him. But really, don't we take chances in leadership positions every day? We take chances because we work with people, and people are unique. This individuality can be a weakness or strength to your organization, depending on how you perceive it…and yourself. Hearty self-reflection hones your instincts as a leader. Because I trusted my instincts, and the insights of peers I trusted, our organization gained a valuable, intelligent employee; one who questioned, and studied, and was never satisfied with the status quo; a leader who has continued to grow and live the lessons he spells out in this book. He is the quintessential Servant Leader.
Enjoy!

Preface

Living your Leadership®

The very fact that leadership is an art should discourage your becoming a mechanical leader. Leadership does not provide formulas, rules, or methods which will fit every situation. Leadership is an intangible quality which cannot be seen, felt, or measured except through its results. Moreover, you cannot predict the results with mathematical accuracy. If you have skill as a leader, however, you can predict results within the limits of your objectives. Air Force Manual (AFM) 35-15. Air Force Leadership, December 1948.

I had no idea what I was doing.

Standing there, in the Detachment 207 headquarters underneath the Busch Memorial Center at Saint Louis University, freshly graduated from high school, I was so excited to start my leadership journey. I just hoped to work hard and absorb as much as I could from those around me. Since pouring my heart and soul into my coursework had been the measure of success in school, I was convinced that was mostly what it took to attain leadership success. I didn't have a real plan for future growth. It was a major blind spot I didn't realize I had until it leaped into my consciousness right at that moment. I'll explain why this realization occurred to me a bit later in the text. Everyone needs a leadership development strategy; one that should start within.

Living your Leadership[1] starts with *self-leadership* to discover, understand, and improve oneself. Then the focus moves to *transformational* and *servant leadership*:

---

[1] Figure 2.

empathetic and follower-centric practices that complete the progression of this focused leadership strategy. *Living Your Leadership* enables managers to grow in their leadership practice in a deliberate and structured fashion. I will demonstrate how to develop *your* leadership style to match authentic servant leadership through individual discipline and critical reflection of character.

We strive to remain faithful to ourselves, maintain our integrity, and accept those we lead for who they are while recognizing both strengths and limitations. As you progress in *Living your Leadership*, you will cultivate a space where every person can be genuine, feel safe, and trust one another. *Living your Leadership* is something we practice, not just with others, but within ourselves as well.

As this book started to take shape, it became clear that it should first focus on self-knowledge as the foundation of leadership practice. Living *your* Leadership implies a thorough understanding of self and choices that grow from that understanding. Owning your journey starts with an acknowledgment of your characteristics and values. From self-knowledge, you can work toward an empathetic stance on leadership by shifting your focus onto others.

Dan Rockwell, one of the *leadership gurus* I greatly admire said it succinctly: "The first pressing challenge of leadership is focusing on the thing that matters most. People matter most. Nurture and develop you as much as you nurture and develop others."[2] We are morally obligated to recognize that we are all humans. We wake up, work and play, and go to bed each night. Despite our economic status, title, or popularity on this earth, we are all one human family.

My leadership development started the day I arrived at orientation for Air Force Reserve Officer Training Corps (ROTC) at Saint Louis University. As I looked around at

---

[2] Rockwell, 2012.

the sophomores, juniors, and seniors, I was more than intimidated; I was scared. I knew I didn't have what they had; the ability to lead, to command respect, to fill the room with their presence. As I look back on it, those whom I feared were themselves still terribly young; just beginning their journeys as well.

It was and still is, a joyous experience to be able to learn from other leaders. *What kind of books do they read? What meditative exercises do they practice? What are their philosophies on personal growth and team leadership?* It can be truly amazing to connect and gain insight from other leaders.

Many of my leadership lessons came from my undergrad classroom professors – the Jesuits[3] who instructed me in philosophy and the arts and sciences. I learned that growth begins with an intentional focus on the self. Growing as a person, maturing in wisdom and insight, learning about the connections between various academic fields and how theory relates to practice in so many areas were all essential to my journey. Through the gifts of the Holy Spirit,[4] I have been blessed with the wisdom, knowledge, and understanding that I have prayed guide me in right ways during my growth and development in faith and virtue.

There is a wealth of readily accessible information available on self-help topics – quotes from famous people, pop psychology texts, free online courses, and more. I am more than happy to direct readers to other useful works by experts in their respective fields.[5] Several of the topics discussed in this text are profound in their depth and

---

[3] Originating in the 16th century by St. Ignatius of Loyola, a *Jesuit* is a member of the Society of Jesus (SJ), a Roman Catholic religious order.
[4] CCC 1831 & The Holy Bible, 1984, Isaiah 11:2-4.
[5] Check out "Additional References and Recommended Reading" at the end of the book for preliminary suggestions. Also, you can reach out to me via LinkedIn at https://www.linkedin.com/in/chrisjewing or email at profcewing@gmail.com.

impact, and thus, deserve to be explored further. As a lifelong learner, I hope that you engage with the material on a personal level.

Rather than manage, we should strive to lead.

Both Transformational and Servant Leadership styles encourage leaders to inspire and cultivate their followers so that they grow as people. In turn, followers are more likely to choose to become leaders, which inevitably benefits the entire organization. It is a prerequisite of effective social interactions in a leadership capacity that a leader must understand themselves, deeply. That work leads to the smooth transition from the firm foundation of self-knowledge to other-focused leader behavior. Individual leadership progress occurs when the needle moves from an internal to an external focus. Effective leadership must be built on personal integrity and character before a leader can attempt to influence others.

Starting with an internal focus does not mean the leader is of any greater significance than their followers. It certainly doesn't mean that caring for your subordinates is a secondary responsibility. Rather, you have to be whole and competent, capable of Self Leadership before you should engage in the solemn duty of leading others. Should these steps be taken out of order, or performed concurrently, the result can be leadership built on a less than solid foundation. Starting the fight from a position of weakness is unwise, to paraphrase Sun Tzu[6] in his seminal work on strategy and military leadership, *The Art of War*.

Living your Leadership emanates from a place of altruism. It stems from a clear understanding of the self, gained through critical reflection, and fully manifested in servanthood.

Authenticity is the key to trust in relationships.

Along the journey of *becoming* through self-

---

[6] Tzu, 1971.

knowledge, you can consciously encourage others to be genuine, in turn. This model is not the end-all-be-all; as Miyamoto Musashi[7] tells us, there is more than one path to the mountain's peak.[8] Perseverance in the journey toward effective, ethical leadership is required. Unless you persevere on the road, you will not reach that peak. In *The Eclogues* of Ausonius,[9] his character laments over the decision of what path to take (*quod vitae sectabor iter*)[10] in this difficult life, fraught with choices, danger, and pain. Iron will, coupled with genuine humility[11] and the passion to improve are necessary traits in your journey; wherever you choose to go.

Leadership is the bedrock of organizational effectiveness. Bryant and Kazan note that "one of the main reasons that the study of leadership development is necessary is that people with a strong sense of self lead lives that are both self-actualizing and self-transcending."[12] Striving toward individual self-actualization and sincere authenticity is essential to *Living your Leadership*.

I've worked for several (The United States Air Force (USAF), Kaiser Permanente, Duke University Health, and AdventHealth Medical Group, Divine Mercy University, and Touro University Worldwide) distinctly different and successful organizations that depend on flexible and credible management. They provided me with a unique and useful set of knowledge and experiences. Working in a call center function at Duke[13] Primary Care has imparted a strong patient-focused customer service orientation that I now impart to my skilled and dedicated

---

[7] Miyamoto Musashi (1584-1645) was a legendary Japanese samurai and founder of the Niten-ryu sword style.
[8] Miyamoto & Harris, 1974.
[9] Ausonius, 1919
[10] Often mentioned in association with René Descartes' 1619 nightmares
[11] See Jim Collins' *Good to Great*
[12] 2013, p. 31.
[13] https://www.dukehealth.org/

staff. As a regional director in the service-driven continuum of care at Kaiser Permanente,[14] a premier healthcare delivery system, I led through influence, supporting hundreds of thousands of vulnerable patients and their family members. The USAF, my initial place of employment, likewise functions at the highest level of efficiency based largely upon its ever-ready middle managers (officer and enlisted alike).

    My insights are derived and inspired from working with - as well as observing - senior executives in these operating environments. I have a great deal of experience influencing and collaboratively executing business strategies and process improvements. My passion for research has been honed by my time as a student and professor. I have been teaching in higher education for the better part of a decade, recently taking on the challenge of starting up a Masters in Human Resource Management program at Touro University Worldwide. Imbuing the pages of this text with my hard-won knowledge, I am reminded of the author of one of my favorite works of literature.

    Sir Walter Scott described the perils of writing solely Scottish novels (the reading of which *is* quite perilous, as any student who has been in a literature class that featured his work can tell you) while explaining his romp into English history in his book, *Ivanhoe*:

> ...he was not only likely to weary out the indulgence of his readers, but also greatly to limit his own power of affording them pleasure. In a highly polished country, where so much genius is monthly employed in catering for public amusement, a fresh topic, such as he had himself had the happiness to light upon, is the untasted

---

[14] https://healthy.kaiserpermanente.org/

spring of the desert: but when men and horses, cattle, camels, and dromedaries have poached the spring into mud, it becomes loathsome to those who at first drank of it with rapture; and he who had the merit of discovering it, if he would preserve his reputation with the tribe, must display his talent by a fresh discovery of untasted fountains. *Sir Walter Scott*[15]

Scott's message implies that in order to keep people coming back, one must have the newest, and therefore, best ideas, lest the ideas become stale and as unappealing as a can of flat soda, or in Scott's case, a dried-up mud puddle from which no one wants to drink. The same can be said for the subject of leadership; people often look for the flashiest and newest idea – the idea that appeals to the latest fashion.
Just because something is shiny and new, does not necessarily mean it is of value.
Freshness can be said to count in things like our can of soda and the water from a natural spring. Innovation and originality are outstanding leadership traits, but leadership theories must also be steeped in deep knowledge of what came before. The theory should build on past practice and lessons learned from mistakes, and grow on a foundation of success. Leadership touches all of us and can be as conceptually difficult to define as loyalty, responsibility, or honor.
Since deciding to write this book and after the publication of the first edition, I have been surprised, but not necessarily in a good way, by the criticism of my refusal to deal with current events; with technological advances, and the huge impact they have had on the business landscape. I think that Christopher Kolenda said it

---

[15] Scott, 1997, p. xiv-xv.

best in his book, *Leadership: The Warrior's Art.*

Certainly advances in technology and organization have made the challenges and techniques associated with leader competency somewhat different. Yet, while the technologies have changed, the very human dimension of leadership has remained constant. The task of a leader, then and now, is to inspire the best in others so they could contribute meaningfully to the overall good of the organization.[16]

While *Living your Leadership,* humane treatment of others is essential. People are too often pushed to the margin and recognized solely in terms of their financial contributions to an organization. It is incumbent on leaders to recognize individuals are more than just cogs in the business machine.[17] They have feelings and a sense of self-worth that is constantly at war with the persistent, negative cultural reinforcement of their identities as anonymous drones. It is seductively easy to go into staffing planning meetings and refer to employees as "FTEs" and not think of them as people.

I am not saying that managers intentionally dehumanize employees, but the temptation to do so is always there, beckoning. Why not take the easy way out? As a manager, you are obligated to serve your company and staff according to business needs. People are messy. Their lives are complicated and they often bring their issues to work. I have seen managers insist that home stays at home and that they would not listen to 'whining' from employees about their lives outside of work. How callous!

---

[16] Kolenda, 2001, p. 4
[17] Reference Kant's extensive works on the universality of law and categorical imperative that humans be treated as an end, not a means to an end.

There is an inherent human dignity in work[18] and labor is a fundamental human task.[19] Just because it is an easier path to ignore the humanity of your employees does not make it right or good. In fact, like the stoics of old and perhaps the ancient Buddhists before them, you have to realize that what stands in the path, is the path.[20] When you care, when you show interest, that is when people will go over and above.

Recognizing and publicly emphasizing the intrinsic value of others by tangibly recognizing their myriad contributions renews and reinvests in your personnel. They can again see that your success, the success of your organization, and their success are all deeply connected. Transformational Leaders know, and employ, methods to positively motivate and support employee morale.[21] The foundation of the practice of *Living your Leadership* is to value those you lead.[22] [23]

As the legendary Jack Welch intimated in his best-selling book, *Winning*,[24] the key to progressing, and ultimately, succeeding, is understanding your particular industry from as many perspectives as possible. It is important to realize that experience alone is not enough when it comes to leading. I am sure you have come across people who have been in a field for decades but could never inspire followers. Experience can make a great frontline worker or even first-level supervisor, but even subject matter experts need education, training, and mentorship to grow.

Leadership is a field of study all on its own. It is a field that cuts across many domains, from psychology

---

[18] Pope St. John Paul II, 1981.
[19] Pope Leo XIII, 1891.
[20] Marcus Aurelius.
[21] Kiel & Watson, 2009.
[22] Vadell & Ewing, 2011.
[23] Northouse, 2004.
[24] Welch & Welch, 2005.

to business and philosophy to education.

I do not think, sir, you have any right to command me, merely because you are older than I, or because you have seen more of the world than I have; your claim to superiority depends on the use you have made of your time and experience.
- *Charlotte Brontë, Jane Eyre*

    A leader must be more than experienced, a leader must be credible. They learn through multiple modalities: experience, reading, education, and socialization. Throughout this text, you will see references to useful leadership books aligned with successful leadership theory and practice, often drawn from my Jesuit, USAF, academic, and healthcare leadership experiences.

    As an admitted leadership studies aficionado, one of the first things I do when I am invited into the office of a leader is to check out their book collection. It isn't uncommon for someone at the upper management level to have a small, curated collection to impress others, visibly represent their leadership philosophy, and potentially read in moments of peace or passion. In some cases, the books are fairly generic; ubiquitous to an organization. Other times, the books I've seen on the shelves of military commanders and civilian senior leaders have shocked me. I knew, for example, that I probably wouldn't get along with the base commander who had Niccolo Machiavelli's *The Prince* prominently displayed on his shelf. Therefore, it was not a surprise when he applied the principles of that amoral, conniving, political being in his leadership practice.

    You* should read about *Living your Leadership.

    You bought or borrowed this book, and you have read at least this far into the text. Thank you! Most likely, you are a self-determining and autonomous individual. You recognize the importance of leadership development and accept the idea that reading books like this one will benefit you.[25]

If you have identified the importance of study for self-improvement, perhaps you have progressed to examining yourself and have found this action to be in alignment with your values and needs. The next steps are to believe you are capable of improving, to do the hard inner work necessary to improve,[26] and to cease doubting yourself and your ability to lead. Inner work should naturally precede our outer work.

> *Our doubts are traitors,*
> *And make us lose the good we oft might win.*
> *By fearing to attempt.*
> *- William Shakespeare* [27]

A homogeneous mixture of leadership talent or uniform knowledge is never found in any pool of employees or almost any company. From an organizational standpoint, the idea behind leadership training is to increase the cumulative knowledge of a group. Training provides for a shared leadership language and improves those individual leaders who will lead the company into the future. Using a single text to align the educational efforts pushes the envelope of leadership development in a uniform direction. A single text might accomplish what you want to instill in your organization, but an individual leader should know better than to trust a single source for wisdom. That being said, leadership development will become a diffused and confusing effort if multiple texts are recommended. The time it takes to read and train new leaders, coupled with the potential for mixed messaging will cause frustration and confusion in your employees.

---

[25] Ryan & Deci, 2000.
[26] George, 2015.
[27] "Measure for Measure," Act 1, Scene 4.

In agreeing to pursue an aligned leadership development paradigm, an organization ensures a majority of personnel - both managers and employees - increase their knowledge level. This knowledge increase constitutes a virtual leadership sea change; a tidal shift that raises all ships. No one's leadership style is the same as another's, but if a theoretical structure is built for anyone and everyone, it is possible to see dividends in the leadership development of an entire group.

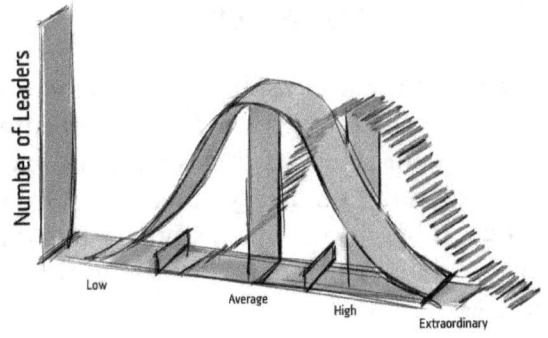

Figure 1. Moving leadership competency to the right

The notion of 'leadership capacity' is extremely important. It is not simply a
function of the number or quality of individuals in formal leadership roles, rather,
it implies a system of leadership, if you will, that can ignite leadership
wisdom, insight, and behaviors from many more individuals. Thus, it fuels the

continuing search for different kinds of leadership approaches, both individual
and joint, at all levels of the organization. In fact, many downsizing, restructuring,
and reengineering efforts are actually reducing the number of leadership and
management positions in the formal structure. The objective function of all this is
to expand the capacity for leadership and independent initiative without having to
increase the number of individuals in formal leadership roles. *Jon R. Katzenbach*[28]

The Model: *Living your Leadership*

There are as many leadership models as there are recipes for chili in Texas. *Living your Leadership* combines carefully curated existing theories; it is an organic and grounded model that relies on theory but is meant to be put into daily practice. It begins with the assumption that Peter Drucker[29] so cogently summarized: "Leaders grow; they are not made."

---

[28] Katzenbach, 1997, p. 84.
[29] (1909-2005) Austrian-born American management consultant, educator, and author; celebrated by BusinessWeek magazine as "the man who invented management."

Figure 2. The *Living your Leadership* Theoretical Framework

Leadership development should include a theoretical framework that provides an underpinning and sense of direction for the work that will be done. A theoretical framework is something leaders use to define their leadership styles and also inform their leadership interactions. In most cases, the theoretical framework, even those advertised as solve-all models, are not flexible enough and do not take into account the emotional and organically evolving realities of the world we live in.

Living your Leadership employs a unique, holistic approach that encourages authentically aligned behaviors informed by the theories outlined in this text. The *Living your Leadership* paradigm primarily incorporates the tenets of Self-Leadership, Transformational Leadership, and

Servant Leadership. This paradigm offers a highly *individualized* path to developing leaders, as the natural talents and orientations of the individual leader are discovered, reinforced, and expanded in a process that gradually orients the leader toward a servant disposition.

The uniqueness of the model is based on the development of a leader's traits and characteristics during the mastery of Self-Leadership. It also provides a sounding board for accomplished leaders with the tacit understanding that anyone *can*[30] lead, but not just anyone *should*. It recognizes that as people mature their motivations move from a *carrot and stick*, external motivational context, to an intrinsic orientation.[31]

> *Leaders need an inner focus to be aware of their own feelings, values and intuitions, and to manage themselves well. A focus on others allows a leader to read people well, which is key to managing relationships – the art of leading itself. And an outer focus lets a leader understand the larger forces and systems that she must navigate, and determine the best strategy going forward.* –Daniel Goleman

Decision-making processes tend to grow more self-directing over time, per the human need to be autonomous.[32] This process of internalization yields adaptive[33] social advantages and an enhanced well-being.[34] *Living your Leadership* infuses traditional leadership philosophies with the most current research in leadership to help individuals mature toward self-actualization.[35]

---

[30] Sinek, 2011.
[31] Chandler & Connell, 1987.
[32] Ryan, 1995.
[33] Ryan, Kuhl, & Deci, 1997.
[34] Ryan & Deci, 2000.
[35] Maslow, 1943.

Leading Yourself

Conquer yourself and the world is at your feet.
- Saint Augustine

Saint Augustine by Philippe de Champaigne (c. 1645)

Grow Intentionally

Most of the significant things done in the world were done by persons who were either too busy or too sick! There are few ideal and leisurely settings for the disciplines of growth.
— Robert Thornton Henderson [36]

    My active-duty time in the USAF launched in the nuclear missile field. Smartphones weren't a thing yet, and you weren't allowed to bring devices that could store or transmit information onto the missile site. To keep track of what happened on our shifts, missileers would keep an unclassified journal called an alert log. Our shifts ranged from twenty-four to seventy-two hours on-site and we called these shifts "alerts." A two- or three-person team manned the launch control site from which intercontinental nuclear missiles were targeted and could be launched at the direction of the President.
    Captain Jimmy Winters took me on my first alert. The drive to any alert facility from the military base was a minimum of 45 minutes one-way, with nothing to see but snowy plains in the winter, and well-tilled fields in the summer. After a few trips across the Northern Tier plains, the novelty started to wane. The long trips with little else to occupy the time meant the two crew members always had a great deal of time to talk. Capt. Winters was a solid mentor who believed in training his deputy crew commanders by first getting to know them. He used these long drives as a time to do just that.
    My first trip out to the site was an overwhelming experience. I was nervous about memorizing the security phrases we needed to transmit over the radio before being

---

[36] American author, pastor, and Presbyterian denominational leader.

allowed to drive through the gate onto the complex. Capt. Winters rehearsed the verbiage with me over and over before I had to make our radio call. My voice quavered a bit, but in the end, we reached the site successfully. We checked in with the machine gun-toting security controller and I rode down the industrial elevator to the capsule for the first time. The solemn weight of isolation seemed to increase as it creakily descended 50-feet down into the junction between the launch control center (LCC) and the launch control equipment building. For the uninitiated, it was like entering a buried, prehistoric starship. The sights and faint chemical smells, the oppressive darkness broken by intermittent incandescent bulbs; it was eerie.

The crew worked out of the launch control center[37] and were responsible for carefully checking and maintaining the attached structure holding the equipment that sustains basic functions of air, power, and water for the underground capsule. There are two eight-ton blast doors formed of solid steel and concrete; one door led from the elevator into the junction between the launch control center and the equipment building and the other led directly into the LCC where the off-going crew was waiting to be relieved.

The sequential blast doors served a dual purpose – they protected the crew and equipment from blast overpressure, and also provided security against hostile intrusion. The first door is hand-operated by spinning a manual crank and then using a latch. I nervously worked the hand crank on the blast door, and it silently and grudgingly swung open, expelling a gust of stale air.

After we conducted a thorough crew changeover, when the off-going crew and the oncoming crew verified classified material disposition and signed over control of

---

[37] For a more detailed description of the facilities:
http://npshistory.com/publications/mimi/srs/sites.htm

the facility and its associated nuclear warheads, I was officially on my first alert.

Capt. Winters and I went over various checklists and procedures for several hours and then settled in to watch some B-movies before he took his turn in the bed-mod – the coffin-sized, curtained enclosure where one of the two ICBM[38] crew members were allowed a modest amount of privacy and sleep during predetermined rest periods.

I vividly remember being scared to death that I would mess up a seemingly insignificant detail and ruin my career before it even started. Thankfully, that didn't happen. In my time at Minot AFB, I pulled over 300 of these alerts during three years.

When I reached out to Jimmy on social media and asked what he remembered about our time together in the missile field, he replied, "The thing I remember most about you was your drive. You were different from most. You had a clear vision of the path you wanted to take and where you wanted to end up. I remember talking to you in the office about your goals and what you wanted to accomplish."

He went on to say it is a leader's responsibility to accept the personal ambitions of followers; that the leader must encourage followers in their development. He believed that one should never cut corners on the path to self-development. He taught me the importance of giving my best and never losing focus on my goals; this allowed me to establish perspective. Jimmy encouraged me then, that, wherever I saw chances to learn and grow, even if others only saw them as distractions, I should avidly pursue them.

Change is inevitable. Growth is optional.
John Maxwell

---

[38] Intercontinental Ballistic Missile.

In the course of my professional and personal life, I have experienced very little free time to sit back and reflect, to take the time to read professional literature, and apply those principles in a low-stress environment. There hasn't been a time in my adult life that I haven't worked at least two jobs and had a family to care for.

The professor I chose to be my dissertation mentor decided to accept the position as chair of my dissertation committee because he remembered I had taken his class during my combat deployment to Mosul, Iraq. I suppose he figured if I could pass social psychology under those conditions, researching and writing a dissertation would be a piece of cake in the time frame allotted.

Despite how difficult it has been to carve out time for critical reflection, I recognized the value of choosing to make the time. Fitting reflection into my daily schedule gave me the chance to think about the choices I'd made that day, to consider their outcomes and antecedents, and to incorporate contemplative understanding into my mindfulness practice. As part of my mindfulness practice, I choose to take a Jesuit approach[39] each day; conducting a mini-Examen at least once, during my meditation time. While turning my thoughts on my day, I start with gratitude, remind myself of my goals and purpose, and try to think of the things that went well and the things that did not go my way, focusing particularly on those things that I could control (i.e., my reactions and decisions).

Mindfulness is a powerful practice. Studies have shown that employees who lack transformational leaders can, in some small way, make up for that lack and inspire intrinsic motivation through mindfulness practice.[40] It is telling, however, that even a mindfulness practice on the

---

[39] Saint Ignatius of Loyola originated the twice-daily mindfulness practice called the Examen.
[40] Kroon, van Woerkum, & Menting, 2017.

part of employees does not bridge the gap entirely; good leadership is needed to increase intrinsic motivation and drive an organization.

One of the major benefits of a mindfulness practice is being present in the moment, circumstances as they are, and the opportunities for growth and joy in our lives. Most of the time when we're awake, our minds tend to wander, but the practice of mindfulness allows our minds to slow down. Constant demands on our attention - from smart devices to emails to meetings and appointments - clutter our consciousness. Mindfulness encourages focus, improves our decision-making capability, eases our stress, and is positively correlated with leadership adaptability[41] and decision flexibility. Wally Schmader emphasizes that focus is the new IQ.[42] He insists that a leader has to maintain their focus intentionally.

I've learned that leaders should always take full advantage of the present moment; that they should use each moment to thrive by learning and growing intentionally. Mindfulness and leadership are alike in that way; both are developed intentionally.[43] It is through focused striving that leaders flourish in all environments; from nuclear launch facilities to deployments in Iraq to leading biomedical engineers and call centers in hospital systems and even in academic leadership.

Consciously commit to your personal growth.

Learning is not attained by chance,
it must be sought for with ardor and attended to with
diligence.
- Abigail Adams

---

[41] Baron, Rouleau, Grégoire, & Baron, 2018.
[42] Wally is the founder of the Exceptional Leaders Lab, Vistage CEO Advisory Board Chair, & a best-selling leadership author.
[43] Atkins & Reb, 2015.

For leaders, time for relevant reflection must be built into the day...at the beginning or the end. Reflection allows the leader time to organize short-term priorities, prioritize your daily actions, and validate the coherence between your inner desires and outward decisions. Demands on our time are ever-present, especially in our data-driven, technologically advanced workplaces. Managers today are required to know more, to have access to more information, and to interact faster (and yet meaningfully) with employees. You may not *have* time to develop your leadership, though you will most likely have to *make* the time.

> *Time is an equal opportunity employer.*
> *Each human being has exactly the same number of hours and minutes every day.*
> *Rich people can't buy more hours.*
> *Scientists can't invent new minutes.*
> *And you can't save time to spend it on another day.*
> *Even so, time is amazingly fair and forgiving.*
> *No matter how much time you've wasted in the past, you still have an entire tomorrow.*
> *- Denis Waitley*[44]

Remember that diamonds are nothing more than lumps of coal that persevered through the heat and pressure:

> Just as the diamond requires properties for its formation—carbon, heat, and pressure—successful leaders require the interaction of three properties—character, knowledge, and application. Like carbon to a diamond, character is the basic quality of a leader...But as carbon alone does not create a diamond; neither can character alone create a

---

[44] International best-selling author, consultant, and motivational speaker.

leader. The diamond needs heat. Man needs knowledge, study, and preparation...The third property, pressure—acting in conjunction with carbon and heat—forms the diamond. Similarly, one's character attended by knowledge, blooms through application to produce a leader. *General Edward C. Meyer*[45]

The law of intentionality describes growth as an active process.[46] It is not something that *just happens*; rather, it is something that is *intentionally* pursued. John Maxwell's[47] *15 Invaluable Laws of Growth* outlines the law of intentionality as having several traps. He describes these traps as gaps in our perception that stop us from becoming our best selves or from making crucial decisions.

For example, the assumption gap is the idea that you will grow without any real effort. However, critical reflection and discernment are necessary for growth. The knowledge gap says you don't necessarily know *how* to grow; you go about your day-to-day life without having to worry about the question "How do I improve myself?" or "What are the steps required to become a better person and a better leader?" The knowledge gap can easily be addressed by reading some of the excellent books out there. Finally, the timing gap: the idea that there is an easier time to grow than right now. We all face these gaps, knowingly or unknowingly.

The practice of *Living your Leadership* addresses these gaps head-on, allowing the leader to grow with intentionality and direction.

---

[45] US Army Chief of Staff, 1979-1983.
[46] Maxwell, 2014.
[47] John C. Maxwell is an NYT bestselling author and leadership *guru*. He has sold more than 26 million books in fifty languages and has trained more than 6 million leaders.

> *There are no office hours for leaders.*
> *- Cardinal J. Gibbons*[48]

A lack of intentionality and personal accountability are two reasons many people who lead busy and happy lives do not stretch themselves and develop their potential fully. They tell themselves that tomorrow will be easier and the next day they will have X, Y, or Z done. Or they say they are far too busy just now to worry about this (seemingly) immense challenge in their lives. Perhaps they believe that success will just happen, refusing to acknowledge their agency in their lives. Adopting a defeatist attitude, a person may consider the steps to success so large as to make the climb impossible. My hope is, as you read this book, you will realize the only possible kind of steps are small, but not insignificant.

A paradigm shift in your thinking is not achieved instantaneously upon the acquisition of new information. As awesomely powerful and as quick as your neurons may fire, you still have to take the time to integrate, to reflect, and to act, for those actions to become habitual. Becoming the leader you hope to be is a revelatory, and often, difficult journey. This challenge will not come to a resolution in a day or a month or even a year. It is a gradual process through which we develop as authentic and active leaders wherein we synthesize and integrate our knowledge and experience. Even *'ah ha'* moments do not typically occur without self-reflection and prior knowledge playing a large role.

There is a simple realization from which all personal improvement and growth emerges. This is the realization that we, individually, are responsible for everything in our lives, no matter the external

---

[48] Archbishop of Baltimore (1834-1921).

circumstances. We don't always control what happens to us. But we always control how we interpret what happens to us, as well as how we respond. Whether we consciously recognize it or not, we are always responsible for our experiences. It's impossible not to be. Choosing to not consciously interpret events in our lives is still an interpretation of the events of our lives. *Mark Manson*[49]

So, take the time to read leadership books and blogs, listen to podcasts, attend seminars, lectures, and conferences,[50] connect with other managers, spend those extra few minutes a day, encouraging your employees using the techniques you learn. All of these practices are essential. Leadership growth activities are more valuable pursuits when considered together than they seem to be individually. Improving yourself pays dividends significantly greater than the effort it takes; it is a force multiplier. Use your infrequent free moments. Build small islands of deliberation. Meditate on your actions and your plans. Engage with your followers on a more profound level. These small steps lead to self-development, collaboration, and solidarity.

Personal development is a belief that you are worth the effort, time, and energy to develop yourself.
- Denis Waitley

Leadership development should not start right from the *leading others* aspect of leadership. You need to crawl before you walk and walk before you run! It is a grave error to skip over what is a truly rich and underappreciated,

---
[49] 2016, p. 94.
[50] Pfeffer & Sutton, 2000.

foundational issue – development of self. Leadership training that does not emphasize critical reflection is shallow, but all-too-common in the world of self-help and leadership development. Without critical reflection, disciplined thought, and understanding of oneself, it is not possible to recognize, modify, and grow your virtues, vices, and attributes and to ensure truly authentic interactions with others.

The conscious act of *being authentic* can preclude attaining authenticity.[51] In the attempt to be authentic, a leader "puts on" a persona that they hope will mimic *their* perception of the ideal leader. This is indicative of a leader who has not taken the time to critically reflect. They refuse to do the hard, small steps – the necessary work of developing authenticity from the inside out. People see through the charade for what it is and they resent the attempt at deception. People want to respect their leader; to know who they are.

> *Those who try to make life better for everyone without having learned to control their own lives first usually end up making things worse all around.*
> *- Mihaly Csikszentmihalyi* [52]

The glaringly obvious issue, in this particular progression, is those leadership courses that do not begin with an understanding of the individual. Not many people have a solid grasp of who they are. As Dr. Jordan Peterson tells us in the *12 Rules for Life*, we are exceptionally complex beings; we are the product of millions of years of evolutionary processes. It can take people years and therapy to come to terms with their upbringing. Leaders

---

[51] Caza & Jackson, 2011.
[52] 1990, p. 191. Dr. Csikszentmihalyi is a Distinguished Professor of Psychology and Management Founder, Co-Director, Quality of Life Research Center (QLRC).

don't need to be perfect (far from it) but they must at least have done the work to understand where their shortcomings are; to know where they need to focus their efforts to clear the lens of self-perception and to frame their past in such a way that it contributes positively to the tapestry of their persona. By persona, I do not mean to imply something that a leader "puts on" or "takes off," rather, persona in this context is intended to mean 'who they perceive themselves to be and who they choose to show the world.'

Learning the skills associated with self-knowledge will pay great dividends as a leader grows in their journey. A leader must think of themselves as capable and worthwhile, and able to meaningfully contribute to personal and organizational goal attainment. That belief is self-efficacy. Positive self-efficacy beliefs start with an evaluation of yourself and acknowledgment of your self-worth. Building self-esteem[53] serves as the starting point of Self-Leadership.[54]

As I mention in the chapter on Authentic Leadership, a leader is always on display. Psychological and psychosocial issues are often amplified in leadership positions based on the fact that leaders are visible to their subordinates in all of their actions. If a leader is an overt narcissist, their narcissism is on display. Conversely, a leader possessed of a humble, compassionate nature will be recognized as well. "Self-leaders, therefore, live by a mantra - 'there is no failure, only feedback for improvement' - because they have the confidence that they learn from mistakes and move forward."[55] This mantra should extend throughout one's organization. All levels of personnel should have access to clear and concise feedback and be treated fairly in the context of *learning from mistakes and moving forward.*

---

[53] Rosenberg, 1979.
[54] Bryant & Kazan, 2013, p. 32.
[55] Bryant & Kazan, 2013, p. 69.

As you continue your self-improvement journey, keep in mind that resilience is a key trait in self-improvement. There are always solutions to problems, though they may not immediately present themselves or have a satisfactory resolution. Additionally, problems sometimes linger. Issues you are working on may not be resolved in a timeframe anyone thinks is reasonable. Reasonableness is not a prerequisite for personal issues including trauma response, healing, or grief, just to name a few social and emotional issues that often seem unreasonable, irrational, or incomprehensible.

> *Do not try to excuse your faults, try to correct them.*
> *- Saint Giovanni "Don" Bosco*

Your improvement journey may take several years; some say the self-improvement journey never ends. With specific milestones in mind, it will be easier to judge your progress along the way. When the going gets tough, the resilience you have developed will allow you to face the difficulties along the way. You will learn to thrive under internal and external pressure, making mistakes and celebrating successes. Part of growing in resilience is being able to learn from your failures.

> A human being is not one thing among others; things determine each other, but man is ultimately self-determining. What he becomes—within the limits of endowment and environment—he has made out of himself. In the concentration camps, for example, in this living laboratory and on this testing ground, we watched and witnessed some of our comrades behave like swine while others behaved like saints. Man has both potentialities within himself; which one is actualized depends on

decisions but not on conditions. *Viktor E. Frankl*[56]

---

[56] 1963, p. 157.

Chapter Recap

Consciously commit to personal growth. It is an active and intentional process.
- Make the time to reflect, especially when it is difficult.
- Consume material that will aid your growth journey by reading leadership books and blogs, listening to podcasts, and attending seminars, lectures, and conferences.
- Connect with other managers and respected leaders. Ask probing questions and notice the areas that you differ from them in practice and character.
- Encourage your employees to use the techniques you learn. Practical application is key.
- Do not expect immediate results. Personal change takes time and effort.

Temet Nosce (Know Thyself)

> *The key to becoming an effective leader is not to focus on making other people follow, but on making yourself the kind of person they want to follow.*
> *- John C. Maxwell*

I was bereft.

The airplane trip to St. Louis from Sacramento on TWA seemed like I had been shoved through a portal onto a different planet. I had no friends. I was one of only a handful of students from the West Coast who had been admitted to Saint Louis University. ROTC was only one day per week, but even that marginally social activity seemed intimidating to a newly displaced introvert like me.

Naturally, I clung to what I knew; I clung to what I had previous mastery experiences in that had informed my self-concept. I excelled in my studies. Upon entering my philosophy classroom on the first day of school, I found it was a traditional lecture hall setup, just like I had seen in the movies! Our professor, a seemingly ancient Jesuit priest, greeted us warmly as we entered. He started our first lecture of the semester with the story of the Oracle at Delphi and the principle of *Temet Nosce*.[57]

We spent the next several weeks deconstructing our conscious and unconscious cultural biases. We learned to question all of our previously lived experiences. We were taught to critically examine those experiences and our previously held beliefs. We learned to see our lives and our beliefs anew, through a lens of critical self-reflection. We worked to evaluate and incorporate them into our newly emerging understanding of self. The geographically

---

[57] *Temet Nosce* or "Know thyself" is a Latin translation of a popular ancient maxim traced back to ancient Egypt and chiseled in stone on the Temple of Apollo at Delphi in Greece.

enforced isolation, coupled with the Jesuit philosophical training, kick-started my process of self-understanding.

Self-Leadership is the theory underpinning *Living your Leadership*. It requires "having a developed sense of who you are, what you can do, and where you are going, coupled with the ability to influence your communication, emotions, and behavior on the way to getting there."[58] A foundational understanding in Self-Leadership practice is that leaders can be grown and nurtured.[59] Though certain desirable leadership traits might naturally occur in certain people, the lack of an inborn propensity toward leadership is not a barrier to the rest of us developing and enhancing our leadership characteristics through study and practice.

A leader who truly values people makes a deliberate choice to behave as a servant. The choice to serve is grounded in "an accurate understanding of his or her self-image, moral conviction and emotional stability."[60] His Holiness, the Dalai Lama recognizes there has been a lack of inner development in the last 50 years. People rarely consider compassion, spirituality, and humanity's inner life, preferring instead to focus on the external signs and symbols of success.[61]

Lack of self-knowledge and failure to appreciate one's own worth make for faulty judgement in all other matters; If you are not able to understand (and accept) your own self, you will not be able to understand (or accept) what is beyond you.
- Saint Bonaventure [62]

---

[58] Bryant & Kazan, 2013, p. 85.
[59] Thompson, 1995.
[60] Sendjaya & Sarros, 2002.
[61] Bstan-'dzin-rgya-mtsho, 2011.
[62] A Franciscan in medieval Italy, Giovanni di Fidanza was a scholastic theologian and philosopher.

Understanding your strengths, weaknesses, belief system, and motivations is the only way to master Self-Leadership. You have to know yourself before you can lead yourself.

Satinder Dhiman reminds us that "Socrates believed that 'an unexamined life is not worth living' and declared cultivating *gnothi seauton*, Self-Knowledge, to be the most important purpose of life."[63] You have to be able to lead yourself before you can be expected to lead others.[64] Be sure to develop a thorough understanding of the emotional self in a purposeful and deliberate process.
But how do we know ourselves?

> *You can only find out what you actually believe (rather than what you think you believe) by watching how you act. You simply don't know what you believe, before that. You are too complex to understand yourself.*
> *- Jordan Peterson*[65]

The path to understanding takes stamina and determination since it involves an evolutionary change. Each piece of understanding builds upon the last, and each piece of understanding is hard-won. Saint Augustine describes the tendency of man to avoid (or at least not choose to seek) interior knowledge in his *Confessions*, "Here are men going afar to marvel at the heights of mountains, the mighty waves of the sea, the long courses of great rivers, the vastness of the ocean, and the movements of the stars, yet leaving themselves unnoticed."[66]

Self-knowledge is one of the most important

---

[63] Dhiman, 2009, p. 56.
[64] Manz & Sims, 2001
[65] Dr. Peterson is a best-selling author, professor, and clinical psychologist.
[66] 2006, X, 8, 15.

intangible assets of a leader.[67] The concept of Self-Leadership purposefully mirrors what it takes to effectively lead others: understanding, effort, and focus. Living *your* Leadership requires a compassionate and empathetic connection with your followers. It stands to reason that you would need a compassionate and empathetic connection with yourself before you are prepared to offer that part of yourself to others.

The idea of being compassionate with yourself may sound silly initially. Compassion flows from one person to another, doesn't it? As an exercise to demonstrate how someone can be compassionate to oneself, take a moment and try to think of times when you have not been especially kind to yourself. Were you angry or sad about something, an event, or a situation, but you did not know exactly why? Have you ever used negative self-talk when you feel like you failed at something?

Constructive self-talk is an important skill to develop.[68] Verbally nailing an employee to the wall for a mistake is not an effective motivational technique, and it does not do much for you, either. Be willing to forgive your own mistakes. As an indication of how important this concept was to Dr. Jordan Peterson, he included it as the second rule in his book *12 Rules for Life,* "Treat yourself like someone you are responsible for helping."[69]

> *The greatest of faults, I should say, is to be conscious of none.*
> *- Thomas Carlyle* [70]

Acknowledge that you have faults. Yes, I know this seems basic and maybe even insulting to a learned leader

---

[67] Montgomery III, 2007.
[68] Figure 3.
[69] 2018.
[70] Scottish philosopher, satirist, historian, and teacher (1795-1881).

such as yourself...do it anyway. We aren't perfect, and it is hubris to think otherwise. Perhaps you are too quick to judge, perhaps you have let your job become your identity, perhaps you lack compassion with challenging employees. Whatever the case, identify those faults. Write them down.

Once you acknowledge your faults, you have to be willing to do the hard work to mitigate them. This isn't a one-time effort, either. Chances are good that your faults are habitual, that they have become automatic to the point where constant and consistent attention must be paid to recognizing and counteracting them. As any home renovation expert can tell you, it takes dedication and determination to restore or refinish something pre-existing; building new is easier, but as humans, we only get one start to our journey. We deal productively with where we are and who we are in our life path. The work, then, is *becoming* who we choose to be.

As you think of yourself as a leader, you must be willing to forgive yourself for not fulfilling your mental model of the perfect leader. None of us is perfect. The idea of a leader is much like any other deceptive idea. We idealize constructs like "the perfect leader," often pointing to one or another historical or actual leader to fill that role. Even if we know a great deal about that person, we do not know everything. Our ideal leader is still a person with faults, flaws, and emotions that accompany humanity.

Negative self-talk is not useful. It feeds into the self-talk loop and degrades your self-image and your performance. As a technique to prevent mistakes in judgment, self-condemnation does not help your mental health. In much the same way, condemnation does not encourage willing or enthusiastic followership, either. The only way that negativity plays out with followers is to encourage fearful compliance.

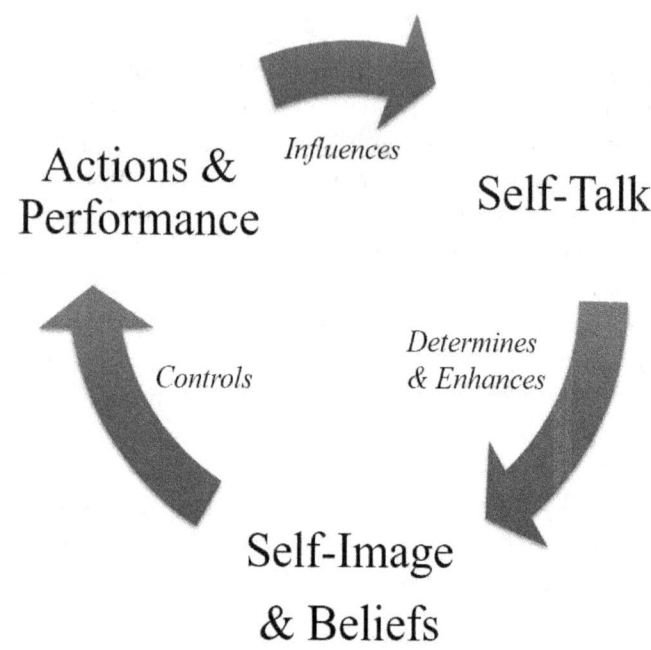

Figure 3. Self-Talk Loop[71]

Fear is a poor motivational tactic.[72] It employs psychological bullying and often results in decreased motivation and loyalty after its initial effects wear off. This fact is true when it comes to the self as well. You will not encourage yourself to examine issues causing mistakes through self-degradation. Negative self-talk will not change your habitual thinking; it will only make you feel bad and start to solidify a lack of self-esteem which will invariably crush developing positive leadership attributes.

Few things are more harmful to your psyche and eventually to your actions than negative self-talk.

Behavior flows from our thoughts. Ancient

---

[71] Galanis, et al., 2016.
[72] Treasurer, 2014.

philosophers understood this, and the psychological community agrees that even habitual actions flow from ordered or disordered thought. Self-recriminatory thoughts produce hesitant behavior. Hesitant behavior then causes the mind to anticipate failure. Anticipating failure makes it more likely that you will fail since behavior flows from thoughts and may cause unwanted stress, anxiety, and the negative health effects that those emotions have, as well. It is a self-destructive cycle.

Forgive yourself rather than using negative self-talk. Resolve to correct the behavior that failed to meet expectations and move on. Practice compassion with yourself by generously forgiving your own mistakes. Forgiveness creates a safe mental space to learn from those mistakes. Without a safe mental environment, it is easy to devolve into the cycle of self-recrimination.

Turn your compassionate focus outward.

Man is now not only a social being;
his social nature transcends national and regional limits,
and whether we like it or not,
we must think in terms of one human family,
one world.
- Thomas Merton [73]

The lenses with which we view ourselves and the world around us are often shaped by our differences rather than by what makes us similar. The Dalai Lama notes that there are many aspects to focus on when we view others. There are so many things that make people different: race, gender, religion, national origin, occupation, and level of education. These tangible characteristics moderate the way we interact with our social environment. Focusing on visible differences to the exclusion of that which brings us

---

[73] A Trappist monk, poet, and social activist (1915-1968).

together negatively influences behavior toward *the other*.[74]

Rather than focusing on all of the things that make people different, turn your lens on our common humanity. People too often see external characteristics and stop thinking. This lazy thinking places cognitive emphasis on ourselves. We attend to that which makes us different, rather than what we share in common, our ability to love, our desire to forgive, to love, and be loved. Even well-meaning people do not take the time to pause and reflect[75] before saying the first thing on their mind.

There is nothing wrong with recognizing the differences between people, just as there is nothing wrong with identifying, internalizing, and incorporating the immutable characteristics that influence our self-concept into our psyche. Failing to recognize the individual makeup of others does show a distinct lack of empathy. It is through recognizing and respecting[76] the inherent dignity of others that we are united. We share our human dignity, regardless of our physical characteristics.

Respecting our shared human dignity[77] raises a leader above common pettiness.

Respecting others is a crucial aspect of leadership development.[78] Considering others and our interconnectedness inexorably shifts the focus from our interests to compassion for all people. We acknowledge that for one of us to succeed, we all must succeed. This frame of thought encourages empathy and increases our ability to self-lead with compassion.

---

[74] Bstan-'dzin-rgya-mtsho, 2011.
[75] Figure 8.
[76] De Pree, 1989.
[77] CCC 1700.
[78] Firth-Cozens & Mowbray, 2001.

The most important single ingredient in the formula of success is knowing how to get along with people.
- Theodore Roosevelt

Good leaders tend to be highly emotionally intelligent. According to Daniel Goleman,[79] emotional intelligence (EQ) is both established at birth and can be learned.[80] In his view, EQ is the *sine qua non*, indispensable component of leadership. His research strongly suggests there is a genetic component to emotional intelligence, even though the EQ can be attained and honed through study and dutiful practice. Verwey, Miriam, and Mooney insist that emotionally intelligent leaders lead themselves first. They "monitor their moods through self-awareness, change themselves for the better through self-management, understand their impact through empathy, [and] act in ways that boost others' moods through relationship management."[81]

Psychological research in the field of human development indicates that nurture plays a role in growing empathy and other-centeredness that are hallmarks of EQ. This makes perfect sense, as nurture involves healthy relationships built over time that require reciprocal trust, positive reinforcement, and consequences for bad actions. Emotional intelligence is a key component for flourishing in relationships. As Colonel Deranger noted in her introduction to this text, leadership is essentially a relationship.

> It is better therefore that two should be together, than one: for they have the advantage of their society: If one fall he shall be supported by the other: woe to him that is alone, for when he falleth,

---

[79] 2004.
[80] Goleman, 1998.
[81] in Veldsman and Johnson, 2016, p. 356

he hath none to lift him up. And if two lie together, they shall warm one another: how shall one alone be warmed? And if a man prevail against one, two shall withstand him: a threefold cord is not easily broken. Ecclesiastes 4:9-12[82]

We are not wholly able to constructively use our emotions to understand the emotions of others and consistently employ appropriate emotions to support healthy interactions without emotional intelligence.[83] Developing EQ causes us to grow as people, to accept ourselves leading to positive self-efficacy beliefs,[84] and to more fully align our inner beliefs with our outer behavior.

What we achieve inwardly will change outer reality.
- Plutarch

---

[82] Holy Bible, Douay-Rheims 1899 American Edition
[83] Goleman, 2005
[84] Canadian College of Health Leaders, 2010.

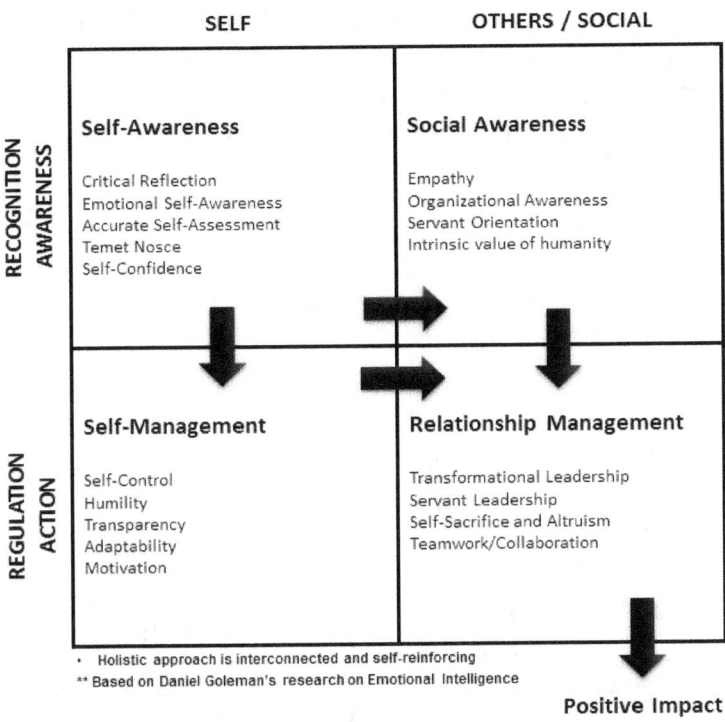

Figure 4. Emotional Intelligence

The Dalai Lama identifies compassion as a foundational human emotion. He insists that compassion can be learned through experience[85] and that through compassion, ethical behavior can be informed and practiced. In order to put others' needs first, you must exercise a certain level of EQ and engage in dialogue, fully participating in relationships to ensure you are accurately assessing how others want to be treated. This relationship is a form of interpersonal leadership.

By delving into literature, reflection, meditation, and by connecting with others, empathy is increased. Extensive social contact with people who are different from

---

[85] Bstan-'dzin-rgya-mtsho, 2011.

us facilitates an understanding of the diversity of emotions and experiences others face and increases our ability to experience and embody true compassion.
Compassion is developed through shared understanding and social experience.

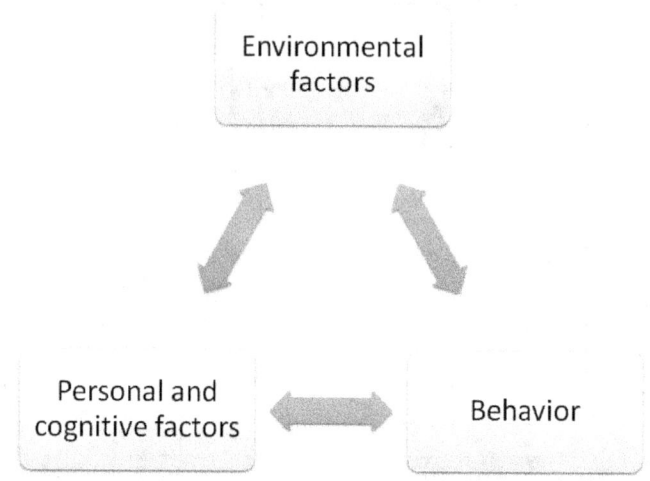

Figure 5. Triadic Reciprocal Determinism[86]

Albert Bandura's theory of social cognition[87] is a groundbreaking way to understand the cause of behaviors in the context of a reciprocal model. Human behavior had before been explained as resulting from a single causal factor, either environment or their internal dispositions.[88] In triadic[89] reciprocal determinism, behavior is influenced by cognitive and environmental factors. The interaction between a person and their environment determines behavior, as does the influence of a person's internal characteristics. Behavior shaped by this reciprocal

---

[86] Bandura, 1978.
[87] Bandura, 1986.
[88] Bandura, 1989.
[89] Three, closely interrelated factors.

determinism informs the beliefs that a person develops. Therefore, beliefs are inextricably linked to the social environment.

Table 1. Positive Leadership Attributes

Self-Awareness	Understanding one's emotions, strengths, weaknesses, [90] and driving forces; they are neither overly critical nor unrealistically hopeful; they are honest to self and others; they are self-regulating; they have an inner conversation with the self, helping to keep emotions and feelings under control or *in check*.
Motivation	Driven to achieve beyond expectations of themselves and others; they are full of passion for what they do, achieve, or learn.
Social Skills	They can communicate and authentically interact with others; they find common ground with almost everyone.
Empathy	The ability to understand the emotional makeup of others; they are thoughtful and understanding of others' feelings.[91]

There is a distinct lack of studies quantifying the detriment or benefit of Emotional Intelligence to an organization; such studies are often focused on too many variables to return unmixed findings. Some highly emotionally intelligent leaders may be manipulative and

---

[90] August, 2001.
[91] Mehrabian & Epstein, 1972.

use their abilities for personal achievement or organizational gain with little attention to social responsibility.[92] The relationship between EQ, moral reasoning, and ethical behavior is a question for potentially fruitful research.

It seems apparent that how EQ is used by leadership within an organization is dependent on the individual. The leader's moral worldview and organizational cultural beliefs should be in close alignment to forgo the possibility of ethically questionable leadership behavior, but it would be helpful if more organizations developed and thoughtfully internally promulgated a mission that was aligned with ethical practices so that it was easier for aligned decision making on the part of individual leaders.

Morals are often culturally defined and black and white,[93] whereas ethics involves the reasoned approach to moral conundrums. There are many formulae[94] for determining the ethical disposition of a situation or a decision. This is why ethics can be examined and debated, but axiomatic truths tend to be regarded as sacrosanct, depending on sociocultural and historical context.

Here again, we see the connection between leadership and an individual's values. One must understand one's belief system before attempting to lead others or risk alienating others due to a narrow moral worldview.

---

[92] Sivanathan & Fekken, 2002.
[93] Morals are axiomatic to the individual. That is, they are self-evident. This is why morals tend to vary depending on social norms.
[94] Examples include: Aristotelian, Kantian, utilitarian, Nichomachean, and virtue ethics.

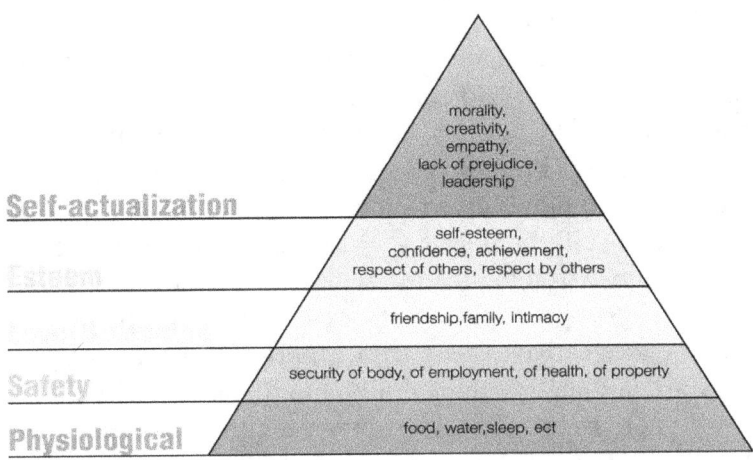

Figure 6. Modified Maslow's Hierarchy of Needs[95]

Maslow's hierarchy is a graphical representation of the pattern that a person generally follows in their behavioral motivation. If the approach is not followed from bottom to top, Maslow argued that physical or psychological illness would result. A person deprived of love and belonging may experience the attainment of esteem as a distorted or improbably process, for example.

You cannot reach a level of self-actualization, whatever your interpretation of the hierarchy of needs, by relying on others to get you there. As children, we are provided with the first few levels by our caregivers. It is up to us to develop ourselves and seek the good of others to continue the climb. Self-actualization is a level of the hierarchy that must be developed internally, through success, mastery experiences, and by learning from failures over time. Being aided in the journey toward self-actualization by effective mentorship allows leaders to

---

[95] The hierarchy of needs is a popular motivational theory in psychology that was originally proposed by Abraham Maslow in his 1943 paper "A Theory of Human Motivation."

ascend the hierarchy more efficiently.[96]

Ideally, individuals move through their lives on a path that is a clear and consistent approach to self-actualization.[97] Chemers, Watson, and May claim "high levels of dispositional confidence and optimism, [are] gained through graduated success experiences that help to build such self-perceptions."[98] In many cases, we take steps away from self-actualization with negative self-talk and fail to learn appropriate lessons from setbacks; traumatic experiences can also be detrimental to self-actualization if they are not dealt with healthily and therapeutically.

There is a fine line between arrogance and healthy self-confidence. Sometimes that line is twisted by the observer's preconceptions.

Arrogance has often been described in a negative light, but it is, in many cases, nothing more or less than self-confidence fearlessly presenting itself via outward expression. Socially acceptable pride is a rare thing and when it is on full display it can be inspiring. When a person has self-confidence, when they have high self-esteem, they are more likely to be high achievers. A healthy dose of self-confidence is necessary in good leaders.

One of my best friends that I met in my undergrad time at Saint Louis University ROTC is the son of a 3-star USAF General. He had quite the swagger in college if you catch my meaning. I don't mind admitting that I looked up to Dave. He was my roommate for a few years, and we were the best man at each other's weddings. I am introverted and independent but was lacking in the kind of confidence he routinely displayed. Dave was very self-assured; confident in his abilities, and secure in his personhood. I learned a great deal from his influence on my life.

---

[96] Burns, 1978.
[97] Maslow, 1943.
[98] Chemers, Watson, & May, 2000, p. 274.

Dave was often accused (generally by those envious of his success) of being arrogant and privileged. He never denied his background, rather, he is proud of his upbringing and his father. It was because of the strength of his nuclear family that he established his well-grounded personality. While some may maintain that Dave was arrogant, I know that he was self-possessed and confident. These traits have been crucial to his continued success as a squadron commander and pilot of F-22 fighter jets in the USAF.

Living your Leadership requires self-confidence and self-respect. Self-respect is a prerequisite for earning the respect of others. How can you respect and desire to follow an individual who does not have confidence in themselves? Confidence is achieved through the recognition and celebration of personal strengths and positive attributes; this is ideally only after deeply questioning yourself to understand your faults. In the continual search for humble, approachable, credible leaders,[99] we may discredit authoritative, confident individuals. The prideful approach to leadership is never to be desired; rather, a leader should recognize and respect the innate value of all people by being willing to humbly serve.

That is the line between confidence and arrogance in a leader. An arrogant leader believes in themselves to a fault; they fall prey to the perception gap identified by Kruger and Dunning.[100] The opinions of others are not valued by the arrogant leader. A confident leader, on the other hand, seeks meaningful feedback. They deeply feel that they are meant to serve, rather than be served. They are willing to be vulnerable; to admit that there is much they may not know and should learn, and that wisdom may come from anyone.

Much has been written about the Dunning-Kruger

---

[99] Motto of the USAF Weapons School at Nellis AFB, NV
[100] Kruger & Dunning, 1999

Effect, and I highly recommend that you check out relevant literature. Credibility rests on the curve defined in the Dunning-Kruger model below. Credibility is a combination of vulnerability, wisdom, and experience. Leaders must be honest and vulnerable because we need to trust the integrity of their decisions. Leaders must be willing to earn their credibility. This is accomplished through experience, particularly by learning from their mistakes.

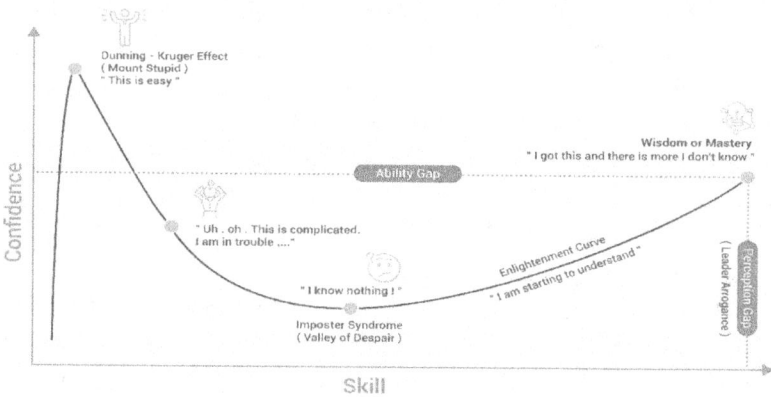

Figure 7. Dunning-Kruger Effect

Leadership is not a state of being, but the actions taken by individual people. You are only as 'leaderly' as the last action you take. Even if your last action was a mistake, owning that mistake is a 'leaderly' decision. Leaders are built, grown, nurtured... not born. They are formed from the constant pressure and refinement, consisting of the actions they have taken and the lessons they have learned from those actions.

Whether leadership is good or bad often depends on the receptiveness of a leader to learning new approaches, engaging in and integrating feedback, and their innate level of authenticity.[101] Self-awareness is the precursor and the foundation of authenticity. It is impossible to be your authentic self if you do not possess self-knowledge.

---

[101] http://brenebrown.com/videos/

Chapter Recap

Knowing yourself is necessary to lead yourself and leading yourself is a prerequisite to leading others.
- Understand your strengths, weaknesses, belief system, and motivations.
- Give yourself time and compassion. Develop positive self-talk to build upon self-image and work on complementary actions.
- Work to understand and grow your emotional intelligence. Starting with self-awareness and regulation, EQ encourages positive social interactions and is a key enabler for effective and compassionate leadership practices.
- Recognize that beliefs and actions are informed by your environment.
- Healthy pride shouldn't be confused with egotism or arrogance. An appreciation of self applies to the 'esteem' category of Maslow's hierarchy.

Integrity and Mentorship

Show me a successful individual and I'll show you someone who had real positive influences in his or her life. I don't care what you do for a living—if you do it well, I'm sure there was someone cheering you on or showing the way. A mentor.

- Denzel Washington

My wife was bone-weary and scared that night, as she had been almost every single day for months. Our infant son was sick. We had been told by a specialist that he needed to be seen out of state. The base's lead pediatrician, acting as the base hospital commander, refused to send him. During the prayer meeting, the kind wife of a high-ranking officer recommended that we speak to my commander to see what could be done.

The emotional toll of my son's illness on our family was indescribable. We were helpless to get him the treatment he needed. My commander was a man of great integrity. You could always go to Lieutenant Colonel Jed Davis with anything, and he would really listen. I met with Lt. Col. Davis the next day. He immediately went into action on our behalf. He recognized that we had tried to solve the problem ourselves and that we had reached the limit of what we were able to do on our own. Although we never heard the full details, after a meeting between the hospital commander and Lt. Col. Davis, that pediatrician immediately signed the paperwork to get our son the treatment he needed. In the space of a week, we went from being completely helpless to having special medical orders to a specialty hospital across the country. Lt. Col. Davis acted with integrity and grit, saving my son's life.

None of the principles outlined in these pages exist in a vacuum. A precursor to servanthood is humility. A prerequisite to productive critical reflection is being a person of integrity, and integrity is more than just rule-following. A person of integrity acts in a predictable manner that is dictated by the alignment of their values and actions.

Leadership is a potent combination of strategy and character.
But if you must be without one, be without the strategy.
- Norman Schwarzkopf

Take a minute and try something in your workplace. Ask your peers to define *integrity*. You will learn there are many different ways to define this simple word. Many leaders believe others should know what this word means, but there always seem to be significant variations. Why is this?

The United States military is an outstanding organization that places incredible value on leadership. The United States Air Force lists integrity as its primary core value. Unfortunately, the definition of this desirable trait is subject to dispute. One of the more common, sarcastic, comments one often hears about *integrity first* in the Air Force is that *integrity* is a force that holds objects together.[102] Though this notion is tongue-in-cheek, it draws attention to an important point – trait words are not as specifically defined as they should be.

If a good reputation is like gold,
then having integrity is like owning the mine.
- John C. Maxwell

General Lorenz described integrity in terms of the

---

[102] Like electromagnetic structural integrity or tissue integrity; integrity as a physical descriptor, rather than a moral characteristic.

strength of a building. He noted that the USAF as an institution is built on the collective strength of its members' integrity. He wrote those words during a difficult political climate in the USAF. Despite difficult times, some leaders rise to the occasion and embody - rather than simply exhibit - transparent and just leadership behaviors. Having served under Colonel Davis, I know that he shares General Lorenz' perspective that transparency is foundational to integrity.[103]

> *Excellent leaders stand for absolute integrity, absolute honesty. They preach the concept of honesty in the organization. Excellent leaders practice integrity in thought, word, and deed. And they insist upon integrity and honesty on the part of their subordinates.*
> *- General W. L. Creech* [104]

Acting with integrity is often described as doing the right thing when no one is looking, and not doing the wrong thing when no one is looking. But what is the *right thing*? How do we define the right thing? The right thing can be argued to be culturally or situationally dependent. No book of rules or flowchart can adequately capture the entire realm of leadership experience that would dictate what the *right thing* would be in any given circumstance. Millennia of ethics scholars have tried, and we still do not have a consensus. At least, in the case of the Air Force, the right thing can often be recognized through the lens of regulations and technical orders, the organizational mission, and the rules of engagement. In a non-military setting, things can get even more convoluted concerning

---

[103] Lorenz, 2012.
[104] General Wilbur Lyman Creech commanded the USAF Tactical Air Command 1978-1984.

what is right. Happily, this book is not written to answer that question, rather, as leaders we must use our best judgment, heavily informed by our compassion, to determine the rightness of our actions.

Acting with integrity rightly leads to a culture of transparency in an organization. You won't find transparency without the willingness of ethical leaders to expose processes and outcomes. An opaque culture is typically a culture in ethical disarray. Predictably ethical leaders act following obvious principles. Everyone knows it is uncomfortable being scrutinized. Having a bright light shone on you and your actions can also be freeing if you act conscientiously! Being open to criticism and having your methods and character on display allows for more authentic interactions. Having your actions and character on display is a humbling experience because no one is perfect. We strive to live in accordance with our values, but we all fall short. That being said, an authentic and transparent leader is likely a humble leader.

> *My advice to new leaders is this: if you want to be a good leader, start by being a good person. Leadership is an inside job. Before you can lead people outwardly, you have to lead yourself inwardly. Leadership starts with internal goodness, in other words, integrity.*
> *- Bill Treasurer* [105]

Fairness not only reflects on the leader but also means that the direction the organization is taking is transparent. Secrets are not guarded; their use in political power plays is curtailed, and cooperation is increased when the leader can articulate their philosophy through consistent, ethical action. "Public opinion is a weak tyrant

---

[105] International bestselling author and Chief Encouragement Officer at Giant Leap Consulting.

compared with our own private opinion. What a man thinks of himself is what determines, or rather, indicates, his fate."[106] Integrity is a very personal matter. A leader acting with integrity acts per their internal, predefined set of morals and values.[107]

> *The supreme quality for leadership is unquestionably integrity.*
> *Without it, no real success is possible, no matter whether it is on a section gang, a football field, in an army, or in an office.*
> *- Dwight D. Eisenhower*

A seasoned leader has lived experiences and knowledge, which have provided opportunities for growth and insight, and have led to a more nuanced understanding of self.[108] Many of the greatest leaders have had their character and leadership refined by passing through a crucible. The term 'crucible' refers to intense and meaningful experiences that leaders continually draw from to gain insight.[109] It is metaphorically derived from using clay or another heat-resistant bowl to melt metals or alloys and, by the application of heat, to refine those liquified metals by separating impurities that rise to the top.

Crucibles are described as a place, time, or situation characterized by the confluence of powerful intellectual, social, economic, or political forces.[110] It is a severe test of patience, belief, or both.[111] There are four types of crucibles: (1) mentoring relationships, (2) enforced reflection, (3) insertion into foreign territory, and (4)

---

[106] Thoreau & Levin, p. 10-11.
[107] George, 2015.
[108] Vitz, Nordling, & Titus, 2020.
[109] Bennis & Thomas, 2002a.
[110] De Pree, 1989.
[111] Bennis & Thomas, 2002a.

disruption or loss. The leader does not look at a crucible as a tragic event, but as a learning experience; as an opportunity. True leaders see what they can learn from crucibles, not how to use them as a reeking pond of self-pity in which to wallow.

One of the crucible events for my marriage and personal emotional resilience was dealing with my son's health challenges that I described at the beginning of this chapter. We learned so much, and with great struggle, the importance of community, of perseverance, of mentorship, and of love for one another. How we persevere through, learn from, and rebound from difficulties defines our resilience and molds character in ways that sailing along the smooth waters of life cannot do.

One of the benefits of passing through crucible events is that they tend to develop and refine one's integrity. Crucibles put a leaders' integrity to the test. Leaders with integrity possess four key character strengths: consistency, honesty, morality, and trustworthiness. Leaders with integrity show how consistent they are in their actions and words and always demonstrate who they are and what they stand for when faced with difficult trials.

The immediate influence of behavior is always more effective than that of words.
- Viktor Frankl [112]

Leaders at the top of the organization are figureheads (by this, I mean that they are highly visible, not ineffectual) who should be role models, demonstrating organizational values. Leaders with integrity also demonstrate bravery: having the strength to speak up even when opposition exists;[113] perspective: understanding the

---

[112] 1963, p.101.
[113] Peterson & Seligman, 2004.

strengths and weaknesses of their competitors; and social intelligence: sensing what makes themselves and others tick.[114] Many leaders will show bravery and stay true to their values, which makes them stronger than most; they must also have the courage to stand alone when it is necessary.[115]

It can be difficult to maintain your principles in the face of pressure from your superiors or your subordinates. Bill George[116] warns leaders not to be swayed by expediency in the face of that external pressure. Taking a traditional view, Bill advises that a leader should ignore the prevailing wisdom, not following the crowd; that a leader should take care to adjust their methods slowly, over time, in a bid to best suit their own *True North*.[117]

> *Regard your soldiers as your children,*
> *and they will follow you into the deepest valleys;*
> *look on them as your own beloved sons,*
> *and they will stand by you even unto death.*
> *- Sun Tzu*

Team members are not Amazon.com packages. Followers do not come with gift receipts; you cannot just return them. Although Jim Collins asserts that getting the wrong people out and the right people in[118] is the way to get started toward a good-to-great organization, it is not always possible. In those cases, it is the ideal time to exercise your empathy.

Terminating or transferring a difficult (but coachable) employee is often the easy way out.[119]

---

[114] Peterson & Seligman, 2004.
[115] Center for Creative Leadership, 2008.
[116] Senior Fellow, Harvard Business School and former Chairman and CEO of Medtronic.
[117] George, 2015.
[118] Collins, 2001a.
[119] There are always reasons (illegal, immoral, or unethical behaviors) to

However, you must know that if you are building a team, there are always going to be conflicts. Sometimes, a negative personality trait rears its ugly head in a follower, and it catches you completely by surprise. My first opportunity to mentor an employee in a civilian leadership position happened at my first healthcare management position.

One of my employees was an ambitious young man who seemed to rub people the wrong way. Let's call him George. I'm proud to say that George is now a leader both by position and action. Our mentor-mentee relationship started when I caught George with his feet up on his desk midday. That was obviously an unacceptable behavior, given the amount of work that we were behind on at the time. I saw my opportunity in a moment of clarity: I could go the disciplinary route or the mentorship route. Choosing one over the other was easy because my mentor in the organization always told us to err on the side of compassion. I was motivated to follow his example and use the clear organizational vision that he had communicated as a guide.

I walked into the office, closing the door behind me. I started with the 5 why's[120] to determine the reason why he wasn't contributing. George was especially well-educated and certified for his position. His talents were underutilized by the company and by the former management team. I concluded that he needed an opportunity to excel and use the skills and abilities that we had collaboratively identified in him during our one-on-one mentoring sessions. Within the constraints of the union contract, we put George in charge of a process improvement project during the time he used to put his feet

---

terminate an employee. Here, we are talking about a difficult employee.
[120] Gemba Gembutsu, or *place* and *information* in Japanese refers to the practice of asking *why a failure occurred* 5 times to come to a more complete understanding in simple root cause analysis (RCA).

up on the desk. He excelled. George's co-workers were stunned at his transformation. His attitude and his performance were exceptional.

That seemingly simple change was an *ah-ha!* moment for me. A leader must *choose* to care, whether or not her followers seem to care. A leader *always* cares. I realized that a leader must always lead with individualized compassion. The natural extension of that compassionate and caring choice is to invest the time to mentor followers so that they can become leaders themselves.

Leadership interactions are further informed by any mentor a person happens to choose. Let me take a minute to emphasize the importance of choosing mentors, and of choosing the right mentors for your personal and career[121] development. Mentors are crucial for leadership development.[122]

Setting an example is not the main means of influencing others; it is the only means.
- Albert Einstein

Mentorship involves diligent work.

When setting out on a journey, do not seek advice from someone who has never left home.
- Jalal al-Din Rumi [123]

Ideally, a mentor will have experience. However, experience is not the end-all-be-all. Experience is a qualification to be a subject matter expert (SME) and a prerequisite to be a trainer. When we talk about experience, it does not automatically mean that a person has done the self-improvement and critical reflection necessary to have

---

[121] Zachary, 2005.
[122] De Pree, 1989.
[123] 13th-century (1207-1273) Persian Muslim poet and Sufi mystic.

developed themselves as leaders. It does not mean that person is a leader with integrity. A mentor must behave in a manner that is internally and externally consistent.

A mentor is not simply a trainer. They are a coach, and a coach develops relationships with their team members. If you want to be a leader with integrity, then find a mentor with integrity. No one can enhance skills within you that they do not possess.

Mentoring is a brain to pick, an ear to listen, and a push in the right direction.
- John Crosby [124]

None of us knows it all. There is nothing wrong with not knowing everything; leveraging your mentors will provide a necessary springboard to propel you into previously out-of-reach skills and abilities.[125] Mentors should engage in scaffolding[126] with their mentees. Scaffolding is a commonplace concept in the classroom. If a student is not able to perform an academic task, often, a teacher will assign another student to assist. The gap between the two students' knowledge of the subject is less than the gap between the student and teacher. The smaller gap between the two students makes what would have been a leap from a lower level of knowledge to a fuller understanding to a short hop from current state to a deeper understanding.

Scaffolding provides that extra support needed to reach a new level of performance. Using a mentor to *pull* you past your current capabilities shifts the Zone of Proximal Development as learning occurs. A capable mentor will be able to identify the gaps in knowledge and assist the mentee to overcome those gaps using scaffolding.

---

[124] (1859-1943) American politician from the state of Massachusetts.
[125] Vygotsky, 1978 (Concept of the Zone of Proximal Development, p. 86).
[126] Wood, Bruner, & Ross, 1976.

Just as it is not possible to have too many mentors, likewise, you shouldn't limit the number of people that you are willing to mentor.[127] Giving or receiving mentorship shapes not only someone else's leadership capabilities but their entire outlook on life.

*The delicate balance of mentoring someone is not creating them in your own image,
but giving them the opportunity to create themselves.*
- Steven Spielberg

---

[127] Lorenz, 2012.

Chapter Recap

Integrity increases transparency. It is based on individual values and requires coherence between those values and leadership actions.
- Leaders must act with integrity. Always.
- Crucibles aid in the development of leadership characteristics and serve to refine a leader's commitment to acting with integrity.
- Mentors are crucial to leadership development.
- Mentors are coaches.
- Mentors scaffold leadership behaviors and practices for their mentees.

Critical Reflection

We don't see things as they are. We see things as we are.
- Anaïs Nin

It's 1999. *The Matrix*[128] has just premiered in theaters and I'm obsessed. The digital effects were awesome, the soundtrack was edgy and the motif was exciting. What caught my interest was an existential question originally posed by Morpheus. He offers Keanu Reeves' character, Thomas Anderson/Neo, the red pill or the blue pill. *You take the blue pill, the story ends. You wake up in your bed and believe whatever you want to believe. You take the red pill, you stay in Wonderland, and I show you how deep the rabbit hole goes.* Neo has a choice to make.

René Descartes originally described the philosophical underpinnings of being skeptical of our physical sensations in his 1641 work, *Meditations on First Philosophy.*[129] He was followed by several other influential philosophers in this vein of thought.[130] To be clear, I don't believe we exist in a computer-generated reality, like in *The Matrix*. However, that scene with Morpheus and Neo was an eye-opening realization for me. I needed to be mentally prepared to examine and potentially reject my mental preconceptions. I had to question my reality to learn about myself and the world that I inhabited.

In essence, my choice was the same as Neo's: 1. to continue to live a life devoid of critical reflection – the easy route, or 2. to walk the more cognitively and emotionally uncomfortable path – to choose the red pill. I was pre-

---

[128] Wachowski & Wachowski, 1999.
[129] 1979.
[130] See Peter Unger's *Evil Scientist* and Hilary Putnam's *Brain in a Vat.*

configured for my journey of self-development by a blockbuster movie. Though the Wachowskis' film may have introduced the idea to my mind, the real work of critical reflection had yet to begin in me.

As anyone who has suffered from depression can tell you, a loss of perspective can allow even healthy emotional responses to spiral out of control. Being calm, at peace, is when we are able to make our most rational decisions. A healthy sense of detachment, a higher mental state that allows us to passively observe and thereby regulate our emotional responses[131] is something toward which we should strive daily.

As Miyamoto Musashi said, "If you wish to control others, you must first control yourself."[132] Developing self-control is necessary for any leader. Having self-control means that you are not subject to the whims of your emotions. Awareness of your emotional state is a necessary first step in controlling your emotional response. Controlling your emotional response[133] is a facet of self-control. Subduing emotional responses in favor of a long-term goal is willpower.[134] To maintain control of emotional responses, you must first hone the skill to monitor them.

---

[131] Chan, 2007.
[132] Miyamoto & Harris, 1974.
[133] See Figure 8
[134] Willpower is one of the key requirements in Jim Collins' 5th Level Leader.

> *The fundamental step every leader needs to take now enables him or her to manage their own emotional state. That means changing your relationship to your feelings – recognizing them rather than just being pushed around by them. And once you know what you are feeling – particularly if it's fear, anxiety or worry – the next step comes down to managing those feelings.*
>
> *– Daniel Goleman*[135]

As humans, we have the ability, unique in the animal kingdom, to observe our thoughts as they pass through our brains. As we monitor these thoughts, we have the additional ability to control them. This is the simple definition of metacognition.[136] Practice is required to develop the ability to self-monitor. Self-monitoring involves doing difficult mental work. That work commences with monitoring emotionally-driven thoughts. Once the thoughts become distinguishable on the canvas of your mind, it is possible to determine the emotional antecedents of those thoughts. The next step is to choose and modify the thoughts. External pressures too often force reactive, emotional thoughts to the fore.

> *The field cannot be seen from within the field.*
> *- Ralph Waldo Emerson*

Perspective involves an awareness of self. To some

---

[135] Harvard educated Ph.D., award-winning science author, Fellow of the American Association for the Advancement of Science, and thought leader on Emotional Intelligence.
[136] Martinez, 2006.

self-awareness can be frightening and disturbing[137] at times because it opens the leader to a level of empathy and vulnerability that many people are not prepared to handle. Awareness of your own emotions is a prerequisite for understanding others, however. Thus, it is a necessary step in the journey of *Living your Leadership*.

Extend your understanding outside of yourself. Apply your knowledge of self to the needs and desires of others. You can see that there are parallels in some, but others that differ wildly. That is what makes us unique and special as people. Embracing vulnerability, that is part of releasing the need for self-centeredness, to care for others and you have the beginnings of empathy. Self-awareness means that you recognize your triggers and tendencies. If you do not understand those things about yourself, you will not be able to recognize and improve on them.

I think it is very good that you should try daily to increase the depth of your concern for those under you. For to feel surrounded and protected by the affectionate understanding of the one in charge, can be the effective help which is needed by the people you have to serve by means of your governance.
- St. Josemaría Escrivá[138]

A leader must intimately understand their own motives and character. Introspection of a specific kind is called for to do so. Part of gaining an understanding of self is metacognitively viewing and regulating your reactions by selecting and modifying thoughts. A famous quote from Aristotle that you might have read on social media or heard in TED talks indicates that we are what we repeatedly do and that excellence is nothing more than habit. Naturally,

---

[137] Spears, 2005.
[138] St. Josemaría Escrivá, the founder of Opus Dei, wrote these words in his book: *Furrow*, No. 395

this presupposes that you are acting in an excellent manner, which is unlikely unless you have clearly understood your motivations and acted morally. When repetitions of vices like smoking or drinking can be described as a habit, the importance of thoughtfulness in your actions becomes more painfully clear to ensure your actions are, in fact, excellent. Carefully use the emotional distance that perspective gives to practice patience and self-control. Perspective, along with the act of thinking before acting, provide consistency and stability to your environment.[139]

Your past shapes the present. It crafts the lens through which you perceive the world. Were you raised poor? Rich? Middle class? Were your parents left, middle, or center of the political spectrum? Were you raised to cherish a certain concept of morality? Were you raised in a household where education was considered important? Did your parents graduate from high school, college, graduate school? These questions may seem like nothing more than noise to some people, but that could not be farther from the truth.

It requires troublesome work to undertake the alteration of old beliefs.
- John Dewey [140]

Leadership development begins with your family,[141] the family you were born into or the one you have chosen. Understanding how your past influences your character, decision-making, and frame of reference is of critical importance to a clear understanding and regulation of self.

---

[139] Headquarters, United States Army, 2006.
[140] John Dewey (1859-1952) was one of the founders of the philosophical school of pragmatism and was a pioneer in functional psychology and educational reform.
[141] Zaleznik, 1992.

Your past *shapes*, but does not *predict* your present.

I am not what happened to me, I am what I choose to become.
- Carl Jung

Understanding, incorporating, and moving beyond some of the negative things that happened in your past can redefine your vision of the present, offering different choices and re-shaping the lens through which you view your world. All three of them - understanding, incorporating, and moving on - involve the practice of critical reflection. Some of the greatest leaders of any time have had immeasurably sad and traumatic pasts. That did not stop them from realizing their potential. Epictetus, for example, was a slave whose ideas in the school of Stoic philosophy like 'memento mori' have echoed throughout the ages.

Critical reflection takes each of these and many more questions and closely analyzes the impact that they have on your psyche and, by extension, on your fitness to lead. You will find that unresolved emotional issues will lead to leadership pitfalls. The Dalai Lama exhorts us to seek critical philosophical inquiry and ethical living with contemplative practice.[142] Critical reflection is a contemplative practice that incorporates philosophical inquiry. One of the benefits of critical reflection is that you will become more conscious and intentional about your leadership practice.

Once you have incorporated this new understanding into your practice, take a step back. How might your former perspective have limited you previously? What part of your upbringing do you need to carry forward with you because

---

[142] Bstan-'dzin-rgya-mtsho, 2011.

it is valuable? What should you discard or modify? These are all questions that should be answered to fully realize the holistic approach to *Living your Leadership*. You should be able to identify and fully understand where your perspective comes from so that you can modify perceptions at will.

Even if you have initially gone through the activity above, it is something that you will have to do throughout your leadership journey. Novel situations will arise – situations that will trigger emotions from your past. Those emotions will have to be critically re-examined to fully incorporate the emotion around your experience into authentic self-knowledge. You must reconcile the emotions and reactions within yourself when you consider new stimuli, as well. Develop the self-control to cultivate a useful perspective. Your new perspective is grounded in experience since your view of the present is shaped by your memory of the past. The practice of self-control in critical reflection allows you to incorporate emotions, perceptions, and stimuli most ethically and thoughtfully.

Insults, confrontation, and the need for mature perspective.

As anyone who has spent time in retail or food service can tell you, it is not only possible but also necessary to realize that one can take offense to something, while not being offended by it. You are responsible for your response, not for another person's abusive behavior. This is an incredibly difficult thing to do, but the practice of self-control and the development of a healthy self-perception demands the ability.

As the manager for biomedical engineering at a hospital in Silicon Valley, I had ultimate accountability for a portfolio of strategic service delivery, educational, and budgetary initiatives in the service area. With responsibility for thousands of medical devices in the hospital, I was bound to encounter an array of negative and positive customer service interactions, despite the professionalism typically expected in a healthcare setting.

I had been in the position for some months when my first real customer blow-up happened. Evidently, there was a shortage of a particularly expensive medical device in a unit and the manager of that unit needed someone to take their frustration out on. I had learned during my time in Iraq that taking a breath and evaluating a situation before responding was advisable, so I put that into practice as I stood in the hallway, being berated by this person. They contended that my department was ineffective, that I was under-qualified, and that it was *all my fault*.

It would have been easy to take offense and lash out. As a leader in the hospital, I knew that my role was to support patient care and my duties to the inpatient units were clearly defined in the service level agreement. This person was lashing out because she was emotionally immature, not because I had done anything deserving of a dressing down.

When I was a young leader, I had a weakness that is common in new leaders: I was confrontation avoidant. Confrontations are uncomfortable and can feel personal in ways that produce feelings of shame, inadequacy, and fear. Thanks to my critical reflection practice, I had long been aware of my tendency to avoid confrontation and had dealt with the antecedents of the feelings that confrontations produce. I took her 'feedback' and waited a beat to respond. Recognizing her position and her brokenness, I responded with kindness and empathy – offering to help her find a solution to the issue despite it being outside my primary area of responsibility. By weathering her verbal storm and offering to help her find a solution, I built a bridge where there had previously only been a wall.

Something *can* be offensive, objectively speaking. Certain things are morally and ethically deplorable, and thus, *should* offend our sensibilities. Our moral outrage,[143] and our other emotions (e.g., sorrow),[144] are intrinsic to the human person and may even be necessary for moral action[145] to focus, sustain, and execute. An action that does not align with our emotional state may be inauthentic, thus removing part of the human component from our relationships. That being said, control of emotion is necessary to prevent us from being a slave to our passions.[146]

Human freedom involves our capacity to pause between stimulus and response and, in that pause, to choose the one response toward which we wish to throw our weight.
- Rollo May[147]

An additional distinction must be drawn, however, between something being offensive and our being offended by it. As a self-aware and self-confident leader, you should possess the moral objectivity and perspective to be able to isolate and examine your emotional reaction to an objectionable situation. You should employ your hard-won self-control to view the potentially upsetting scenario and respond to it in a professionally unemotional and appropriate way without allowing emotions to cloud your judgment.

---

[143] The Holy Bible, 1984, John 2:15.
[144] The Holy Bible, 1984, John 11:35.
[145] LeDoux, 1998.
[146] Augustine, 1972, IX.4.
[147] 1975, p. 100.

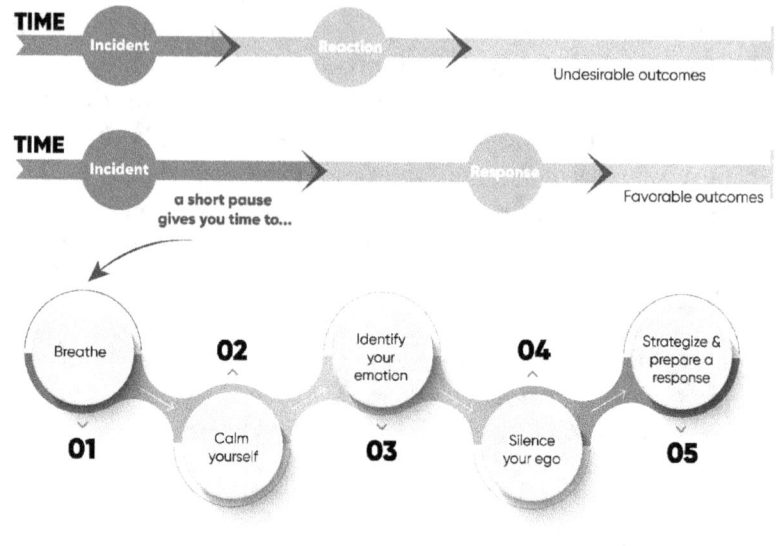

Figure 8. Take a moment to reflect before responding

We all run into situations where someone accosts us with an outburst that seems exaggerated beyond all reason. As a leader, *regulating* your response to that over-emotional outburst is a practical aspect of emotional intelligence.[148] Determining the cause of the outburst involves empathy, while not taking immediate offense requires active humility and self-control which can be attributed to a deliberate mindfulness practice.[149]

Taking the time to breathe, calm yourself, identify your emotional antecedents, silence your ego, strategize and prepare your response before delivery will give you the time you need to turn a reaction into a considered response.

---

[148] Figure 4.
[149] Carroll, 2007.

You must learn to resist the temptation to engage in the culture of immediacy and respond when you are adequately prepared to advance the conversation. Self-regulation is an EQ-related trait that needs to be exercised by leaders[150] in difficult situations so that they do not simply allow their brain-to-speech filter to spew whatever they are thinking. **Leaders do not have the luxury of being offended.**

Offense is taken because leaders fail to understand that most criticisms are not about them; criticism is often just someone venting. Developing a humble, empathetic mindset and responding through self-regulation does not happen overnight. It takes practice and internal work to develop self-control.

Choose not to be harmed—and you won't feel harmed.
Don't feel harmed—and you haven't been.
- Marcus Aurelius

More on the subject of objectivity: perspective and objectivity should not be used interchangeably. This is more than a simple semantic difference, in that, objectivity implies your emotions have been disconnected from the subject. While this is appropriate in some circumstances, it is not appropriate when dealing with the human side of leadership. I'm sure you have experienced someone who describes themselves as a 'numbers person' when what they often mean is that they are not interested in hearing about the issues and dealing with the messy details of human interaction and relationship building that is an integral part of the leadership process. Beware of those leaders; their emotionally unhealthy and immature understanding of self and lazy approach to relationships all but guarantees they will not support their team in times of

---

[150] George, 2015.

interpersonal (or personal) crisis. These situations may represent crucible moments. In neglecting to respond properly to these crucibles, the team misses an opportunity to learn and grow.

In contrast to objectivity, perspective is a mental exercise that provides distance between an event and its emotional impact. Perspective allows the incorporation of the experience into our mental models so that it can be analyzed and learned from. Perspective does not detach emotional consequence; rather, it tempers our reactions.

Most leadership decisions affect your followers in one way or another. The intrinsic value of humanity and the recognition that you exist to serve your followers should supersede your desire to be objective, rather than apply perspective, in your decision-making processes.

Self-reverence, self-knowledge, self-control.
These three alone lead one to sovereign power.
- Lord Tennyson [151]

Crucial business considerations have to take precedence,[152] but the human factor should never be overlooked. That is why it is appropriate to use the word 'perspective' instead of 'objectivity' when describing how to make decisions as a leader. The use of *perspective* when making leadership decisions allows you to remove the immediacy of the negative emotional response. Taking a step back, metaphorically speaking, means that the leader retains useful emotions when dealing with the care of followers; emotions like pity and love.

Among the other things for which he was famous, Marcus Aurelius was one of the great stoic thinkers of his day. His fame spread as he pursued the German campaigns

---

[151] Alfred Tennyson (1809-1892) was Poet Laureate of Great Britain and Ireland during the Victorian era.
[152] (i.e., legal and contractual concerns).

in the later Roman Empire. He was perceived by many as one of the Five Great Emperors of Rome[153] and was also influential in philosophical circles. One of the practices that Marcus Aurelius swore by was taking a few moments at the end of each day in contemplation.[154] During those few minutes, he would critically reflect on his actions, their impact, and contemplate the future.

Our lives are composed of decisions and the consequences of those decisions. Realizing that the color of your thoughts shapes the day that you're going to have makes the idea of meditating on those thoughts more palatable – even desirable. Your thoughts impact the relationship you have with those around you. Meditation is a deliberate act that primes the mind, allowing you to critically assess your thoughts and feelings through focused relaxation.

You need to avoid certain things in your train of thought: Everything random, everything irrelevant. And certainly, everything self-important or malicious. You need to get used to winnowing your thoughts, so that if someone says, 'What are you thinking about?' you can respond at once (and truthfully) that you are thinking this or thinking that.
- Marcus Aurelius

Meditation is often seen in some conservative Western societies as inadvisable or incompatible with Judeo-Christian values, but this could not be further from the truth.

---

[153] The Five emperors in unbroken (not blood) succession were Nerva, Trajan, Hadrian, Antoninus Pius, and Marcus Aurelius.
[154] Similar to the Jesuit Examen practice mentioned elsewhere in this text.

It is vitally important to withdraw to the desert [a calm place in your mind/soul] in order to combat the dictatorship of a world filled with idols that gorge themselves on technology and material goods, a world dominated and manipulated by the media, a world that flees God by taking refuge in noise. It is necessary to help this modern world to have the experience of the desert. There, we get some distance from everyday events. We can flee the noise and the superficiality.
- Cardinal Robert Sarah [155]

The profound rest you can achieve during meditation results in a needed refreshment of mental and emotional resources,[156] not to mention that it is easier to examine the world and your place in it while outward distractions are minimized.

We must be silent before we can listen.
We must listen before we can learn.
We must learn before we can prepare.
We must prepare before we can serve.
We must serve before we can lead.
- William Arthur Ward [157]

There is practicality in taking time during our busy days for reflection.
Lieutenant Barker was miserable. He'd been disciplined for being late, had missed questions on his monthly classified missile test, and worst of all, he had

---
[155] The Power of Silence: Against the Dictatorship of Noise, section 103.
[156] Cashman, 2008.
[157] Quoted in Leadership...with a human touch. June 1, 1999. p .11.

been geographically separated from his active-duty wife during their long-distance move, despite assurances that they would be stationed together. Barker was one of my subordinate officers. He was a good guy; young and intelligent, with a facility for making others feel welcome. His test scores and behavior weren't indicative of the type of officer that he could be. I had been tasked with writing the paperwork that would ruin his career.

It wasn't a task that I wanted to do. The hesitation was grounded in more than just my preference for education and training than punishment; the situation felt wrong. As I walked into the headquarters building from the frigid North Dakota winter, I knocked the snow off my boots and entered my office, fully intending to do as I had been instructed. I shut the door, frustratedly shucked my parka, and tossed my gloves into the corner of the room. As I sat there, staring at the computer screen, I breathed slowly in and out, taking the time to calm myself.

I was Lt. Barker's boss. What were my responsibilities as his leader? His mentor? I hadn't taken enough time to talk to him, to ask him about his troubles. As I sat in my quiet office, I formed a plan.

This brief pause was the time I needed to develop perspective. Rather than seeing Lt. Barker as a problem or a task, I saw him as a person. He was struggling and needed guidance. I decided to "go to bat" for my subordinate. I formed a plan and scheduled some time with my boss to talk about the situation. After I got his buy-in, I was able to mentor Lt. Barker and worked closely with him for the rest of my time as Flight Commander.

Though he didn't remain an active-duty member of the Air Force, Barker's time at Minot became much more bearable. We developed a close relationship and went on dozens of alerts together. It was that reflective time that allowed me the mental reorientation necessary to make the 'leaderly' decision.

How should I go about meditating?

There are several recommended ways to start a meditation session. One of the first things to do is to clear the physical area around you if at all possible. Chaos on the outside can negatively impact the mental stillness that you are trying to achieve. Disarray in your surroundings is often echoed by disorder in your thinking; your outer circumstances can be a mirror for your inner mental state.

You should also remain still. Sitting in repose will allow you to most effectively clear your mind because you are not using muscles in your body that could be otherwise used in productive activity. You do not typically feel as connected to the world around you if you are not moving about in your physical space. When I meditate, either in prayer or in thoughtful reflective practice, I like to close the door to my office, dim the lights, and turn on a fan to dull my auditory sense with white noise.

Meditative practice is enhanced by dulling our sensory perceptions. Consider lowering the lights or closing your eyes. The eyes are our primary means of gathering information about the world. They can distract your inner calm by attempting to process visual stimuli during your attempt at relaxation. Meditation will encourage you to cultivate, appreciate, and use mental solitude to benefit your spiritual, emotional, and physical well-being.

There is no need to go to India to find peace.
You will find that deep place of silence right in your room,
your garden or even your bathtub.
- Dr. Elisabeth Kübler-Ross

The next step is to relax. Relaxation is not a physical or mental process, per se. If it helps you to think of it that way, then I would encourage you to do so. Ideally, you should be able to simply let go. You sit down and detach cognitively from the world around you; actively surrendering. This cognitive detachment does not mean that you are no longer thinking. Rather, you will be attentive to the world around you in a different way. A mindful reflection is what you hope to attain when you relax in this manner.

There are many books about meditation and relaxation techniques - this is not one of them. I hope that this brief overview gives you a quick dip of the toe into the still waters of meditation. Just remember that in order to reap the greatest benefit from practicing critical self-reflection, it should be performed in a relaxed mental state.

You will find that once you can achieve a practice of mindfulness - present state awareness - you will have greater control over your attention. And by attention, I mean that you will be able to control what you will and will not spend your time thinking about,[158] and ultimately have a higher level of control over your mental and emotional state. With the practice of mindfulness, you will find that actions flow more authentically[159] from a place of repose and groundedness.

As described, this meditative practice stands in opposition to automatic, knee-jerk responses to external stimuli.[160] Those reactions are to be avoided at all costs because, without knowledge of what is motivating your emotions or actions, you lose control of your reactions and cannot authentically lead others. Loss of self-control is not something any leader wants. Emotional mistakes can have long-lasting repercussions and are best avoided. As Rudyard Kipling wrote: "If you can keep your wits about you while all others are losing theirs, and blaming you... The world will be yours and everything in it, what's more, you'll be a man, my son." Ethical decision-making, a crucial skill for leaders, also demands a certain level of

---

[158] Posner & Boies, 1971.
[159] Dhiman, 2009.
[160] Bryant & Kazan, 2013, p. 51-52.

mindfulness.[161] Mindfulness requires self-awareness, self-acceptance, and self-control.

To what should we devote our attention?

It seems that every day we are inundated with ideas, images, and sound bites. We live in a world that expresses itself 140 characters at a time, all the time, day and night. Posts on social media are pictures of idyllic lifestyles and wise, pithy quotes. The successes of others are constantly available to us on LinkedIn, Twitter, Facebook, and Instagram. These stimuli enter through our eyes and become rooted in our skulls. With the sheer amount of information (read: noise) available to us, it is extremely difficult for us to focus our attention on what is important; that which adds value to our lives.

Critical reflection and meditation are two ways that will encourage your brain to understand what is value-added in your life. They will allow you to direct your attention to those things that are meaningful and impactful. Rather than automatically reacting to anything that occurs to you externally, your mindfulness practice will mature into the ability to step outside yourself. You should be able to allow those experiences and stimuli to pass in front of your mind's eye so that you can choose what to react to. This ability requires a great deal of control and patience. Critical reflection, questioning ordinary external stimuli, is not common.

It is far more common for people to automatically, almost subconsciously, process and react in preconfigured ways. Past experiences have informed our minds to respond in these highly templated ways. There is immense survival value to these schemas that have been developed over millennia. The human mind is a complex and beautiful creation; it can automate an enormous number of reactions.

Part of the responsibility that comes with

---

[161] Sauer & Kohls, 2011.

civilization is curbing automatic responses that may have a deleterious effect on others. Part of the journey toward self-actualization is controlling our base impulse and ingrained responses to ensure we are in control of our actions, not a biologically predetermined routine. These schemas,[162] templates, or scripts that allow us to more quickly and effectively respond to outside stimuli must be picked apart. They should be analyzed and questioned. Even though a situation might look similar to a past situation, that does not necessarily mean that it needs to be reacted to in the same way – or even reacted to at all.

In general, we spend far too little time examining what we consume experientially, and not enough time examining the process by which it penetrates our consciousness. We seldom even consider the reactions that we have to our experiences. Understanding our mental processes allows us to have a firmer grip on our emotional reactions. Control is eminently desirable, in that, it leads to a high level of rationality and self-control.

The ability to subordinate an impulse to a value is the essence of the proactive person.
- Stephen Covey[163]

Self-control is achieved once we can more closely regulate what enters our minds, rather than simply absorbing it. With that regulation comes a better understanding of our values and a firmer knowledge of what is likely to motivate us as leaders. Regulation implies the ability to process external stimuli, questioning them against previously held beliefs and self-knowledge. Using

---

[162] The study of schemas as templates for understanding behavior, contradictory to the popular study of behaviorism at the time, was initiated by Frederic Bartlett in the early 1930s.
[163] (1932 - 2012) American educator, author, businessman, and leadership consultant best known for writing *The 7 Habits of Highly Effective People*.

the techniques described above, those experiences should then deliberately be incorporated, discarded, or modified in our mental models.

An added benefit to self-knowledge and control in mindfulness practice is that it opens us up to a better understanding of others. Control over our thought processes allows us to identify a lack of control in others. Einstein believed that the only way to gain knowledge is experience. Experience, from successes and from failures, leads to wisdom. It is the hard-won experience that allows the properly formed leader the wisdom and insight to perceive and negotiate the emotions and motivations of others.

Paired with this wisdom must be mercy and compassion. While this skill can be heady in its implications for daily practice, being able to identify weaknesses in others does not grant you the license to condescend. Observing weakness in others with a caring heart allows you to embrace a greater degree of empathy. Your ability to help them in very specific ways is improved through this increased understanding.

Empathy will be discussed in a later chapter; however, one of the important aspects of mindfulness - of observing and regulating our thoughts - is to cultivate a practice of non-judgment. Refusing to judge and condemn is part of self-control. Knowing that you have advanced in a fashion that is superior to your fellow man does not mean that you are, in fact, superior to your fellow man. Appreciating the inherent dignity of humanity and practicing humility means that you understand at a deep level that self-improvement can only be meaningful if it is used to lift others.

Any critical reflection of self should involve the definition of the self. What do we mean by *I*? A possible definition is that it is that entity that detachedly examines your thoughts as they pass through your mind. Still, others describe *I* as a collection of successive perceptions, a bundle of perceptions like humanist David Hume.[164] "When I enter most intimately into what I call myself, I always stumble on some particular perception or other....and never can observe anything but the perception."[165] For the purposes of this text and critical self-reflection, *I* will be defined as The Ego; that part of ourselves that is eminently in our control to modify at will.

Let us take a moment to discuss a piece of the lexicon for this book that could be confusing. One of the words in this book that has a dual meaning which I hope not to use inappropriately is "ego." *The Ego* - the proper noun (in the Jungian and Freudian sense) - refers to the mental or inner self. However, in this book, *egotism* or *ego* - the common noun - refers to an inflated or selfish sense of self.

Though egotism is not a desirable leadership characteristic, I do not mean to imply that ego is unacceptable. At its most basic level, a healthy ego is the result of natural mental development. Having a robust sense of self allows us to develop self-confidence and esteem. As social animals, a limited amount of ego allows us to be evolutionarily competitive with one another. As the Dalai Lama states, however, once egoism reaches the point where you start to disregard the good of others in favor of your interests, that is where the line is drawn between healthy and unhealthy ego.[166]

Part of achieving self-actualization is the realization that you are not the most important thing around which the universe slowly turns. Your thoughts should center on others. Developing yourself is necessary, but without the effort of the community, it is unlikely that the journey to self-actualization will ever be fully realized. Serving others means that they will have the benefit of your help on their

---

[164] Hume, D., 2000.
[165] Treatise, 1.4.6. para. 3.
[166] Bstan-'dzin-rgya-mtsho, 2011.

path. This reciprocal relationship is the bedrock of community. To focus beyond individual needs and concerns, a leader must stop worrying about themselves to the exclusion of others.[167] The subordination of your ego to the needs of others is a crucial step in the journey toward self-actualization.

One of the reasons it is so hard to understand oneself, to achieve self-mastery, is that a person is *more* than just the accumulation of experiences. It is narrow-minded to take a snapshot in time and define a person based on that solitary picture. People can choose to think about thinking, plan their actions, or allow instincts to have control. People grow and change. "Self-mastery is a long and exacting work. One can never consider it acquired once and for all. It presupposes renewed effort at all stages of life."[168]

In any case, the environmental and social factors that play a part in a person's life, their emotions, and their experience-based schema all contribute to the choices a person will make. A person is acting out Living *their* Leadership if their choices are based on predetermined priorities and values while taking into consideration a thorough knowledge of self. Concurrently, a leader must not neglect the needs and concerns of others.

Metaphor and mindset.

Imagining life as a race is a typically Western idea. Saint Paul says, "Do you not know that in a race, all the runners run, but only one gets the prize? Run in such a way as to get the prize."[169] St. Paul is speaking metaphorically about the way to live a life that will lead to rewards in heaven, but the metaphorical meaning that many people choose to see is that winning is the important thing.

Living your Leadership is a journey, a distance race that "is about training and being prepared for opportunities

---

[167] Hayward, 2007.
[168] CCC 2342.
[169] 1 Corinthians 9:24 (NIV).

when they come – you don't train for a marathon in the same way you train for a 50-yard dash!"[170] The process of human development is a lifelong effort.[171] It is easy to picture a swift footrace of several hundred meters when *winning a race* is mentioned, but like so many metaphors, our first impression of it falls woefully short of its true meaning. There is a deeper and richer significance to being a follower (runner) of Christ in the life of St. Paul. His daily acts of grit and perseverance, of charity and love, are monumental and resource-intensive.

St. Paul works. Every day, he understands himself and his mission better than the day before. As he works (races), his struggles shape his psyche. The world he lived in was incredibly harsh by modern standards. St. Paul didn't run his race wearing high-tech, gold Nike running shoes on a rubberized track with a Gatorade stand at the finish. He also wasn't wearing an Armani suit, sporting a Rolex, or strutting around in highly polished Salvatore Ferragamo shoes while rushing to an executive stakeholder meeting in his many-windowed high-rise office building. Paul wore sandals in the desert. His occupation for some time was *tentmaker*. He used the money he made to support his mission of preaching the good news. He served the poor and infirm, knowing his most likely earthly outcome was a martyr's death. It is a bleak picture of the *finish line* of his earthly race, isn't it? That is why equating a quick race with the defeat of other runners is shortsighted.

St. Paul, like all of us, is running a distance race. We pause to help those along the way. We show respect, mercy, sportsmanship, and kindness to other runners. We sacrifice our petty needs for others as we lead the way. We push through our pain and celebrate successes. It doesn't matter where you are in your personal journey, your life

---

[170] Lorenz, 2012, p. 12.
[171] Baltes & Reese, 1984.

will not start when you reach some arbitrary finish line.[172]

Sit with your thoughts. One of the more difficult practices the leader has is being able to sit with their thoughts. It can sometimes seem like a maelstrom venturing into your workplace. You take requests, hear complaints, strategize and perform daily tasks. Oftentimes, one of the solutions to this problem is attempting to give immediate answers and solutions to any problems that crop up.

Immediate (meaning knee-jerk) solutions should be avoided at all costs.

When a situation arises that requires some strategic thought, the leader should take the time necessary to review that thought in their mind. This is almost universally applicable to any major decision that a person has to make. A leader should always have at least one contingency in mind, but even the best strategic thinkers among us are not able to immediately come up with tertiary stratagems at a moment's notice. Indeed, it will make you feel vulnerable to sit with your thoughts and give them the time that they need to properly percolate in your mind. Being at ease with feelings of vulnerability is a strength in leaders.

The fallacy of the immediate decision is something that I often see in new leaders. They feel like their job is to get out in front and start making decisions. Except in cases of life-or-death immediacy, there is nearly always time to take a breath and consider decisions critically. More seasoned leaders typically take the time to suss out various second-order effects of the decisions that they plan to make. They pause to validate that those decisions are in alignment with the strategic mission, vision, and values of the organization.

---

[172] Sinek, 2011.

We can make, to ourselves, very much stronger suggestions than anyone else can, whoever that person may be.
- Émile Coué de la Châtaigneraie [173]

The bedrock of interpersonal skills is self-knowledge. Achieving a solid understanding of self - strengths, weaknesses, and personality - is required before effective communication can occur. This is harder than it sounds. The goal is to fine-tune self-knowledge while helping others move forward. A good way to determine whether you understand yourself in a practical way is to practice asking yourself behavioral interview questions.

A simple internet search will yield some excellent behavioral interview questions. Behavioral interview questions involve scenarios that will yield concrete examples of how you have reacted in real-world situations. For example:
- Give me an example of a time that you worked well under pressure.
- Tell me about how you work with others.
  - Do you take the lead in team scenarios? Why? Why not?
- What does being a leader mean to you?
  - What skills do you have that make you a good leader?
  - What skills do you have that make you a good follower?
- How do you handle mistakes at work?
  - Tell me about a situation where that happened.
- Recall a time you disagreed with a superior.
  - How did you handle it?
- How would you describe your strengths and

---

[173] French psychologist and pharmacist (1857-1926) who developed the psychotherapeutic method of conscious autosuggestion.

weaknesses while working on a team?
- Give an example of how your strengths and weaknesses have played out in your experience.

How does one become more self-aware? It is a lifelong effort, though it can be accelerated by critical self-reflection (discernment) and focused intellectual effort. Some people are naturally more self-aware than others. Valuing objective dialogue about strengths and weaknesses within a family unit, effective mentorship, or an introspective disposition can provide a boost to self-awareness. Consequently, working in those directions will increase your self-awareness, and self-leadership emerges from self-awareness.[174]

Perhaps you are interested in developing a practice that catalogs your progress. You are interested in learning, through reflection, in what areas you have grown and in documenting your "ah-ha" moments. I would suggest taking up the practice of keeping a journal. I've described my process using the Examen to reflect on my day and prepare for the next; a journal is a great tool to document that reflective and planning time.

Great leaders keep journals. Research has consistently documented that outstanding leaders take time to reflect and what better way to memorialize those thoughts and reflections than in a journal? Leadership success depends on the ability to access your unique perspective and bring it to bear on your decisions every day.

If you are considering taking up a journaling practice, start small. Commit to reflecting for 15 minutes 2-3 times a week. Choose the right time, preferably the same time each day when you won't be disturbed. Pick a time that works for you, but keep those 15 minutes carefully guarded in your agenda. A journal's blank pages invite you

---

[174] Bryant & Kazan, 2013, p. 13.

to hold an honest conversation with yourself. Permit yourself to follow your stream of consciousness without judging, censoring, or trying to direct your thoughts. Your reflections are priceless. They are what all the world's experts, advisers, and executive coaches combined can't offer you: your unique perspective.

Remember: "vincit qui se vincit," he conquers who conquers himself.[175]

---

[175] Said to be a derivation of a maxim written by Publilius Syrus in the first century BC.

Chapter Recap

Critical reflection is a skill that encourages perspective, leads to better decision-making, and reduces cognitive bias. Critical reflection involves building connections between critical leadership skills and your interior life - your skills, abilities, and proclivities. Reflect on past performances and attitudes - determine which to carry forward and which to change through repetition. Understanding requires reflection and change requires work! Give yourself time and compassion. Develop positive self-talk to build upon self-image and in which will result in complementary actions. Understand your strengths, weaknesses, belief system, and motivations.

- Perspective is not the same as objectivity. Perspective is gained through experience and reflection.
- An understanding and acceptance of your past leads to the positive integration of values and experiences that give shape to the lens with which you perceive the world.
- Do not let the criticism of others detract from your self-worth or dictate your actions.
- Consider a meditation or prayer practice to increase focus and mindfulness.
- Grow beyond thinking of yourself.
- Self-actualization results in empathy and compassion as the attention shifts to others.

Optimism and Gratitude

Perpetual optimism is a force multiplier.
- Colin Powell, General, United States Army

I was always interested in the mission of the ICBM fleet. Strategic deterrence made sense to me. During the evening and early morning hours, while there was little to occupy my time on alert, I would sit and read the technical orders and manuals so I could better understand the weapon system. One of my goals while in ICBM operations was to be nominated and sent on a *Glory Trip* to test launch the Minuteman III. These test launches happen roughly three times a year. They were a necessity, given the importance of validating the effectiveness, readiness, and accuracy of the weapon system. I wanted to be part of the crew to physically turn the launch key and watch the trail of fire as it ascended into the atmosphere.

I got my chance. Six crewmembers traveled from North Dakota to California's lush Central Coast in February of 2007. My crew partner and I were the ones to provide the final key turn that sent the unarmed Minuteman III intercontinental ballistic missile into the sky. The test flight was code-named *Glory Trip 193GM*. The unarmed reentry vehicle re-entered the atmosphere on a ballistic trajectory to a predetermined target in the Marshall Islands. It was one of the most unique and exciting experiences I participated in while I served in the military.

My selection to the test launch team was more than just a reward for my performance during my crew time. During the trip, I had the opportunity to learn from engineers and specialists about the missile: its fuel, its internal structure, the launch configuration, and how it appears on the weapon's system display console. Gaining that deeper understanding, coupled with my internal desire to do more and serve better aligned my personal goals with an extrinsic motivator.[176] I had an inherent satisfaction with my job that I had not experienced before the trip.

One of the more neglected areas of personal and professional development is focusing on moving motivation, our passion to achieve, from an external to an internal locus. Our natural inclination to be motivated toward a certain activity is central to our social, cognitive, and physical development.[177] Without the natural drive to pursue our inherent interests, it is unlikely that anyone would bother developing themselves...or doing anything other than fulfilling our basic needs, for that matter. Humans were wonderfully and mysteriously made, however. We were imbued with a sense of wonder, of curiosity, that causes us to desire knowledge and to perform creative acts. When we are free, when we have our basic needs taken care of, that is when we can unleash our most positive and creative selves.

Virtually nothing on earth can stop a person with a positive attitude, who has his goal clearly in sight.
- Denis Waitley

Leadership is challenging[178] and, at times, demoralizing and difficult. It, like everything else in life, is harder if you whine about it. Complaining, even if it is just in your mind, is poisonous. Internally, it casts a pall over your view of the world. People are unlikely to be inspired to follow a downcast leader. Externally, if you complain about your duty as a leader, you let your followers know that you cannot be trusted with their well-being. How would you feel as a follower if your leader complained about his tasks? You would probably think twice about

---

[176] More on motivation in the chapter on Control and Autonomy.
[177] Ryan & Deci, 2000.
[178] Lorenz, 2012.

asking that leader for help or advice since you know it would just be one more thing for them to complain about and for them to tackle in their long and (seemingly) arduous day. Complaining erodes trust and faith in your leadership.

Cheerfulness prepares a glorious mind for all the noblest acts.
- St. Elizabeth Ann Seton

Dale Carnegie[179] wrote one of my personal favorite leadership self-help books: *How to Win Friends and Influence People*. In it, he talks about a dog -- the animal that is always happy to see you, who has a perpetual smile, who wags his tail and makes the world a happier place. Though taking lessons from a pet might seem like an oversimplification, try it out sometime and measure the results by the number of positive interactions you have in your office. When you greet someone with a smile, they will probably smile back.

I learned from Dale Carnegie and from my own practice that smiles are infectious; so are frowns. This wasn't always easy for me since I'm a natural introvert and my resting facial expression has been adequately described as looking like a 'disappointed professor.' I work hard on this because it is obvious from literature and from practice that true leaders convey *enthusiasm* and *optimism*.[180] A leader who comes to work happy and excited to tackle the challenges of the day will inspire and motivate their followers to achieve.[181]

However, metaphors like the grateful puppy tend to break down. They are useful tools to get your message across, but if they are stretched too far, they become

---

[179] Carnegie, 1998.
[180] Maister, 2014.
[181] Cockerell, 2008.

cumbersome or unrealistic. The happy dog does not understand the difference between realistic and unrealistic optimism. A dog is pretty happy almost all the time! **Only a fool walks around with a smile plastered on her face all the time.**

With all of life's various challenges, its ups and downs, gravitas is often required in place of mindless optimism. Realistic optimism involves the acceptance that good and bad things happen, but there is an opportunity to make *good,* regardless of the circumstances.[182] The leadership behaviors that you demonstrate will be your legacy. What legacy would you prefer to leave in your workplace?

I always like to look on the optimistic side of life...
- Walt Disney

When I think of examples of optimistic leaders the one that immediately comes to mind is the unlikely character played by Sean Astin in the 1985 cult classic *The Goonies.* An underprivileged kid at the head of a group of misfits searching for pirate treasure, he employs his unflinching optimism and *joie de vivre* with his crew as they meet with obstacles along their way to One-Eyed-Willy's treasure ship. At the point of giving up, when offered a way out, he makes a heartfelt speech at the wishing well that changes their hearts and minds. It isn't the last time that Sean Astin played a character with aspirational leadership traits. He shares his enthusiasm, love for growing things, and unfailing friendship in his role as Samwise Gamgee in the 2001-2003 film adaptation of the literary masterpiece: *The Lord of the Rings.* The quiet supporting hero, Sam is the bulwark that supports Frodo during his perilous journey into Mordor to destroy the One

---

[182] Bryant & Kazan, 2013, p. 23.

Ring. His steadfast heart, love for (and service to) his friend and master, and continuous optimistic outlook see them both through difficult times and grant him the courage and moral fortitude to do what is right even in the darkest times.

Having an attitude of gratitude is useless without corresponding action.

The question that should accost you daily is how do you put your gratitude into practice? Accosting is *meant* to be an uncomfortable term. Being accosted by gratitude, by humility, by selflessness, means that you are caught unawares; that you are forced to come face-to-face with an idea that you had not been prepared for. Being forced to sit with that discomfort is a sure motivation for action on your part.

Brené Brown, in her series of talks about *The Power of Vulnerability*, compares having and wearing yoga clothing to being asked to perform yoga. Her engaging oratory style imparts humor to the comparison. So many folks choose to wear gym clothes, like yoga pants, because they are comfortable and familiar, but they do not have any intention of doing exercise. She draws attention to how commonplace the misunderstanding of the importance of practicing gratitude is for mental health and happiness in our daily lives. I don't mean to say that an *attitude of gratitude* is not a positive mental state or something that shouldn't be aspired to. Getting to a place where you can genuinely feel an *attitude of gratitude* requires work to achieve. The rather pithy, Hallmark greeting card idea of gratitude cheapens the deep and meaningful emotions and actions that underscore the importance of gratitude in our daily lives.

When you arise in the morning, think of what a precious privilege it is to be alive - to breathe, to think, to enjoy, to love.
- Marcus Aurelius, Meditations

Service is a meaningful opportunity to live gratitude. In a business setting, a leader needs to give appreciation to employees who are having a difficult time. A leader can often turn around employees who are failing to meet goals, that are having interpersonal issues, or that seem to be contrary for no good reason. Gratitude confers esteem on others. True gratitude implies humility and self-knowledge. It requires that a leader must understand the intrinsic value of others, rather than just how their work serves the organization.[183]

Being thankful for work done by your employees is useful, only inasmuch as you communicate it to the employees. You should express genuine gratitude by recognizing them in front of others. Granted, you don't want to cheapen your praise by giving it too freely or too often, but using good common sense, rewarding meaningful achievement, and thanking people for their work goes a long way toward making people feel appreciated. An employee will be more motivated by receiving positive feedback based not only on routine performance but also on extraordinary achievements. Meaningful, positive performance feedback enhances intrinsic motivation[184] and is the basis of a positive, autonomy-supporting work environment.[185]

It is easy to get stuck in a tree full of monkeys when you are at work.

Envision the tree as a hierarchy. The lowest level of the tree is full of the front-line employee monkeys. The next level is front-line management monkeys, then middle management monkeys, executive monkeys near the top, and C-Suite monkeys occupying the uppermost reaches of the tree. A dictatorial monkey leader makes sure that

---

[183] (i.e., your power, ego, and reputation).
[184] Deci, 1971.
[185] Vadell & Ewing, 2011.

everyone at the top of the tree, looking down, sees only smiles looking up at him through the leaves. He uses coercion and the threat of retribution to keep people in line. Those miserable monkeys in the bottom branches of the tree looking up at their bosses see only monkey butt.[186] Every monkey (employee) deserves to have their day in the sun. If you have gotten to the point where you are an angry, dictatorial monkey in a tree, you have failed to understand and practice gratitude and servanthood.

Take the time to take a step back and reflect. Recognize that the employees that you have hired and trained are your most important asset. Without them, you would not be in the leadership role you enjoy. Be actively grateful for their work *and* of them as individuals. If you embody that perspective, your actions will be inspired by the positive outlook you have trained yourself to experience.

As a nuclear Missile Combat Crew Commander, operational knowledge is constantly tested. In the nuclear field, *there is no room for incomplete knowledge or substandard performance.*[187] Regardless of the passing score of 90 percent on monthly tests, there was an implicit standard of perfection. Any missed questions on critical questions could mean the loss of countless lives if applied in a real-world operational scenario. One of the knowledge areas missileers are tested on is Weapon System Safety Rules (WSSRs). WSSRs served to validate that each nuclear operator knew how to launch nuclear weapons, or was versed in the safety of such weapons.

One month, on a routine recurring test, an operator missed one of the questions. He shrugged it off since missing only one still allowed for a passing grade. The next

---

[186] Sinek, 2011.
[187] Saying from Lt. Colonel Timothy Murtha, 741st Missile Squadron Director of Operations, on or around 2006. Later officially adopted by the 91st Space Wing.

day, the member was called into the unit commander's office to answer for the missed question. The member explained that a passing grade was achieved, so all was well. The commander quickly corrected the member. He asked, "What part of nuclear knowledge, particularly safety-related knowledge, don't you need to know?" As it turns out, the question missed was about the safing of the weapons. If the safing procedure was performed improperly, it could result in an inadvertent nuclear missile launch.

The commander ordered the entire unit to be re-trained on WSSR knowledge. That disciplinary measure was necessary to reinforce the necessity of the weapon's safety rules and testing competence. It provided a lesson after failure. The emotional struggle that the operator had to endure should have forced self-reflection, given him a chance to learn from failure, and acted as a catalyst to move motivation toward integration and identification.[188] Had the operator been more internally motivated to understand the material and dedicate himself to excellence, the need for retesting and training would have been nullified.

An argument could be made that the punishment was punitive out of proportion to the error and that punishment of a group for the actions of a single individual is unethical, but that person, in this instance, suffers from a misapprehension of the crucial nature of the ICBM mission and the team culture that had to be developed and maintained there.

---

[188] Figure 16.

Chapter Recap

Part of being the kind of leader that people want to follow is embodying an unstoppable force of will and optimism.
- Cultivate realistic optimism, then grow it!
- Practice gratitude until it becomes a mindset.
- Appreciate the people you lead and show them that you do in tangible ways.

Leading with Humility

Remain humble, remain simple.
The more you are so, the more good you will do.
- Saint John Vianney

Code change time had come again. Code change in the ICBM community meant that two crews, and four total missileers, were required to spend five days on alert in the missile field. It is one of the most stressful and technically demanding operations we conduct during the year. The crews are required to not only swap the codes used in the LCC but also are required to coordinate with the maintenance and security teams out in the field performing the complementary code swap-outs at the ICBMs themselves.

These complementary code components comprise the system that ensures command and control; the ability to launch or inhibit the launch of nuclear weapons. There are hundreds of documented actions and phone calls in that narrow space of time that the crews are responsible for. Pieces of the actual launch console are even physically removed and replaced during the operation. There are many technical orders and instructions that must be followed perfectly during code change, including the unclassified AFI 91-114.

> 9.1. Do not let an individual, a code courier team, or an installation team handle, have access to, or have any combination of codes or encoder or decoder devices, at the same time that reveals the information needed to enable or launch a nuclear weapon. A Two-Person Concept team must control any device containing operational code data until the data is overwritten, superseded, or destroyed.

AFI 91-114[189]

Our best crew commanders were scheduled as primary, daytime crew for the code change each year. There were enough individuals to have taken the code change duty without touching some of the primarily command-level, training, or evaluation crews. Each year, there were several of those officers who would volunteer for the duty, out of an obligation they felt to train the next generation of missileers.

This was a big sacrifice for these members and their families. While five days doesn't sound particularly onerous, the level of scrutiny that they have to endure, coupled with the amount of time in preparation and on-site, made for a challenging week. In addition, these senior-level individuals were committed, based on their positions, to a mostly Monday-to-Friday work week. While they still pulled alert, they were more likely to be found in an office, teaching, evaluating, building tests or simulation scenarios, or performing the routine management side of the ICBM business.

I had always admired the folks who would volunteer for code change when they didn't have to. I managed to be involved in a code change each year I was on the crew, despite my position as Flight Commander during my last code change. Having the humility to happily work side-by-side and train our youngest, up-and-coming missileers was something that the best leaders in the ICBM community would do routinely and I wanted to emulate that behavior. The leaders that were not interested in taking code change because they felt entitled were so obvious, one could almost point them out; they felt they were too important to perform this annoying *crew dog* task.

While *Living your Leadership,* recognize that

---

[189] 2015, p. 6.

humility is foundational to leadership practice. Humility is closely related to the practice of self-sacrifice since, as a humble leader, you are willing to make sacrifices for those you serve. Humility recognizes that none of us are perfect and that those who wish to be great, must become servants.

One thing is certain in business.
You and everyone around you will make mistakes.
- Richard Branson

You will make mistakes. There will be times you do not know what to do. This is normal; *embrace* the vulnerability that your mistakes and ignorance inspire in you. Vulnerability allows you to authentically lead your followers, instead of oppressing them. It provides needed perspective and opens the door to empathy. Similarly, it is normal not to know everything. You don't need to devalue yourself or your contributions to be humble; rather, humility acknowledges that leadership success depends greatly on the success of others.

Humility involves being accountable to others; it is listening and being other-centered to the point of personal sacrifice.[190] Humility is not self-effacement. Humility hinges on accurate self-appraisal. Do you remember the chapter on self-knowledge? Self-knowledge is a fundamental requirement in the development of that crucial leadership virtue: humility.

---

[190] Poon, 2006.

"To know oneself is, above all, to know what one lacks. It is to measure oneself against Truth, and not the other way around. The first product of self-knowledge is humility..."
- Flannery O'Connor[191] from Mystery and Manners: Occasional Prose

A humble leader freely gives affirmations without expecting any in return. A humble leader critically examines how they are perceived by others and ensures, through their considered actions, that they value others above themselves,[192] as a true servant. Servanthood is something that will be discussed in a later chapter, but that goes hand-in-hand with the practice of humility.

How do others see the leader? As a leader better understands the perceptions of others, they become more socially aware. This perceptive ability is like a mirror. A self-aware leader will seek to align the perception of themselves to who they authentically are. Changing behavior to align values with perception is the opposite of play-acting or putting on a façade.

Everything will line up perfectly when knowing and living the truth becomes more important than looking good.
- Alan Cohen [193]

The feedback a leader gets from that mirror should be mindfully incorporated into their self-concept. Truly humble leaders value feedback from others to the point where they will seek it consistently. Humble leaders are

---

[191] Mary Flannery O'Connor (1925 - 1964) was an American novelist, short story writer, and essayist who was widely considered one of America's greatest fiction writers and a stalwart apologist for Roman Catholicism.
[192] Philippians 2:3.
[193] Prolific American author and internationally recognized speaker.

lifelong learners. They do not deceive themselves by thinking they are all-knowing or that there is nothing left to learn about themselves. Intellectual honesty is a hallmark of a humble leader.

Leadership cannot exist without Humility.
This single trait opens the leader to learning, trust, and engagement,
which represent the foundation of all great achievements.
- Cameron Morrissey [194]

Practicing genuine humility will be recognized by your followers and will grow that behavior in those followers, creating a "shared interpersonal team process (collective humility)."[195] With the pervasiveness of instant gratification, particularly evident in our *selfie culture,*[196] often incoherent attempts at individualism, genuineness and humility can be difficult concepts for some people to comprehend. It is culturally understood that the way to get ahead is to project excessive self-confidence; to be a loud, charismatic leader. Those at the forefront of the pantheon of American leaders are larger than life and are rarely known for their humility and other-centeredness.[197] This is a generalization, and it is certainly not intended to imply that any culture is more or less able to produce leaders that follow the paradigm outlined in this book.

The rare people who do become truly exceptional at something do so not because they believe they're exceptional. On the contrary, they become amazing because they're obsessed with improvement. And

---

[194] Best-selling author and management thought leader.
[195] Owens & Hekman, 2015.
[196] Meant broadly as digital narcissism; the obsessive need to compete by constantly posting enviable, exciting, or scandalous pictures on social media.
[197] Though that is not always the case, as with leaders like Harry Truman or George Washington and more.

that obsession with improvement stems from an unerring belief that they are, in fact, not that great at all. It's anti-entitlement. People who become great at something become great because they understand that they're not already great – they are mediocre, they are average – and that they could be so much better. *Mark Manson*[198]

How does a leader know that they are being ego-driven rather than humble? There are several indications to be on the lookout for. When talking to followers, a leader should not be focused on what she wants to get out of the conversation. She should not hold in her mind what she wants to say. A humble leader makes the conscious decision to listen in order to understand, not to respond.

When people talk, listen completely.
- Ernest Hemingway

Most people do not listen with the intent to understand;
they listen with the intent to reply.
- Stephen Covey

Listening is one of the most important skills a leader can develop. Followers have both things that they say and things that they *mean to say* when they speak to you.[199] There are generally acknowledged stages of the listening process. The three stages are sensing, processing, and responding.[200] Sensing involves the active use of empathy through observation of body language and unspoken cues and using that observation to understand how the other person feels. Processing is analogous to active listening where you remember what is said to you, and ask clarifying questions. You also must exercise self-

---

[198] 2016, p. 61.
[199] Cockerell, 2008.
[200] Bodie, 2011.

reflection during processing. This involves assessing what is said and comparing it to your memories and mental models. When you engage in the third part of the process – response, you do so using your body language and non-verbal cues, summarize what you heard and ask open-ended follow-up phrases like, "Here is what I heard you say" and, "Please, tell me more."

> In order to listen, it is necessary to keep quiet. I do not mean merely a sort of constraint to be physically silent and not to interrupt what someone else is saying, but rather, an interior silence in other words – a silence that not only is directed toward receiving the other person's words but also reflects a heart overflowing with a humble love, capable of full attention, friendly welcome and voluntary self-denial, and strong with the awareness of our poverty. The silence of listening is a form of attention, a gift of self to the other, and a mark of moral generosity. It should manifest an awareness of our humility. – Cardinal Sarah [201]

Active listening allows for the generation of ideas, the empowerment of followers, and the development of an inclusive atmosphere in an organization.

---

[201] The Power of Silence: Against the Dictatorship of Noise, section 143.

"I carry this card with me at all times," he said, "to remind me about the most important attribute of a leader." The card reads: **When was the last time you allowed a subordinate to change your mind about something?** *"I want you to remember this as you leave here today and rejoin the regular Army: Be a good listener."*[202]
- General Glenn K Otis [203]

    Once again Dr. Jordan Peterson's work is spot-on. His fourth rule: "Compare Yourself To Who You Were Yesterday, Not To Who Someone Else Is Today"[204] is a very powerful perspective to take. The sentiment has been shared in different forms and from many thinkers, some clichés that you probably recognize are: the grass is always greener on the other side of the fence or stop trying to keep up with the Joneses.

    Do you feel like you are competing with others? You should not. You are a leader; self-aware and grounded. Participate in healthy comparison with this maxim in mind: comparison is the thief of joy.[205] You can use comparison to your advantage with the right mental framework. The aspirations and successes of others should not make you fearful or jealous. Instead, you should celebrate their successes.

    When you compare yourself to others, ensure that the gap is realistic. If you are a casual golfer, for example, it is probably unrealistic for you to compare your last tee shot with the way that Tiger Woods crushed it off the 9th tee. If you are a casual gym user, you probably will not feel great about your progress if you compare yourself to fitness models on Instagram. Set realistic goals for yourself, but at

---

[202] Dempsey, 2017.
[203] Glenn Kay Otis (1929-2013) US Army four-star general. Quote from speech at mid-career school graduation, Fort Leavenworth, Kansas.
[204] 2018.
[205] Most often attributed to Teddy Roosevelt.

the same time, do not be afraid to aim high. Focus on strategies that will work for you to get you to that target state, rather than envying the rippling biceps and toned abs on that professional athlete. Neither of you started at peak performance. Remember to reflect on where you came from and how much work that other person put into achieving their success.

> *Don't bother trying to be better than your contemporaries or predecessors. Try to be better than yourself.*
> *- William Faulkner*

Seeking to compete with successful people, even if it is only in your mind, often means that you feel you are not good enough. If that is the case, it is time to reflect on your value system. How are you measuring your success toward embodying the values you hold dear? Everything should be measured against your value system. Does your planned improvement serve to advance your moral being? Will you be a more capable and humble leader after undertaking the work to close the gap between you and the person you are comparing yourself with? If your metric for success is a comparison to others, you have chosen an unhealthy way to measure the attainment of your goals.

> *Don't undermine your worth by comparing yourself with others. It is because we are different that each of us is special. Don't set your goals by what other people deem important. Only you know what is best for you.*
> *- Brian G. Dyson* [206]

As I was researching the subject of feedback, I

---

[206] President and CEO of Coca-Cola Enterprises. From his speech at Georgia Tech's 172nd Commencement Address 9/6/1996.

encountered an interesting perspective from Kim Scott, former director at Google and faculty member at Apple University. She is also a CEO Coach in Silicon Valley. Her impactful book on *Radical Candor* is an eye-opening narrative. One of the most impactful takeaways that relates to *Living your Leadership* is the understanding that *feedback* is annoying, but candid *guidance* is something we continuously strive to give, receive, and encourage.[207]

If you feel attacked or derided when receiving accurate guidance, then you are experiencing an excess of ego. A humble, self-aware leader knows that most feedback is not a personal attack. Most feedback is nothing more than well-meaning guidance. Whether we refer to it as feedback or guidance, it is a gift. Always seek to give and invite constructive guidance. There is a natural urge to protect oneself from difficult facts and negative feedback; that is self-importance speaking.

Humility and tenderness are not virtues of the weak, but of the strong.
- Pope Francis

Remaining connected to your people will help you stay humble as you practice *Living your Leadership*. Ensure that you know about your followers and, as often as you can, visit the frontline to understand the work that you are asking your followers to do.[208] As you practice management by walking around (MBWA),[209] you will find

---

[207] Scott, 2017.
[208] In Lean system methodology, this is known as *going to gemba*, where gemba is a Japanese term meaning *the real place*. A manager goes to the real place, observes, shows respect, and seeks to understand before seeking to improve or meddle.
[209] MBWA is often credited to Hewlett Packard (HP) founders William Hewlett and David Packard, though it is a popular organizational practice and mirrors troop inspection procedures that have been in use for hundreds of years in military organizations.

problems that need solutions. Viewing the work that is done, and where the work is done, is a key leadership technique.[210] This is part and parcel of being a servant, which we will discuss in greater detail in the second half of the book.

If you wait for people to come to you, you'll only get small problems.
You must go and find them.
The big problems are where people don't realise (sic) they have one in the first place.
- W. Edwards Deming [211]

Several buzzwords have become popular over the last few decades in leadership research. Highly successful people, people like Richard Branson and Lee Iacocca, are undeniably big personalities. Entrepreneurs like Elon Musk have more than their fair share of charisma and perseverance in the face of long odds. It would be a logical mistake to assume that charisma or perseverance are the defining characteristics of successful business people or leaders.

Just because we don't see the multitude of failed big personalities, those highly motivated people that tried and failed to become the next Elon Musk, does not mean that there were not thousands of failures for every monumental success. It is a characteristic of the human mind to remain blissfully unaware of things that remain unseen. This is a form of cognitive bias.[212] You will read more about the Pareto principle later in the text, but related to that principle

---

[210] Peters & Waterman, 1982.
[211] William Edwards Deming (1900-1993). American engineer, statistician, professor, author, and expert in the field of quality management.
[212] We are all subject to cognitive biases - one of the reasons to develop our critical thinking skills is to avoid them as much as possible. Cognitive bias describes systematic errors in your mental processes that affect your perception.

is a common heuristic[213] we tend to apply unconsciously: the availability heuristic.

If you have heard of something and it comes to mind easily, then it must be representative of that circumstance. For example, I live in Florida on a lake. When I speak to any of my friends or relatives about fishing on my lake, they warn me about the prevalence of crocodiles and the danger they pose in Florida. Crocs are big and scary! They have lots of teeth! I saw the movie *Lake Placid* and man, I don't want to encounter one of those in the wild! If you did the most basic internet search, you'd find that there are roughly 3 serious crocodile incidents per year in the entire state of Florida. That is something like a 1 in over 3 million chance of a crocodile attacking you. Granted those numbers are escalated when you are near a body of water, but also consider that the lake in question is landlocked and that the small community has had their kids swimming, fishing, and otherwise playing in it for years and no one has even seen a reptile larger than a gecko in there and you can start to dispel the idea that a crocodile attack is likely.

Given a heightened understanding of cognitive bias and dangerous mental shortcuts like heuristics, it is easier to avoid them. You must understand that the world we live in is a complex place and that your mind is trained to think in ways that maximize your evolutionary chances of survival and reproduction. Faster decisions mean food on the table in lean times and a better chance in the competitive and fast moving work environment. If you fail to recognize and question your mental processes, you will likely fall prey to cognitive biases. In a world that markets

---

[213] A mental shortcut. It is lazy thinking, but something we all do. Our brains are efficient and tend to simplify whenever convenient. Heuristics allow us to make faster decisions and simplify the complex. They can be especially dangerous when considering nuanced situations like politics, leadership, or ethics.

products and strategizes political campaigns to appeal to implicit bias, critical thinking is more necessary than ever before.

Getting back to glossing-over the fact that there were an enormous number of failed entrepreneurs for every one successful Elon Musk, it becomes more obvious that, given the well-publicized information on the highly successful and crass or egotistical leaders, we are more likely to believe that success for this type of leaders is the norm, rather than the exception. Consequently, the attributes of the famous leaders we know about must be representative of all successful leaders and should be emulated to attain their level of success. That is lazy thinking.

> That same brutal principle of unequal distribution applies outside the financial domain— indeed, anywhere that creative production is required. The majority of scientific papers are published by a very small group of scientists. A tiny proportion of musicians produces almost all the recorded commercial music. Just a handful of authors sell all the books. A million and a half separately titled books (!) sell each year in the US. However, only five hundred of these sell more than a hundred thousand copies. Similarly, just four classical composers (Bach, Beethoven, Mozart, and Tchaikovsky) wrote almost all the music played by modern orchestras. Bach, for his part, composed so prolifically that it would take decades of work merely to hand-copy his scores, yet only a small fraction of this prodigious output is commonly performed. *Jordan Peterson*[214]

---

[214] 2018. In the section on Price's Law, p. 26-27

Oliver Burkeman in his excellent book, *The Antidote*,[215] notes that there are probably more unsuccessful people with those types of characteristics than there are successful people. People who are exceptional risk-takers fail more often than they succeed. How many people visit a casino, gamble a large amount of money on a long shot, and win substantial sums of money? The answer is, of course, far fewer than those who lose at least their initial stake. Otherwise, casinos would go out of business.

Charisma is not, in and of itself, a bad thing. Transformational leaders rely on charisma and enthusiasm to motivate their followers and obtain a groundswell of support;[216] although, possessing charisma alone does not make a transformational leader.[217] Charisma is not the dark side of humility; narcissism and egotism are. Many charismatic leaders are also humble. They grew up out of humble beginnings or they understand the importance of others over self.

It is often easier to follow a leader who has an excess of charisma because they are inspiring. One of the things to look out for, though, is that charismatic leaders may use this power of influence to gain a following based on their cult of personality. Followers may be more focused on their desire to please and to follow their charismatic leader than do what is best for the organization or its mission.

I do not mean to imply that all CEOs will be successful because they are charismatic. Many charismatic leaders fail miserably. In his book, *Good to Great: Why Some Companies Make the Leap and Others Don't*,[218] Jim Collins describes several of the CEOs of his *Good to Great* companies as humble. They are fifth level leaders; leaders

---

[215] Burkeman, O., 2012.
[216] Stone, Russell, & Patterson, 2004.
[217] Parry & Proctor-Thompson, 2002; Bass, 1985.
[218] Collins, J., 2001a.

that have several attributes that are well-defined by Collins.[219]

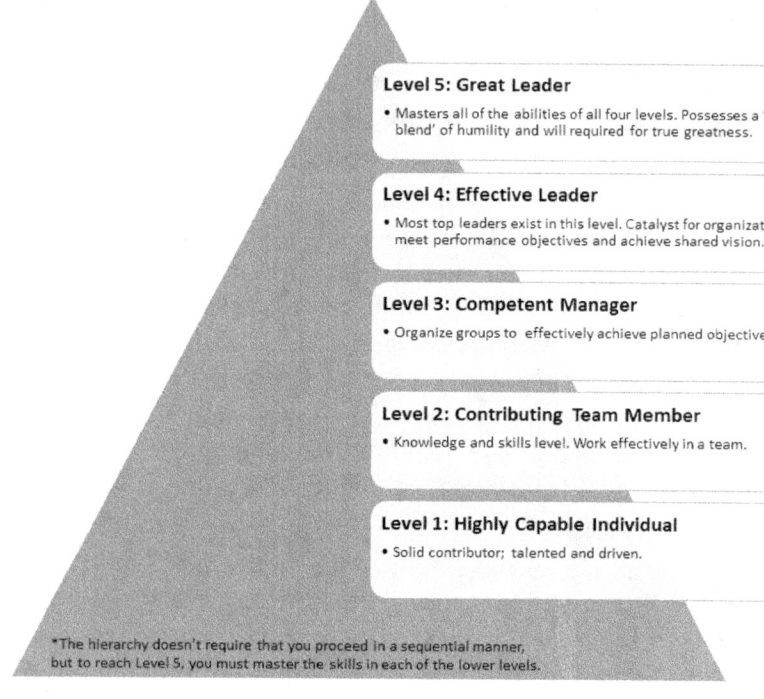

Figure 9. Collins' Level 5 Hierarchy[220]

Level 5 leaders combine *deep personal humility with intense professional will* and are not typically in-your-face, large-and-in-charge celebrities, but are *mild-mannered, steely leaders.*[221] Collins stops short of providing a detailed list of steps that lead to Level 5 Leadership. Rather, he asserts that a leader with the *seed* of Level 5 leadership should endeavor to implement the other conditions he identifies in his *Good to Great* companies.

There is a close relationship between humility and

---

[219] See figure 9.
[220] Adapted from Collins, 2001b, p. 5.
[221] Collins, 2001b.

authenticity. These two attributes, humility and authenticity, were rarely mentioned one without the other in the recent past.[222] Thomas Merton wrote extensively on finding and reconciling with one's true self. His theological work identified the need for humility in the face of dialogue with *the other*[223] and the ability to be truly focused on the *other* as a mark of humility in a leader.[224] Humility implies a self-knowledge and consequent self-acceptance that allows a leader to put another's concerns ahead of their own.[225] Humility urges us to understand and accept our strengths and limitations and by so doing, use our strengths in the service of others. A person who achieves the routine practice of humility has surpassed the *esteem* portion of Maslow's Hierarchy and is well on their way to self-actualization.

The great bard, William Shakespeare, through the wise Polonius, bestowed this advice for Laertes before Polonius' journey to France.

> And these few precepts in thy memory
> See thou character. Give thy thoughts no tongue,
> Nor any unproportioned thought his act.
> Be thou familiar, but by no means vulgar.
> Those friends thou hast, and their adoption tried,
> Grapple them to thy soul with hoops of steel;
> But do not dull thy palm with entertainment
> Of each new-hatch'd, unfledged comrade. Beware
> Of entrance to a quarrel, but being in,
> Bear't that the opposed may beware of thee.
> Give every man thy ear, but few thy voice;
> Take each man's censure, but reserve thy judgment.
> Costly thy habit as thy purse can buy,

---

[222] Vergote, 1988.
[223] Merton, 1972.
[224] Spencer, 2007.
[225] Sandage & Wiens, 2001.

> But not express'd in fancy; rich, not gaudy;
> For the apparel oft proclaims the man,
> And they in France of the best rank and station
> Are of a most select and generous chief in that.
> Neither a borrower nor a lender be;
> For loan oft loses both itself and friend,
> And borrowing dulls the edge of husbandry.
> This above all: to thine ownself be true,
> And it must follow, as the night the day,
> Thou canst not then be false to any man.
> *Polonius to Laertes in Hamlet, Act 1, Scene 3*

In traditional fashion, the father blesses his son before a long voyage, often accompanied by well-intentioned advice. This is the same blessing that an overeager and disobedient son, Robinson Crusoe, forfeits when he leaves home for the sea...and we know how that turns out. In his advice, Polonius echoes several tried and true maxims, among them the idea of humility and authenticity.

A brief portion of this text should be dedicated to the idea of the transfer of power, of succession planning. Through the lens of *Living your Leadership,* it is evident that, with the transfer of power, humility should play a major role.

> *Do you wish to rise?*
> *Begin by descending.*
> *You plan a tower that will pierce the clouds?*
> *Lay first the foundation of humility.*
> *- Saint Augustine of Hippo*

Take the history that Herodotus relates to us concerning Cyrus the Great, King of Persia, and Croesus the Lydian king[226] in about 547 BCE. Upon conquering the city of Sardis, Cyrus II sat with his prisoner, who relayed to him the folly of what he observed occurring in his former capital, Sardis. The violent power transfer had taken place. Sardis had been taken and Cyrus was allowing his Persian forces to sack the city and take away its treasures.

After some time in thought, Croesus questioned Cyrus about what Cyrus was seeing when he looked at the occupied city. Cyrus answered that he saw his victorious army taking the prisoner king's wealth. Croesus looked at him and said that was not what he saw. He saw Cyrus' Persian soldiers taking Cyrus' newfound wealth from his conquered city.

This historical tale, related to us by one of the preeminent historians of the time, should be a cautionary tale for any leader that takes over a team. As they assume the reins of leadership, the leader should not try to immediately destroy the existing culture or plunder the works of the organization that they are going to lead. Rather, they should look at the accomplishments and the follies of their new organization and give due credit for the current state to the old leader. In humility, the new leader should assume the reins of leadership with their new vision of the organization firmly in mind. Oftentimes, that would mean attempting a culture change. The culture change might even mean firing and hiring new faces.

The gentility with which a leader accomplishes the change will be immediately remarked upon and long remembered.

Is leadership a serious endeavor? Obviously, yes. Your model as a person and as a leader will inspire actions with sometimes grave consequences in your role as a leader. Does that mean that you should be a frowny, stony-faced bore? I should hope not since there is a well-studied

---

[226] Herodotus, 2007.

psychological effect indicating that we tend to distance ourselves from those we consider highly competent and who do not use either self-deprecating humor or make an occasional mistake.[227] Our most beloved and influential leaders in the last few centuries have had a lively sense of humor. Humor in our leaders generates better business outcomes and a more favorable work experience.[228] Too often the prevailing 'wisdom' from leaders is that self-care is an indulgence or that humor is not appropriate because your followers will think that you do not take your role seriously. Tell that to the folks who run Wharton, MIT, London Business School and more - an explicit focus on humor and interpersonal relationships are built into their executive leadership programs.

Use your sense of humor as a leader!

It is easy to take ourselves too seriously as leaders. We are in charge of people and assets, and that can easily imbue a false sense of importance to our work lives. Leaders often take themselves too seriously.[229] Exercising your funny bone is freeing in that respect.

---

[227] For more information, research the Pratfall Effect.
[228] Lynch, 2009.
[229] Vanderkam, 2012.

Do not take life too seriously. You willl never get out alive. – Elbert Hubbard

Figure 10. The humorless boss

Many leaders seem to think that a sense of humor is out of place in business. They would be right if they were only referring to humor that is constantly self-deprecating, inappropriate, or demeaning to others, the organization, or mission.

> *A sense of humor is part of the art of leadership, of getting along with people, of getting things done.*
> *- Dwight D. Eisenhower*

Assuming that you can draw the line between what is appropriate for the situation and what is not, humor has many tangible benefits.
1. It puts people at ease. This can be especially useful in our busy workplace. As we refuse to take ourselves too seriously, we bring a sense of levity

and humility to the office.
2. Your team will benefit from the use of humor. Not only does humor help make the delivery of difficult news more palatable, but it helps get teams over the storming hump by building team cohesion.
3. Leaders who can laugh at themselves are more likable. You do not have to be a comedian to exercise humor. Practicing an appropriate amount of humor ensures that you are not a fool but that you are someone whom people want to be around.
4. Humor can be both motivating and serve to emphasize a point. Smile and laugh, your followers will smile, too.[230] People are more likely to remember a point made with a joke or a quip.
5. Humor can provide mental and emotional distance in a difficult situation. Making light of a tough situation can put the struggle in perspective and allow the release of negative emotion.
6. In addition to perspective, humor can spark creativity. Creativity is a powerful cognitive force that pays huge benefits in work and life.[231]

Using humor can be a daunting prospect, especially to those introverts among us. It involves risk,[232] but the rewards far outweigh them.

When you were made a leader, you weren't given a crown; you were given the responsibility to bring out the best in others.
- Jack Welch

---

[230] Carnegie, 1998.
[231] Csikszentmihalyi, 1990.
[232] Taylor, 2013.

Chapter Recap

Humility is a foundational leadership practice.
- Humility is not self-effacement. It relies on an accurate understanding of self, other-centeredness, and social awareness.
- Humble leaders avoid self-deception and are lifelong learners.
- Listen to others with the intent to understand, not respond.
- Get out to the 'front line' where the work happens.
- Don't be afraid of your sense of humor. You will experience greater connection and efficacy if you show your humanity using humor.

Application of Self-Leadership

Outstanding leaders go out of their way to boost the self-esteem of their personnel. If people believe in themselves, it's amazing what they can accomplish.
-Sam Walton

My first military assignment was to the idyllic central coast of California for space and missile training. As I progressed through my technical training in space and ICBM operations, I began to think about what I needed to do to mold myself into the kind of leader I wanted to be. I started reading various books on leadership and personal growth. I began my master's degree, and I strove to emulate the behaviors I saw in the leaders I admired around me.

Minot Air Force Base, North Dakota was where I would call home for four long years (less my time spent deployed in Iraq). I was an ICBM operator and worked my way from the deputy position up to flight commander. I had operational control of approximately 60 individuals and an extraordinary amount of strategic nuclear assets. The leadership atmosphere at Minot was very much like a pressure cooker. There were constant tests and evaluations, with nearly 300 junior officers vying for the same types of positions. Cronyism and politics undeniably played a large part in promotion. There was a major struggle to recognize merit, but all too often, there is so little quantitative difference between one junior officer and another that other factors tended to play a large role in advancement.

I had the opportunity to view leadership through the lens of high-stakes operational military leadership in Minot, North Dakota. A lot of the commanders had to deal with unenviable situations under intense scrutiny. Watching their reactions to difficult situations was more than instructive; it constituted a major paradigm shift in how I thought of leadership. In many cases, as you can imagine, draconian decisions were made in the pressure-cooker environment. Mistakes often came with consequences (punishments) that were way out of proportion in comparison with their actual impact. Leaders who, in less stressful situations, would have balked from meting out such severe punishment would be responsible for the most heinous degradations of those below them. The thrust of many of the lessons I learned from my time in North Dakota was what *not* to do as a leader.

Of course, there were outstanding examples of humble, authentic leadership – the best leaders rise to the occasion in those kinds of environments. But unfortunately, those examples were not emulated by everyone. I had the opportunity to work with, and for, many of those incredible leaders. The level of self-sacrifice and dedication by several commanders was more than inspirational; it was life-changing.

The most prevalent form of feedback is social feedback. From the moment you step outside you have the opportunity for interaction. In our connected world, you may receive feedback based on your social media presence before you are fully awake.[233] Part of the human evolutionary makeup is the imperative to socially *fit in*. A leader is no different. Self-Leadership imbues the process of self-monitoring with awareness which allows us to notice cues from our social environment.[234] The reciprocal actions and consequences inform our future behavior in the social setting. *Unambiguous, plentiful, and consistent*[235]

---

[233] For best sleep health, it is not recommended to use screens right before you fall asleep or as soon as you wake up. Allowing your body and mind rest from the demands of mobile devices is a healthy practice.
[234] Gardner & Cole, 1988.
[235] Leonard, Beauvais, & Scholl, 1995, p. 323.

feedback contributes to forming solid self-perception.

In the work setting, an employee receives constant feedback from coworkers and supervisors concerning task-specific performance. Social cues embedded in those communications let the employee know if the behavior conforms to acceptable group social norms. That feedback reinforces the employee's role-specific social identity.

Feedback from this secondary reference group[236] is internalized and contributes substantially to the employee's perception of self. The acceptance of the feedback impacts the distance between the perceived and the ideal self, which informs self-esteem in an iterative, social process.[237] [238] In the same way that your self-concept is impacted by the praise, acceptance, or criticism of others, your followers will be affected. With that understanding in mind, you should seek to employ the lessons learned about Self-Leadership for you to effectively lead them.

In his social cognitive theory, Albert Bandura examines self-regulatory processes in a social milieu. He noted that people have greater motivation to change when the results of their social learning are positively appreciated by their social group.[239] One of the most common ways that positive appreciation of change is accomplished is through recognition.

Recognition can be a double-edged sword; it can make people feel good and enhance their intrinsic motivation. However, the extrinsic nature of recognition can have negative psychological ramifications. From a behaviorist perspective, if recognition is administered in a manner that is consistent with a particular desired behavior, then it becomes a contingent reward; transactional in

---

[236] Primary reference groups are typically family units.
[237] Leonard, Beauvais, & Scholl, 1995.
[238] Bandura, 1986.
[239] Bryant & Kazan, 2013, p. 16.

nature.[240] A contingent reward serves to stimulate an individual's extrinsic motivation while causing a movement in the locus of control from an internal one toward an external one. This decrease in intrinsic motivation is an undesirable long-term outcome.

Before rewarding behavioral change, focus on the effect that praise will have on an individual and the group. Attempt to catch a follower in the act that you would like to recognize and reward. If an award is given spontaneously in front of subordinates and superiors, it is more likely to positively motivate.[241] [242]

A reward should be temporally close to the event itself to increase the perception of the relevance of the reward to the action for the individual. Even a small good behavior, when recognized, can have a huge impact on future performance.[243] There can be a transactional element to verbal praise[244] and so we should carefully regulate our offering of praise to make sure it does not become the *carrot* in the extrinsic *stick and carrot* approach to behavior management.

---

[240] Bass, 1985.
[241] Cameron, Pierce, Banko & Gear, 2005.
[242] Deci, Connell, & Ryan, 1989.
[243] Poore, 2012.
[244] Yukl, 1999.

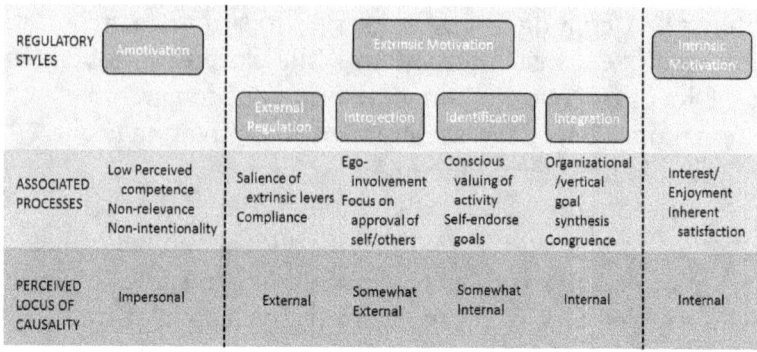

Figure 11. A Taxonomy of Human Motivation[245]

Should an individual receive praise often compared to their peers, then it may be a good idea to encourage them differently. You may choose to encourage the awardee to coach fellow employees in the behaviors that they are routinely praised for, for instance. Encouragement should be more often applied to those who would benefit from it – the mid-low achievers. Although, in all, genuine appreciation should be given freely and often.[246]

Valuing individuals should become ingrained to the point where it is an entirely ubiquitous part of organizational culture, much in the same way as expressed by the Disney paradigm: *Gratitude improves attitude.* Disney renames their employees *Cast Members* and affords them the respect and responsibility to make a difference.[247]

This paradigm shift involves seeing employees with compassion. For example, do not think, "My manning is strained because Larry is taking too much time off." Rather, "Larry has been having a rough time with his custody agreement and needs some time for his family. Maybe we should write him a sympathy card and offer him

---

[245] *Adapted from Ryan & Deci, 2000.
[246] Cashman, 2008.
[247] Poore, 2012.

counseling resources." Recognition works the same way. "Sandy just finished her MA in Education; we should celebrate her life achievement!" Though it is not of any financial value to the organization, Sandy just accomplished something laudable and deserves recognition from her leaders. Small, individualized recognition can make a large impact on an employee's outlook and effort.

When a genuine accomplishment is attained by a high achiever, it is sometimes not credited so that others will not feel unappreciated in comparison. This is a mistake. Failing to recognize that person harms overall morale and motivation. By refusing to acknowledge genuinely impressive accomplishments as they happen, the overall expectations for the group are lowered. Less impressive performance starts to be seen in the same light as truly exceptional performance. This removes the motivational incentive to struggle for exceptional achievement when the simply adequate will earn the same recognition. It makes no logical sense to reward mediocre performance, just as it makes no sense to punish your highly motivated performers.

There is a positive effect when appropriate and timely recognition is applied to low-achievers. Transference of confidence is known as the Pygmalion or Rosenthal effect.[248] A teacher or another adult, who believes in a person's innate potential, causes such a person to flourish based on that positive expectation. This is a transfer of confidence. A leader can have the same effect on their followers. A leader who truly believes and expresses confidence in the potential and abilities of their followers will inspire confidence in those followers.

How leaders handle adversity – their ability to find meaning in negative events and yet push forward – is an indication of perseverance. Take a traumatic situation and

---

[248] Bryant & Kazan, 2013, p. 68.

look at it as a learning experience; focus on the positive effect, if there are any – leaders who can do this and come away stronger are better leaders for it.[249]

Steven Covey popularized the 90/10 rule. He is one of the most popular thinkers in the management and leadership development sphere, having authored several New York Times Best Sellers on those subjects. The 90/10 rule is a bit less complex and more widely applicable than many of the other practical applications of psychological theories for management and leadership. In life and leadership, 10% of what happens to you is out of your control, and 90% of a situation is your reaction to it.

I would be remiss if I didn't mention the 90/10 rule while discussing the choice of attitude, positivity, and motivation. Viktor Frankl understood our obligation to choose and our ability to do so as an exercise of our human freedom. His internment in a concentration camp is certainly a much starker reality than any situation we will ever find ourselves in.[250] Frankl's ideas about the search for meaning gave rise to his theory of logotherapy. Logotherapy revolves around the pursuit of meaning for a person's life.

Leaders are constantly on display. Their reactions to anything - from policy change to criticism, to organizational change - determine what followers' reactions will be. Let's say one of your employees accidentally splashed hot coffee on your shirt as you turned to a corner. Would you curse? Would you glare? Would you take that brief moment described by Victor Frankl and choose to react in a way that will speak to your leadership practice? This is a deliberately easy example.

---

[249] Bennis & Thomas, 2002b.
[250] Viktor Frankl (1905 - 1997) was an Austrian neurologist and psychiatrist; inventor of logotherapy. Between 1942 and 1945 he labored in four Nazi concentration camps, including Auschwitz. His parents, brother, and pregnant wife perished in the Holocaust.

Consider this scenario; your executive has decided not to fund your pet project. You find out about their decision just before your morning meeting. All of your employees and your management team attend this meeting and look to you for leadership. Will you allow that negative situation – that rejection – to color your attitude?

Your first thought before you enter the room full of your followers must be "I am their leader. They look to me for motivation; for guidance." Your attitude at this meeting could very well shape the rest of their interactions for that day and beyond. Reflect on the overall objective of your work unit. Consider that there are always other ways to address rejected ideas, and perhaps solicit ideas from your staff to counter the rejection. This, in turn, involves and empowers your employees. Consequently, involving your followers in the process increases their intrinsic motivation to perform, by increasing their perceived autonomy because they want to help someone who looked to them for assistance.

The 90/10 rule is more than just a reminder to *be on your best behavior*. It is a lesson that you should keep in mind at all times. It is something to ingrain in your daily practice to the point where it becomes second nature. Remember that your response determines the outcome of events, rather than the event determining your response. You are in control of your attitude by choice.

You have the freedom and, as the leader, the obligation to respond appropriately.

As a self-leader, you learn to understand the rules of the social game being played and will be able to determine whether or not you play those games. This simultaneous perception and choice allow followers to see that the leader is demonstrably *authentic*. Exercising that choice, making informed decisions is a hallmark of an effective self-leader.[251]

---

[251] Bryant & Kazan, 2013, p. 41.

Chapter Recap

Self-leaders are humble and authentic. They understand social cues and have an unshakeable understanding and appreciation of self.
- Encourage and practice feedback.
- Employ feedback and reward in such a way that it serves to increase intrinsic motivation in your followers.
- Though your leadership endeavors are difficult, endeavor to persevere.
- Learn to choose your reaction to situations.

Leading Others

*Leadership is all about people.
It is not about organizations.
It is not about plans.
It is not about strategies.
It is all about people--motivating people to get the job done.
You have to be people-centered.
- Colin Powell*

The Declaration of Independence, July 4, 1776 by John Trumbull

Management vs Leadership

> *Management is the most noble of professions if it's practiced well. No other occupation offers as many ways to help others learn and grow, take responsibility and be recognized for achievement, and contribute to the success of a team.*[252]
> *- Clayton M. Christensen* [253]

    Labor negotiations had started. The atmosphere in every Biomed shop in Northern California had been tense for months. Some major, unpopular changes had reduced overtime and impacted fringe benefits like the use of company vehicles. The talk of strike abounded, and sympathy strikes had already garnered more support than typical from the usually-reticent group of engineers.

    I was excited, though. I had been involved in many of the changes that had occurred, planning and executing some of them as the project management lead. My boss - we'll call him Steve - had authorized me to be present during the opening stages of negotiations as a subject matter expert, and I couldn't have been more pleased to learn about the inner workings of the negotiation process.

    After I parked, checked my appearance in the reflection of my car (I was wearing one of the few suits I owned at the time and was nervous about how it looked on me), and grabbed my case full of related files, I walked toward the entrance of the union headquarters. I was met halfway by Steve and his boss (the executive). Without looking at me, the executive turned to Steve and inaudibly spoke to him for a minute before turning away and walking

---

[252] *http://hbr.org/2010/07/how-will-you-measure-your-life/ar/2*
[253] Clayton Magleby Christensen is a professor of Business Administration at the Harvard Business School and acknowledged expert on innovation and growth.

into the building. To his credit, Steve looked chagrined when he told me that I wasn't welcome at negotiations. Despite having been cleared to attend by all parties, the executive had a new plan that did not involve me being present at negotiations.

I was stunned. Not because I wasn't allowed to attend anymore, though that was disappointing, but by the fact that the executive, who I had dinner with in the past and who had sent me to specialized training, didn't deign to speak to me himself. It was the casual dismissiveness that crushed any vestiges of loyalty I held for him at that moment. Steve was not off the hook at that point, either. He didn't speak a word in my defense; he just relayed the message without apology, turned his back, and walked into the building. I was left, holding my injured feelings and my case bulging with union documents in the parking lot.

At least there was a decent dim sum restaurant around the corner.

Thus far, this book has been concerned with the development of self. A leader is not fit to lead if they cannot first lead themselves. The development of self is not a step on the ladder to successfully *Living your Leadership*. It is the *foundation* of your leadership practice. Without it, your leadership would solely be based on external understanding.

Ultimately, leadership is about others. You have to care. You have to want what is best for your followers. In short, you have to give a damn! There is a necessary reciprocal relationship between the leader and the follower.[254] The maintenance of that relationship defines leadership practice.

In *Managers and Leaders: Are They Different?* I argued that a crucial difference between managers

---

[254] Kouzes & Posner, 1989.

and leaders lies in the conceptions they hold, deep in their psyches, of chaos and order. Leaders tolerate chaos and lack of structure and are prepared to keep answers in suspense, avoiding premature closure on important issues. Managers seek order and control, and are almost compulsively addicted to disposing of problems even before they understand their potential significance. In my experience, seldom do the uncertainties of potential chaos cause problems. Instead, it is the instinctive move to impose order on potential chaos that makes trouble for organizations. *Abraham Zaleznik*

Moving on to the study of leadership practices focusing primarily on others, there are several extant, popular theories. In this text, the focus will be on Transformational Leadership and Servant Leadership. Both of these two theories have a deep grounding in scholarly research and literature and are put into practice by some of the world's most successful business and spiritual leaders. Place the focus of leadership practice on others, only after an effort has been made to conform to the theory-to-practice outlined in the *self*-portion of the text.

Before you are a leader, success is all about growing yourself. When you become a leader, success is all about growing others.
- Jack Welch

I had the rare opportunity to serve in Mosul, Iraq as an electronic warfare officer liaising with the Army. Going from a high-stakes, pressure-cooker environment in Minot, North Dakota, to a leadership environment where lives are consistently on the line was an eye-opening change for me. My responsibility was to ensure the proper operation of signal jamming devices that defeated improvised explosive devices that the enemy would set for radio detonation (like a cell phone detonated bomb).

Each time a convoy would drive off the FOB (Forward Operating Base), a piece of my soul would go with them. Knowing that the education I provided those soldiers, operating and maintaining their jamming devices would inevitably either save or - if they chose to disregard it - end their lives, brought the idea of servant leadership sharply into perspective for me. I would often seek the opportunity to *roll out* with convoys so I could see the equipment while it was operating and emphasize the importance of its use.

Management is efficiency in climbing the ladder of success; leadership determines whether the ladder is leaning against the right wall.
- Stephen Covey

There is a foundational understanding of management and leadership that begs wider acceptance and understanding. Management and leadership are two different concepts. There is a simple litmus test for management versus leadership. Could a robot do your job with the appropriate programming? If you answered yes, I have bad news for you if you consider leadership and management synonymous.

Management is doing things right; leadership is doing the right things.
- Peter Drucker

Managers control processes, while leaders empower and influence people. It is a near-universal experience in the working world to have had a boss who acts only as a manager and not as a leader. That does not mean that leadership and management are in opposition to each other, as the title of this chapter may seem to suggest. Rather, they are complementary concepts since "management controls complexity [and] effective leadership produces useful change."[255]

Pure managers were scarce in the Iraqi area of operations. While engaged in combat operations and planning, I met *leaders* at all ranks, from different countries, and different military services. These soldiers *led* from the front. They did not shy away from their duty. I watched some of them bravely perish and others compassionately inspire their troops in the wake of disaster.

> *Leaders have the ability to inspire others to achieve what managers say is not feasible.*
> *- Colin Powell*

One of the main tasks of leadership is developing and communicating vision. Leaders will define the future organizational vision and goals. Management is the transportation system meant to mechanically move the organization from its current state to its future state. Leadership defines the change, shows the way, and sets the organizational destination. Management is task-oriented and works to achieve the vision leaders have clearly defined. There is always a need to manage processes, but leadership is indispensable to a successful organization.

Transformational leadership is one of the two theories that *Living your Leadership* hinges on when practicing other-centeredness. In 1978, Sir MacGregor Burns identified that leaders were either transactional or transformational.[256] The understanding of that concept has evolved to recognize that leaders operate on a continuum from transactional to transformational leadership styles.

---

[255] Kotter, 1990.
[256] Burns, 1978.

Transformational leadership characteristics include many that are also identified as positive characteristics of servant leadership. In those cases of behavioral overlap, the terms 'transformational' and 'servant' may be used interchangeably.

Measures of leadership effectiveness are often outcome measures. Outcome measures are based on profit and loss or other quantifiable measures of organizational success. If you've gotten this far in this book, then you probably understand that organizational success isn't the penultimate measure of success as a leader. A leader must also be able to empathize, treat followers with respect, and lead with humility.

Leaders with high emotional intelligence (EQ) may not be the most successful leaders when it comes to quantifiable goals (i.e. EBITDA, sales performance, etc.),[257] but that may not have anything to do with their high EQ. Rather, it may result from other qualities and habits of that individual. Does a leader need to be emotionally intelligent? Traits that point to high emotional intelligence like self-awareness and empathy are essential to *Living your Leadership*. Leaders with high EQ are passionate and logical, seamlessly combining emotions with intelligence.[258] This is a major point of intersection between the practice of transformational leadership and *Living your Leadership*.

> "Reason is always a kind of brute force; those who appeal to the head rather than the heart, however pallid and polite, are necessarily men of violence. We speak of 'touching' a man's heart, but we can do nothing to his head but hit it." – GK Chesterton[259]

---

[257] Lindebaum & Cartwright, 2011.
[258] Spencer, 2007.
[259] From "Charles II," Twelve Types. GK Chesterton 1874 - 1936 was an English writer, philosopher, lay Catholic theologian, and critic.

A true meritocracy promotes individuals who excel; those who prove themselves through superior performance. Without a meritocracy, an unhealthy skepticism in the abilities of coworkers who may have been promoted for reasons other than performance may develop. Promotion based solely on seniority may appeal to the lazy and entitled, but it is not the hallmark of an effective organization.

In ineffectual organizations, promotion is based on seniority or politicking. Milestones like promotions - or being chosen for specialized training - are a big deal to people! They serve to reinforce positive self-efficacy beliefs when properly celebrated or conferred. When rewards are handed out too often or worse, without an obvious connection to effort on the part of the recipient, the motivational benefits are undermined both for the recipient and for those who bear witness.

Traditional models of leadership are typically vertical and hierarchical. That structure is outdated and detrimental to quick, clear, and effective communication.[260] Siloed structures in the organization tend to lead to the idea that leaders of those silos are kings of their fief. There is little communication between, for example, research and development and manufacturing. All hierarchy is not bad, however. In order to ensure clear lines of communication it is necessary in a heavily matrixed organization to have a clear delineation of those leaders accountable for specific outcomes.

The flattening of the organizational structure and the decentralization of power is critical to empowering followers in an organization. The move toward a more transparent and cooperative organization which imbues followers with the authority, resources, and

---

[260] Cockerell, 2008.

responsibility,[261] while maintaining ultimate accountability in the hands of the leader, will empower employees to achieve organizational outcomes.

Hierarchical, autocratic leadership is an anathema to the *Living your Leadership* paradigm wherein followers are encouraged to participate in decision-making processes.

The Eisenhower Box

	URGENT	NOT URGENT
IMPORTANT	**DO** Get this done ASAP	**DECIDE** Put this on your schedule
NOT IMPORTANT	**DELEGATE** Can someone do it for you?	**DELETE** If you have time...

Figure 12. The Eisenhower Box

The Eisenhower box is a concrete representation of the way that a leader with a sense of priority acts in response to tasks. Every one of us has a lot of things to do; that is an immutable rule of our time. We are no longer peasant farmers ruled by a feudal lord; instead, we are leaders in the information technology age. Many leaders receive hundreds of emails per day, are in charge of dozens

---

[261] Winston, 2003.

of people, and have multiple projects in their primary occupations. Add those responsibilities to the effort and care owed to family, social, and spiritual life and you have a person who would drown in their responsibilities without prioritization.

Leaders are jugglers with too many flaming torches in the air. The Eisenhower box is one way to organize decision-making processes for maximum efficiency. Dwight Eisenhower said, "What is important is seldom urgent and what is urgent is seldom important." This tool allows a leader to address those things that require action in a structured way.

Effective leadership is putting first things first.
Effective management is discipline, carrying it out.
- Stephen Covey

Have you ever sat back and wondered what is important in your life? Of those things, how much time do you spend on each, compared with those things that you immediately reject as unimportant? Would you rank personal growth among those things that are unimportant? That is unlikely.

If we can agree that growth is important, how much time and energy are you putting toward it each day? Each week? Do you have an overall plan or strategy that you were pursuing? These types of questions have a direct bearing on whether you are pursuing your leadership journey with *intention*.

Using absolutes in your language precludes the possibility of alternative solutions or nuance.
A common aphorism for leadership is that leaders take all of the blame and none of the credit. Try to avoid any scenario where the words *all* or *none* are used in most circumstances. It is true that leaders must be in the habit of accepting blame and distributing credit (just not all of it, all

of the time). By accepting blame, a leader shields employees from repercussions and makes them feel safe and trusted.

An employee who feels trusted also feels able to contribute through moderate risk-taking and innovation. These behaviors can raise the level of team performance to new heights while at the same time strengthening the bonds of trust between the leader and the follower. You are already the leader, why do you need credit, other than to feed your ego? Allowing others to have credit for successful initiatives means that they are more likely to take the initiative in future situations.

Paul Zak, in his 2018 study on manager engagement behavior, measured by the production of the brain chemical oxytocin, developed a framework for building teams based on trust that fosters increased productivity, increased energy toward work, increased collaboration, decreased stress using fewer sick days and increased job satisfaction. The key management behaviors that Zak identified as making a positive difference in the culture of trust were: (1) Recognizing excellence. (2) Inducing "challenge stress." (3) Giving people discretion in how they do their work. (4) Enabling job crafting. (5) Sharing information broadly. (6) Intentionally building relationships. (7) Facilitating whole-person growth. (8) Showing vulnerability.

His study reaffirms the positive effect of empowering employees as a method of cultivating trust. Providing direction and delegating meaningful tasks leads to significant, positive team results. Additionally, engendering trust, taking the blame, and distributing credit promote a sense of self-worth and leads to the creation of other leaders, which is one of the distinguishing factors of leadership itself.[262] Advancing your people, expanding their leadership horizons, building them into leaders themselves is not only

---

[262] "...the function of leadership is to produce more leaders, not more followers." - Ralph Nader

a success for them but also a success for you as a leader. Robert Greenleaf established that the best test for servant leadership success, and the most difficult to administer, is asking whether those who are served can grow as persons.

Louis Efron asserts that ensuring a lasting and successful organization means that there must be foundational leadership at the core of the organization. He goes on to describe the three main parts of *foundational leadership* as establishing trust, demonstrating care, and practicing servant leadership.[263] His emphasis on transparency and integrity are crucial to the practice of *Living your Leadership*. Of special note, transparency and integrity both relate to authenticity in this paradigm.

Don't be afraid to show your vulnerability. Be transparent with your team, even when the truth may be unpopular or inconvenient.
- Bill George

You have to be honest and authentic and not hide. I think the leader today has to demonstrate both transparency and vulnerability, and with that comes truthfulness and humility.
- Howard Schultz [264]

Managers and leaders take different approaches to their work. Managers have problems that need to be solved, just like leaders. Managers use an impersonal approach when responding to problems, seeking first to *manage by exception* (MBE). That is, correcting the mistakes in the process as they occur, rather than taking a holistic view of the situation.

Leaders are active instead of reactive.

---

[263] Efron, 2015.
[264] CEO of Starbucks.

A leader sits with chaos calmly, instead of responding immediately. A leader seeks to understand before applying a solution. Leadership demands adaptation of personal approach and maintaining an active posture toward goals and problems.[265]

Systems (Lean) Thinking - Leaders vs. Managers

Managers	Leaders
Busy as a status symbol	
	Stop what you are doing to focus
Make your numbers	Evaluate the validity of your numbers and focus on what will move the needle
Spread your effort - get all your tasks done	
	Take tasks one at a time
Focused on tasks	Focused on processes and outcomes
Management dictates standards	Front line collaborates with management to create standards
Managers don't dirty themselves on the front line	Gemba - Everyone sees where the work is done as a learning and servant experience
Problems look bad - hide them	Problems are opportunities to improve - bring them into the light
Work, work, work.	Plan, Do, Study, Adjust (or Act)

Kotter notes that leadership is about anticipating and managing change, while management is necessarily a more reactionary process that tends to monitor and control complexity.[266] Leaders who focus on strategy look beyond today and set processes in place to prevent negative

---

[265] Zaleznik, 1992.
[266] Kotter, 1990.

outcomes from occurring. Today's volatile, uncertain, complex, and ambiguous (VUCA) environment[267] requires leaders more than it requires the balance to be tipped toward the pedantic and bureaucratic behaviors which are more typical of managers.

Leaders intentionally and actively mentor their employees; they strategically plan, and they genuinely care about the "people side" of the organization. Leaders are not afraid to interact meaningfully with their followers. They know that paying attention to people makes them feel appreciated;[268] it humanizes interactions and serves to strengthen the relational bond between leader and follower as the leader is committed to the interaction mindfully.

A leader is willing to have a difficult conversation when necessary. They can inspire their team, teach, and develop their followers. The competencies of good management are necessary for a successful leader, though. Do not be fooled. Should a leader focus their attention solely on change management and people leadership skills, the day-to-day operations of the complex machine of a large organization can fall into disrepair. Like so many other things in life, balance is necessary. Leaders must be adept in detail-oriented management tasks, while never abandoning their people-centric orientation; thus, a balance must be struck. Thinking back to the example at the beginning of the chapter, if Steve had balanced leadership and management appropriately and reacted to my presence differently - by acting as a mentor would have - it would have affirmed my leadership capabilities and given me an opportunity to tell a positive story about that interaction.

---

[267] Van Zyl, Campbell, & Lues, (2020). Note: the complexity involves the political, economic, technological, cultural, and educational dimensions of leadership decisions made in the VUCA environment.
[268] Atkins & Reb, 2015.

Figure 13. Pareto Graph

If you have had the opportunity to attend any Six Sigma or other process improvement training, then you are probably aware of the Pareto Principle. The Pareto Principle is an observation, not a scientific law. The idea behind the Pareto Principle is that results are not always evenly distributed. Originally, the Pareto Principle was an observation that 80% of the land in Italy was concentrated in 20% of the people.[269] Observing the chart above, you'll notice that roughly 80% of the results are due to only about 20% of the effort expended; categories A1 and A2. This means that 80% of your success during the day is only related to about 20% of your effort.

This principle can apply to almost anything during your day as a leader. It has been said that 20% of the people that you lead will take 80% of your time. Perhaps you have

---

[269] It was named after Italian economist Vilfredo Pareto in or around 1906.

also observed that 20% of your tasks take 80% of your time. After the first 20% of the effort is expended producing 80% of the results, any additional effort makes less of a difference than the first 20% did. In economics, this is referred to as the law of diminishing returns.

It should be noted that the last 20% is not unnecessary. Rather, you should take time when analyzing the tasks that you have to perform to determine which are the most important and which can wait. This is much like the Eisenhower Box: it is a valuable tool to save time for more important tasks.

Chapter Recap

Leadership is ultimately about others. Transformational and Servant Leadership theory guide the second half of this text.
- Manage processes, not people. Leaders have a vision; managers have metrics.
- Traditional leadership often involved hierarchies and direct orders. Transformational and Servant Leaders work through influence, with an emphasis on the needs of others and the character of the leader.
- A leader engenders trust, takes the blame, and distributes credit. She delegates tasks and develops her followers.

Respect and Human Dignity

...the essential qualities and values that enable one person to influence others & the capacity to reach and touch one another as caring, compassionate human beings.
- David Lawrence, MD, Former Chairman and CEO, Kaiser Foundation Health Plan, Inc.

A major change initiative was afoot in the missile operations field. The question raised was whether it would be safer and more efficient to conduct alerts that lasted three days rather than one day. This wasn't the first time this particular question had been raised, but, organizational memory being what it is, the question was asked again. There were concerns before, and there were concerns with this implementation.

Logistically, a 3-day alert would mean that a squadron would send three operators out to each of their 10 missile sites for 72 hours instead of two operators per site for 24 hours. One of the three squadrons in the wing had been volunteered to participate in the pilot effort by its commander. This decision was wildly unpopular with the entire crew force.

There were a lot of unanswered questions about the transition and the execution of the new schedule. One of the major causes of discomfort and fear revolved around concern about the impact on families. This new alert structure dictated a minimum of 80 hours away from home at a time, most often with only a day and a half off, before going right back out on alert.

A commander's call was held before the implementation of the 72-hour alert structure. A commander's call is akin to an all-hands staff meeting. The missile field does not sleep. Each day, there are at least 10 missileers from each squadron, so, 10 people at the meeting and 10 people in the missile field, received the news just before or during their alert activity. At this meeting, complaints regarding the impact on families were raised to the commander. Rather than hearing, empathizing, and validating the concerns of his multitude of followers, he responded with, "If the Air Force had wanted you to have a family, it would have issued you one." Dead silence followed. Whether or not he meant what he said, the words couldn't be unsaid and, more importantly, they couldn't be unheard. He had communicated his lack of respect for the dignity of his followers all too clearly, and the results to performance and morale were catastrophic.

Emotions are an integral part of people. Ignoring or invalidating the feelings of others is a violation of their dignity and constitutes disrespectful behavior on the part of a leader. Feelings do not trump operational requirements, especially in the military. But that is not the point here at all. A leader must take the time to acknowledge, empathize, and thereby validate the emotions of followers. Had that commander taken the time to listen to the concerns of his followers, he would have been able to validate their concerns.

One of the most sincere forms of respect is actually listening to what another has to say.
- Bryant McGill [270]

Empathy and validation may not dictate any change in the actions a leader takes, but they should play a role in the decision-making process. Caring behaviors are inherently ethical[271] and they enhance the growth of employees, in addition to improving the quality of an organization's culture.[272]

---

[270] UN-appointed Global Champion & Nobel Peace Prize nominee.
[271] Brown & Treviño, 2006.
[272] Spears, 2010, p. 26.

There is a deep--and usually frustrated--desire in the heart of everyone to act with benevolence rather than selfishness, and one fine instance of generosity can inspire dozens more.
Thus, I established a stately court where all my friends showed respect to each other and cultivated courtesy until it bloomed into perfect harmony.
- Cyrus the Great

If you took a moment right now to think back to the best leader that you've ever had, would you reminisce about how valued you felt if they yelled at you first thing in the morning? Would you look fondly back on the times that you were berated for not having done precisely what they expected you to do, but never told you precisely how to do it? I think it is far more likely that your ideal leader would have encouraged you, communicated their vision and their expectations clearly, and supported your personhood in addition to supporting your work.

Expectations run both ways. Keeping that in mind, here are some of the important expectations of leaders from experienced followers:[273]

1. Get out of your comfort zone and visit people who are doing the job. A visible leader inspires.
2. Leaders make mistakes; acknowledge and grow from them. Without that acknowledgment of error, it is unlikely that anyone will believe that you are authentic.
3. Leaders communicate with, not to, followers. Communication both up and down the chain of command will result in inclusion and transparency. Exercise and encourage candor, ensuring that you create an atmosphere of trust and non-retribution; forthrightness may be uncomfortable, but it is

---

[273] Goldfein, 1999.

necessary to encourage feedback that fuels change.[274]
4. Empowering individuals by including them and distributing authority appropriately. As you invest authority in your followers, be certain that you are not micromanaging. Micromanaging implies a lack of faith in your subordinates and those that you have entrusted with your authority.
5. Living your values and espousing the organization's ethical standards.

The value of a person (not only to the organization but in and of themselves) should not be based solely on their professional or personal achievements. Of the many follower-oriented leadership theories, both Servant and Self-Sacrificial Leadership share *other-centeredness* as the main subset of the attitudinal dimension with *valuing people* encompassed by that trait.[275]

Intrinsic motivation is built on autonomy. You are unlikely to be self-motivated if you are micromanaged. Being told what to do and how to do it takes away a person's autonomy and makes them feel incompetent. Those feelings are not likely to improve self-concept. Self-concept is based on competency beliefs, ego, and the feedback environment. Employees will exercise autonomy if encouraged by the organizational culture and the leadership style of the management staff.[276]

It is not enough to simply appreciate the work that an employee does. A person is not a product. Their efforts are valuable and they are more than a cog in the wheel of business. While critical to the organization's success, anyone is replaceable. On a purely human level, people are not replaceable. People instinctively and inherently desire

---
[274] Lorenz, 2012.
[275] Matteson & Irving, 2006.
[276] Bryant & Kazan, 2013, p. 34.

respect for their effort and for their individuality.[277]

People want to be cared for.[278] If they have loved ones, those loved ones deserve a leader's consideration, as well. Employees who are cared for will work harder and produce better results.[279] Consequent to your care and compassion, employees will tend to overlook your (probably numerous) faults.[280] Whether they take this into consideration or not, leaders are accountable to those they lead. Leaders are responsible for the consequences of the decisions they make. More importantly, leaders are accountable for followers' decisions.[281] This is something that no leader should ever take for granted or forget.

There is an unspoken, but powerful contract between the leader and their followers. The implicit agreement is that the leader will care for the followers; that their mental and physical well-being will supersede the leader's own. Additionally, the leader is responsible for the promotion and growth of their followers. The idea that the leader is accountable for those that they lead forms the basis of their mutual relational contract.

The leader acknowledges that the basic humanity of their followers is the same as their own. Position may separate the leader from the follower, but a title does not imply anything but hierarchical superiority.

Whatever is my right as a man is also the right of another; and it becomes my duty to guarantee as well as to possess.
- Thomas Paine, Rights of Man

The realization of the equality of leaders and followers should bring to mind humility. Leaders are in the position to positively influence their followers and are placed in a

---

[277] Welch & Welch, 2005, pp. 53.
[278] Noddings, 1998.
[279] Blanchard, & Johnson, 1982.
[280] Lorenz, 2012.
[281] Lorenz, 2012.

position of authority over them, despite their inherent equality. The takeaway here is twofold: 1. leaders should act in humility, understanding that they have the honor of serving their followers and, 2. with the privilege of leading comes the responsibility to lead well.

From everyone who has been given much, much will be demanded; and from the one who has been entrusted with much, much more will be asked.
- Luke 12:48 (ASV)

It is not enough to *say* that you believe in the value of people. *Living your Leadership* embraces the fundamental principle underlying Servant Leadership; that every person is part of a team and is valuable regardless of their title or position.[282] A leader must suit actions to words. If a leader says they value people, their actions must confirm it beyond any doubt.

---

[282] Page & Wong, 2000

Figure 14. Authority crushes autonomy

> *Authority is the last resort of the inept.*
> *- Chip R. Bell* [283]

I was demoted from my position as Flight Commander before being sent to Iraq. Not by my boss, though. My boss's boss decided that an example needed to be made.[284] I was one of three Flight Commanders in a

---

[283] Chip Bell is a customer loyalty consultant and best-selling author.
[284] Side note: If you ever think to yourself, "I'm going to punish someone so that an example of my righteous judgment can be attested to by the rest of my followers," you should critically examine your motivation to lead.

squadron that had just had a serious operational screw-up. None of my subordinates were involved. Since I was the longest-tenured Flight Commander, however, this Colonel decided it would send a strict message to his followers and his bosses to terminate someone.

His rationale was that there had been a breakdown of the ever-important *compliance mindset* and that those in charge (not his boss, or him, or his subordinate leaders, mind you) had promulgated a culture of non-compliance. Under those pretenses, I was demoted and happily accepted my opportunity to go make a difference in Iraq.

I was well-respected, and one of the most trusted leaders in the larger group at the time. My commander had rated me as his top junior officer in the organization. My team had been recognized time and again for performance, and the site under my command had recently been awarded as the best launch control center at the base. None of that mattered to the leader who needed to send a message.

Top-down leadership is not uncommon in the military. Structure and discipline often demand it. When a leader cannot entrust discipline to their subordinate leaders, when a leader chooses punishment to manipulate political perception, that leader has dropped an anvil on their followers.

> Man's personal dignity requires that he enjoys freedom and be able to make up his own mind when he acts. In his association with his fellows, therefore, there is every reason why his recognition of rights, observance of duties, and many-sided collaboration with other men, should be primarily a matter of his own personal decision. Each man should act on his own initiative, conviction, and sense of responsibility, not under the constant pressure of external coercion or enticement. There is nothing human about a society that is welded

together by force. Far from encouraging, as it should, the attainment of man's progress and perfection, it is merely an obstacle to his freedom. *Pope John XXIII* [285]

Ultimately, top-down leadership is detrimental to the Servant Leadership paradigm. Top-down leadership means that authority is applied directly from management onto the employees below (like monkeys in a tree). Just as this metaphorical image suggests, the exercise of that direct control means that followers have very little opportunity to succeed.

You don't lead by hitting people over the head. That's assault, not leadership.
- Dwight D. Eisenhower

Persuasion is the tool of a successful leader. Many call this 'leading through influence.' While many historically successful leaders have used positional authority, especially monarchs and military commanders, leaders in collaborative environments attempt to convince rather than direct. Influence drives consensus more assuredly than a well-reasoned argument. Leaders who choose to lead by external incentives and punishments will negate creativity, passion, and dedication in their employees.

A genuine leader is not a searcher for consensus, but a molder of consensus.
- Martin Luther King Jr.

Negative feedback is necessary for poor performance. Negative feedback does not have to mean

---

[285] Catholic Church, 1963, 34.

punishment. Constructive criticism and redirection can be extremely useful to a person when they are willing to listen and make the necessary changes to their behavior. When a leader believes in the employee and makes that confidence felt, negative feedback will inspire better performance. The willingness of an employee to accept guidance during a negative feedback session and the likelihood of the leader to guide the employee in a positive direction depends greatly on the feedback environment in an organization.

The feedback environment is defined by an organization's leadership. It is more than the sum of feedback sessions and annual performance reports; it consists of both planned and spontaneous verbal affirmation, positional promotions, monetary and other performance-based rewards. More subtle, but no less impactful, the feedback environment is influenced by *Living your Leadership*. The relationships you have developed with your followers color the feedback environment, ensuring that it is authentic and resonant. As a leader, culture is your responsibility. The feedback environment is a key component in the overall organizational culture.

Leading and managing are not synonymous as we spoke about in the chapter on leadership versus management. Another of the major differences you will find in management, as opposed to leadership, is the penchant for appearance over substance. Managers who are more concerned with the political perception of themselves than with their integrity and its consequent reputational effect amongst their followers are more common than anyone would like to believe.

We should be slow to speak and patient in listening to all…
Our ears should be wide open to our neighbor
until he seems to have said all that is in his mind.
   - St. Ignatius Loyola

During my combat deployment to Iraq in 2008-2009, I was required to play host to distinguished visitors (DVs) from the Air Force. This was my duty because I was the senior ranking Air Force officer present on the FOB. This FOB was primarily an Army base that played host to multinational forces and was accountable for the largest area of responsibility (AOR) in Iraq at the time.

Among the DVs who came to the FOB were an Air Force general and his staff. All told, there were nearly ten individuals following the general including his aide-de-camp, a Major. I met them in the late morning, immediately after checking a convoy's electronic warfare equipment so that they could *roll outside the wire*.[286] Based on the job that I was performing at the time - working with electrical equipment - I had to wear flame retardant clothing, and the only pieces I had were Army-issued camouflage. I had emailed and phoned my counterparts and my liaison in-country for Air Force-approved uniform pieces rated for flame retardancy and was told to simply wear whatever the Army provided. I acquiesced happily because it helped me fit in with the thousands of Army soldiers I worked around.

After the several-hour visit was concluded, the Major came up to me and chastised me, on behalf of the General, for not wearing an Air Force uniform during his visit. On a normal occasion, stateside, I might have taken the feedback seriously; no one wants to disappoint a high-ranking officer in their own branch of service, after all. However, in the middle of a combat zone, when wasting my time chauffeuring around a crew of non-combatants, only to have them criticize my choice of apparel, was demeaning and infuriating. His awarding me a military command coin an hour before his departure followed by

---

[286] From the relative safety of the FOB into enemy-controlled, marginal, or contested territory.

secondhand chastisement felt particularly disingenuous. It was a perfect example of the preference for appearance over substance.

1930. Respect for the human person entails respect for the rights that flow from his dignity as a creature. These rights are prior to society and must be recognized by it. They are the basis of the moral legitimacy of every authority: by flouting them, or refusing to recognize them in its positive legislation, a society undermines its own moral legitimacy. If it does not respect them, authority can rely only on force or violence to obtain obedience from its subjects…

1931. Respect for the human person proceeds by way of respect for the principle that "everyone should look upon his neighbor (without any exception) as *another self*, above all, bearing in mind his life, and the means necessary for living it with dignity." CCC[287]

---

[287] Catholic Church, 1995, Part 3, Section 1, Chapter 2, Article 3, 1930-1931.

Chapter Recap

Leaders give a damn about their people. They care greatly about them as individuals in addition to appreciating the work that they do daily.
- Encourage your followers and thoughtfully communicate expectations.
- Leaders are ultimately accountable.
- Leaders grow their people.
- The feedback environment should be defined by the leader. Affirmation of the value of the person does not mean that poor performance should be allowed to persist. Rather, transparent communication about performance deficits is necessary for improvement.
- Leaders prefer substance over appearance; they are authentic.

LIVING YOUR LEADERSHIP®

Leading with Empathy

No one cares how much you know, until they know how much you care.
- Theodore Roosevelt

If I had to choose a leader that I came into personal contact with that embodies empathy and servanthood, it would be Colonel Marné Deranger. I had the opportunity to work for Colonel Deranger after I came back from my combat deployment in Iraq. She did not know me. She only had the word of the person that I worked for at the time, and whatever information she could glean from my performance reports up to that point.

Certain criteria were understood as necessary prerequisites to becoming an ICBM operations instructor. I was not the traditional acquisition for that position. Among those included that I would have been exposed to teaching in an operational position. My career had taken me a different route while I was stationed at Minot, North Dakota and I had followed what is typically referred to as the leadership route, having been promoted from a line operator to Assistant Flight Commander to Flight Commander before being deployed.

I did have the advantage of already having a master's degree in education and had started pursuing my Ph.D. at that point, but because I didn't serve in the training squadron while at Minot AFB, I had surrendered myself to the idea that I would not qualify to take one of my dream positions as an instructor. You can imagine my shock and gratitude when I received my acceptance letter, signed by Colonel Deranger, while I was sitting in my containerized housing unit (CHU) in Mosul, Iraq.

Upon my return to the United States, I started my tenure as an instructor at what was lovingly dubbed "the schoolhouse." I was on cloud nine. Living on the beautiful central coast of California and teaching ICBM operations was a dream come true! I still vividly remember the first time I signed for control of nuclear weapons while on crew duty in North Dakota; I was enthused to imbue my students with that enthusiasm and with the lessons that I had learned in the frozen North.

I knew that there was something different about Colonel Deranger when I first walked into her office at Vandenberg Air Force Base, California in April of 2009. She greeted me at her door, smiling; she was on time for our appointment, and asked me what I needed to make the transition successful, and inquired about my family before she concerned herself with the value that I would add to her organization.

Every chance that I got from then on, I studied her actions and her words and found that they were always congruent. She would remember the names of people's children, solicit subordinates' feedback, want to know our opinion on how best to proceed with operational issues, and make herself available at any time, should an emergency arise.

I count myself as extremely privileged to have served under someone who truly embraced and inculcated a servant leadership culture. Her brand of other-focused leadership seemed at times to be contrary to the nature of our mission, especially in the environment of a teaching institution where we trained warfighters in the world's most destructive technologies. I can personally attest, however, that it was exactly what the new college graduates (our students) and her instructors (myself and my peers) needed most. We felt valued and would have done anything for her personally or for the organization.

People desperately want to be heard; they crave

meaningful leadership[288] that takes their feelings and opinions into account. Empathy is the *secret sauce* that allows leaders to meet their goals while simultaneously caring for those they lead.[289] A servant leader, like Marné Deranger, works hard to understand and empathize with others,[290] feeling *with* their followers, rather than feeling *for* them. Servant Leaders are other-centered; they value people and are oriented toward empathy.[291]

The hearing that is only in the ears is one thing.
The hearing of the understanding is another.

But the hearing of the spirit is not limited to any one faculty, to the ear, or to the mind.
Hence, it demands the emptiness of all the faculties.
And when the faculties are empty, then the whole being listens.

There is then a direct grasp of what is right there before you that can never be heard with the ear or understood with the mind.

- Chuang-Tzu[292]

Daniel Goleman[293] claims that emotional intelligence is a more important determinant for success in management than technical expertise or cognitive ability, and quantitative studies tend to agree.[294] Empathy accounted for 20% of the positive variance in leadership

---

[288] Kriger & Seng, 2005.
[289] Stefano & Wasylyshyn, 2005, p. 6.
[290] Spears, 2010, p. 27.
[291] Matteson & Irving, 2006.
[292] Found in: Rosenberg, 2015.
[293] Goleman, 2005.
[294] Chen & Jacobs, 1997.

scores in the 1954 Bell and Hall Jr. study.[295] Leaders who demonstrate empathy are more likely to be perceived as successful by their peers.[296] Some people, through nature or nurture, already possess a great deal of empathy. Experience, often hard experience, can also inculcate a deep sense of empathy in people. Absent those life experiences, empathy can still be learned through intentional practice and constant inner observation. As you notice empathy growing within you it is time to turn that emotional connection outward - turn it into action. Leaders who are lucky enough to possess high EQ scores still have to operationalize that trait when dealing with others.

If you can learn a simple trick, Scout, you'll get along a lot better with all kinds of folks.
You never really understand a person until you consider things from his point of view, until you climb inside of his skin and walk around in it.
- Atticus Finch in To Kill a Mockingbird

The "Golden Rule" is simple and memorable: Do unto others as you would want to be done to you. Though it works on the playground, it is insufficient advice for leaders who are working toward an other-focused mentality. Rather than the Golden Rule, I would urge you to consider what Dave Kerpen calls the "Platinum Rule."[297] It goes like this: Treat others as *they* would like to be treated. This takes into account individuality in an empathetic and inclusive way. Dave illustrates this with a passage from an outstanding book, *How to Win Friends and Influence People* by Dale Carnegie:

---

[295] Bell & Hall Jr., 1954.
[296] Kellett, Humphrey, & Sleeth, 2006.
[297] 2017.

Personally, I am very fond of strawberries and cream, but I have found that for some strange reason, fish prefer worms. So, when I went fishing, I didn't think about what I wanted. I thought about what they wanted. I didn't bait the hook with strawberries and cream. Rather, I dangled a worm or grasshopper in front of the fish and said: "Wouldn't you like to have that?"

Growing empathy is necessary for leaders,[298] especially in our disconnected world. Despite the perception of a globally-linked, internet-driven society making the world smaller, implying people are more engaged with each other, the reverse is actually true. Though there may be more interactions with more faces over an online meeting, there are fewer meaningful, relationship-building moments.

Interacting through screens is dehumanizing. Just visit the comments on a Facebook post or YouTube video and prepare to be shocked at what "keyboard warriors" are willing to say to another human being when they aren't looking right at them in the flesh. Having worked in a call center for several years in leadership positions, I have been privy to a good number of "customer escalations" that have required me to "de-escalate" the situation. In most cases, the person on the other end of the line has forgotten that the person they are speaking to is another human being; someone with emotions and dignity who is just trying to help.

Absent the majority of our ability to communicate socially (non-verbal cues) we are left without major touchpoints to rely on for interactive feedback. This encourages our brain to objectify the interaction in a way that minimizes the humanity of the 'other' in the

---

[298] Lipman-Blumen, 1996

communication. Over time, we may lose the ability to interact in a humane, relationship-centered way if we are too enamored of our digital communications.

> *If you wanted to design a system to break empathy, you could scarcely do better than the society we've created. And in some ways, empathy has broken. Many scientists believe it's eroding over time. For the past four decades, psychologists have measured empathy. The news is not good. Empathy has dwindled steadily, especially in the 21st century. The average person in 2009 was less empathic than 75 percent of people in 1979. Modern society is built on human connection, and our house is teetering.*[299]
> *- Jamil Zaki*[300]

The first step in curing this malady, to borrow a concept from Lean thinking, is to go to Gemba. Gemba is a Japanese word that translates to "the place where value is created." It is more than a symbolic gesture by a leader; going to Gemba is a way to show respect for the worker and the product, to assess the process, and to engage with the work being done. An over-reliance on data removes the human element from management processes and distances leaders from their people. Going to Gemba is a good start in the training that is necessary to instill a sense of empathy in leaders. A good example of this is President Abraham Lincoln, who used to get out of his office and circulate among the troops.[301] This is the way he, as a leader, could

---

[299] Zaki, 2019.
[300] A professor of psychology at Stanford University & head of the Stanford Social Neuroscience Laboratory.
[301] Phillips, 1993.

perceive, identify, then understand the trials and emotions of those he led. He could then empathically express his own emotions to his followers in a vulnerable and meaningful way.

Get your hands dirty, but do it in an authentic way.

Do it to know the work being done and grow closer to those you lead. Sit side-by-side and perform tasks on the front line. This will endear you to your people and give you a greater sense of what their lives are like on the job.

Never use this as a cynical ploy to manipulate those you lead. Not only would that be unworthy of you, but it would also be an ethical violation of the trust that you owe to those you lead by virtue of your position. Anyone who thinks employees will not see through that charade is fooling themselves, anyway.

When I think of inauthentic braggadocio, I'm reminded of a leader in healthcare that I once reported to. She made a great deal of noise about her self-sacrifice and front-line leadership, despite her executive role. As a naïve person, I took her at her word, only to find out that she had an awful reputation as a deceptive and manipulative leader, who only showed up to the front line when others were watching; later to make demands and criticisms based on what she had observed, rather than offering to help clear obstacles and support lower-level leaders in their tasks.

Engage others with the intent to listen and understand, not respond.

As you work with your front-line workers, ask questions about their work; ask them questions about the department or company. You aren't trying to get anyone in trouble or fishing for damaging information, you are having a genuine conversation. Active listening is a step toward growing empathy, strengthening relationships between people through shared dialogue and genuine concern for the other.

You can read to develop empathy! Not a surprising recommendation coming from the author of a leadership book that emphasizes the role of empathy. Reading, just like traveling, opens the human mind to the shared experience and wisdom of diverse thinkers and can broaden our mental landscape in a way that opens us to a greater shared experience with the whole human family. By experiencing the intimate lives of authors by reading various literature genres, we can open our minds to diverse thoughts, mitigating unconscious bias and bolstering our emotional intelligence.

Authenticity is key.

If you have to teach someone to understand the feelings of another, how authentic can their transformation be? If they were not empathetic before, can their empathy be believed? Is there congruence between their previously held and currently held beliefs, words, and actions? If a leader has not behaved with empathy before, then it is difficult for anyone to believe that empathy is an authentically held belief on their part.

Emotion, learning, and leading are inextricable phenomena. The lack of professional discourse regarding emotion is damaging the formation of trusting relationships, especially in leadership development. It is unclear why these invaluable social skills are not the focus of more management training, but it can be speculated that discussing emotion is a practice that requires vulnerability and, as Brené Brown reminds us, vulnerability is uncomfortable.[302] Too often, we as leaders avoid the uncomfortable but necessary conversations. These situations are opportunities for growth and should not be avoided but embraced! Maintaining focus on the other while remaining open to authentic emotional relationships is necessary and meaningful in both a professional and

---

[302] Brown, 2012.

personal sense.

Perhaps the education to become a leader is more appropriately addressed in a department of philosophy setting than in a business school setting. As we've already discussed, there is a marked difference between leaders and managers. A business program has a necessary focus on accounting and finance. These skills are necessary for running a business, but the temptation to equate a person with a number may be greater for a financier than for a philosopher. The focus in an arts and science program on liberal studies means that a more holistic approach is favored. This doesn't mean that an education focused on science or math is bad, but that those with this educational background may need to more intentionally practice empathy when making leadership decisions. Leadership should emerge as a natural and holistic function of personhood.

It is not enough to know that they see things differently. If you want to influence them, you need also to understand empathetically the power of their point of view and to feel the emotional force with which they believe in it.
- William Ury [303]

Authentic emotions come from the individual. These emotions are unsolicited and are based on in-the-moment reactions. That is not to say that they are untempered. Authentic emotions can be predetermined based on a disciplined understanding and mental models built on experience dealing with such emotions by a wise and experienced person.

You have power over your mind - not outside events. Realize this, and you will find strength.

---

[303] Co-founder of the Harvard Program on Negotiation and the International Negotiation Network with former President Jimmy Carter.

- Marcus Aurelius

Very little is more damaging to relationships, and thus leadership, than narcissism. If you start to feel your ego getting out of check, find your mentor or grab a moment of stillness for critical reflection. Empathy has no greater enemy than self-absorption.[304] Leadership is about others. Focusing on yourself contracts your worldview so you can no longer see past the end of your nose. Thinking of others first lends us the perspective that is so valuable to a leader. Perspective allows us to see the world as it is – absent petty self-absorption. Your world expands when you focus on others. You are more able to connect; to empathize compassionately when you are not at the center of your own universe.

These are leaders who are highly ambitious for the greater good. And because they're ambitious for a greater good, they feel no need to inflate their own egos. And they, according to the research, make the best business leaders. And if you look at these qualities in the context of compassion, we find that the cognitive and affective components of compassion -- understanding people and empathizing with people -- inhibits, tones down, what I call the excessive self-obsession that's in us, therefore creating the conditions for humility. *Chade-Meng Tan* [305]

An amusing article on leadership by Lt. Colonel Dan Ward talks about two views of the iconic villain Lord Darth Vader from *Star Wars*. One person described him as a tyrannical figure who commands obedience while another said he was authoritative and commanded respect.[306] The

---

[304] Goleman, 2006.
[305] Tan, 2010.
[306] Ward, 2011.

Treating employees benevolently shouldn't be viewed as an added cost that cuts into profits, but as a powerful energizer that can grow the enterprise into something far greater than one leader could envision.
- Howard Schultz

Allowing room for failure to teach a lesson means that you should provide leadership guidance. Providing that guidance after a mistake is made means that you must forgive the offense. A difficult conversation has to happen between you and the person who made the error. The conversation will be uncomfortable for you because you must point out the error to the person who made it. It will be embarrassing for the employee because they have to admit fault, repent, and ask for another chance. It is up to you to decide how to respond. When the nature of the mistake allows, choose to err on the side of kindness.

When a mistake is made, a confrontation is necessary. In the same way that leaders must hold themselves accountable, never making excuses for mistakes, they are also responsible for holding their followers accountable.

People deserve compassion and forgiveness.

Never criticize the character of a follower in the presence of other followers. You undercut their future effectiveness and teach those below you that you are not to be trusted. The ripple effects of your lack of empathy serve to destroy your organization from within. It is a pervasive rot that will eventually lead to a complete lack of trust in leadership.

Practice affirmation. Never seek to negate, offer quick solutions for, or otherwise question the feelings of your subordinates. People all have things going on in their lives. In addition to personalities and behaviors, people are shaped by their recent past. A person's attitude is often altered based on the events that have happened to them in distinction between maniacal dictators and servant leaders, among other differences, is their motivation.[307] Servant leaders pursue their vision from a place of humility, empathy, and ethical behavior; a model that is follower-centric, ennobling, and enabling.

Not to carry the Darth Vader analogy too far, but let's discuss patience in the context of the actions and bearing of the Dark Lord of the Sith. Patience is something that should be practiced, not only with yourself, but with your subordinates. Some of you probably remember the scene in *The Empire Strikes Back* where Admiral Ozzel gets Force choked by Darth Vader for coming out of light speed too late. He was in command of the task force that was to root the Rebel Alliance out of its secret base on Hoth. His reversion to realspace too close to the system alerted the Rebels to the Imperial presence, allowing them time to mount a modest defense that led to the escape of the core of the rebellion's personnel. His decision should have been well within the scope of an Admiral's practice, but that didn't matter to Darth Vader. In front of another subordinate, he calls Admiral Ozzell *clumsy* and *stupid*, attacking his character, rather than his action. Vader immediately calls the Admiral and chokes him to death in full view of the bridge crew of the Star Destroyer.

This is an extreme case of lacking empathy and patience. The illustrative nature of the event cannot be undervalued, however. As Darth Vader did not listen to his subordinates, as he failed to exercise patience with failure, managers often fail to allow their subordinates the freedom to fail. As leaders, we serve others. We understand that others will occasionally make mistakes. We are there for our followers when mistakes are made; not necessarily to punish, but to guide.

---

[307] Lad & Luechauer, 1998.

that inside her mind, she might be solving an equation, composing a sonnet, designing a hat. She might, that is, be deploying the powers of quiet. – *Susan Cain*[311]

---

[311] 2012, p. 266.

the last few hours or days.

When *Living your Leadership,* we always strive for inclusivity. By inclusion here I mean that all are welcome. There is room made for those at the margins; the chronically difficult, the impatient, the rude. Inclusivity is a function of compassion. We bring people closer to us, rather than hold them at arms-length. Once again, this is a vulnerable situation for the leader, but leadership embraces vulnerability and shows its authentic heart to all.

When visiting Capernaum, just north of the Sea of Galilee, Jesus is in a packed house, teaching and speaking with both proud religious leaders and common people.[308] The house was so full that when men came to ask for healing of a paralyzed man they had to raise the roof and lower him down to Christ. That is the inclusion we should strive for as leaders. Is your house full? Tear the roof off and let in those on the margins. Empathy, compassion, and inclusion demand that ethical behavior.

Mean-spirited criticism is futile and dangerous.[309] It is unlikely that a critical leader will ever inspire his followers to achieve. Inspiration depends on the leader believing and accepting the follower for who they are. Larry Spears suggests that empathy in servant leadership practice involves assuming the best intentions of coworkers, valuing their inherent worth as humans, while still holding people to standards of behavior.[310]

> Whoever you are, bear in mind that appearance is not reality. Some people act like extroverts, but the effort costs them energy, authenticity, and even physical health. Others seem aloof or self-contained, but their inner landscapes are rich and full of drama. So, the next time you see a person with a composed face and a soft voice, remember

---

[308] Story found in Luke, Chapter 5.
[309] Carnegie, 1998.
[310] 2005.

Treating employees benevolently shouldn't be viewed as an added cost that cuts into profits, but as a powerful energizer that can grow the enterprise into something far greater than one leader could envision.
- Howard Schultz

Allowing room for failure to teach a lesson means that you should provide leadership guidance. Providing that guidance after a mistake is made means that you must forgive the offense. A difficult conversation has to happen between you and the person who made the error. The conversation will be uncomfortable for you because you must point out the error to the person who made it. It will be embarrassing for the employee because they have to admit fault, repent, and ask for another chance. It is up to you to decide how to respond. When the nature of the mistake allows, choose to err on the side of kindness.

When a mistake is made, a confrontation is necessary. In the same way that leaders must hold themselves accountable, never making excuses for mistakes, they are also responsible for holding their followers accountable.

People deserve compassion and forgiveness.

Never criticize the character of a follower in the presence of other followers. You undercut their future effectiveness and teach those below you that you are not to be trusted. The ripple effects of your lack of empathy serve to destroy your organization from within. It is a pervasive rot that will eventually lead to a complete lack of trust in leadership.

Practice affirmation. Never seek to negate, offer quick solutions for, or otherwise question the feelings of your subordinates. People all have things going on in their lives. In addition to personalities and behaviors, people are shaped by their recent past. A person's attitude is often altered based on the events that have happened to them in

Chapter Recap

Empathy is a key component in leadership. A leader must strive to understand, to put themselves in another's shoes, and put that understanding to good use.

- Empathy can be learned, but empathy should never be inauthentic.
- Leadership depends on other focus. Narcissism is antithetical to the practice of *Living your Leadership*.
- Patience and forgiveness are skills that must be mastered for empathy to thrive.
- Affirm the feelings of your subordinates. You do not have to personally feel them or understand the emotions they experience, but that does not invalidate their authenticity.

Live Authentically

> *Being who we are requires that we can talk openly about things that are important to us, that we take a clear position on where we stand on important emotional issues, and that we clarify the limits of what is acceptable and tolerable to us in a relationship.*
> *- Harriet Lerner* [312]

Authentic leadership has been shaped in the public consciousness in the last two decades by some of the earliest popular management literature by Bill George[313] in his book, *Authentic Leadership: Rediscovering the Secrets to Creating Lasting Value.* Self-actualization, the path to self-awareness, is not to be trivialized. You cannot be expected to complete the journey in any specific time frame. An authentic leader is self-aware, and with that awareness, comes the understanding that self-actualization is a journey, though authentic leaders are often described as being self-actualized.[314]

> *Give me beauty in the inward soul;*
> *may the outward and inward man be at one.*
> *- Socrates*

As an authentic leader, self-awareness and self-regulation are necessary attributes.[315] Self-awareness, the knowledge of strengths, weaknesses, and emotions, is a necessary precursor to being able to act in a truly transparent and genuine manner. Transparency necessitates

---

[312] Dr. Lerner is a clinical psychologist and a major contributor to feminist theory and therapy.
[313] George, 2003.
[314] Kruse, 2013.
[315] Gardner, Avolio, & Walumbwa, 2005.

sameness in behavior in public and in private.[316]
Authentic self-regulation processes involve:[317]
1. Internalized regulatory system is driven by the leader's intrinsic self.
2. Unbiased processing of self-related information.
3. Actions that reflect self/core values.
4. Relational transparency.

 The crucial aspect of authenticity as it pertains to *Living your Leadership* is how others perceive the congruency of a leader's behavior with their purported values; their *true self*.[318] Authenticity cannot be developed except in community, in a dialogue,[319] not in isolation. The perception of others may not always be accurate or fair[320] in their assessment of your qualities or behavior as a leader, but developing patience and consistently showing yourself to be as you wish to seem[321] will pay dividends in the perception of your leadership over time.
 Dialogue is a necessary part of developing leadership authenticity. I am not in full accord with Berkovich[322] when he asserts that it is not possible to develop authentic potential through study and critical reflection. His point is that looking back can lead to self-deception, a common cognitive bias. It makes sense that a person would want to cast themselves in the best light possible, but that sort of self-deception runs counter to the correct application of critical self-reflection. Exploring your values, beliefs, and priorities is a necessary first step to developing your authenticity in dialogue with others.

---

[316] Albion, 2006.
[317] Berkovich, 2014.
[318] Kernis & Goldman, 2006.
[319] Berkovich, 2014.
[320] Johnson, 2003.
[321] Socrates.
[322] Berkovich, 2014, p. 246.

Though authenticity can be developed through reflection and study, leadership is a social process. The circle of dialogical pedagogy[323] is a brilliant self-referent diagram to help understand how authenticity is developed in a community.

Figure 15. The Circle of Dialogical Pedagogy[324]

Before attempting to practice authentic leadership, a leader should first develop themselves following the precepts of self-leadership theory. It is not possible to be authentic if you don't know who you are as a person; if you don't recognize your strengths and flaws. You must be

---

[323] Figure 15.
[324] Berkovich, 2014, p. 252 (used with permission)

willing to pursue a path of authenticity that is, above all, internally and externally congruent. Once you know yourself, it is then possible to proceed to the external practice of your leadership.

The privilege of a lifetime is to become who you truly are.
- C.G. Jung [325]

Though authentic leadership is a practice, the focus should not be solely on externally visible actions, but also included in your self-narrative. Authenticity requires the alignment of your thoughts and actions in practice.[326] This is not limited to your personally held beliefs regarding your leadership and moral nature. Actions that align with your internally held beliefs are of critical importance to your followers.

To be nobody but myself
- in a world which is doing its best, night and day, to make me somebody else -
means to fight the hardest battle any human can fight, and never stop fighting.
- e.e. cummings

Aligned actions will ensure that the image you are projecting is the image that is accurate and reliable. A leader should *be* as they wish to *seem*; *be* is meant to be an active verb. *Living your Leadership* is a practice that should be exercised in the open. As General George S. Patton wrote to his son, "You are always on parade." Transparent practice informs who you are as a person and leader. This shows that *Living your Leadership* requires action.

---

[325] Carl Gustav Jung (1875-1961). A Swiss psychiatrist and psychoanalyst credited with founding analytical psychology.
[326] Kouzes & Posner, 1989.

However, it goes further than mere action;[327] it is who you are.

Putting authenticity into practice starts with critical self-examination. Through self-knowledge, a leader will gain an understanding of their strengths, weaknesses, character, and flaws. Without a critical understanding of self, it is not possible to be the best version of yourself. That is of primary utility. Books, training programs, and life experiences must be incorporated and viewed through the lens of critical self-reflection for authentic self-improvement to occur.

When you are living the best version of yourself, you inspire others to live the best versions of themselves.
- Steve Maraboli [328]

Authenticity is not something that you *are* until it is something that you *practice*. Being authentic is only a useful skill if you are acting as the best version of yourself. Some people mistake authentic leadership for just coming out and being who they are in any given situation. What if that person is a jerk? An inauthentic leader will demean, intimidate, exploit, criticize, and belittle their followers,[329] but an authentically mean leader will do the same. Authentic leadership requires that a leader be the best version of themselves.

---

[327] Cashman, 2008.
[328] Dr. Maraboli is a Behavioral Scientist. He writes and speaks extensively on Motivational Psychology, Leadership Dynamics, and the Peak Performance Mindset.
[329] Sutton, 2007.

Authenticity is a collection of choices that we have to make every day. It's about the choice to show up and be real. The choice to be honest. The choice to let our true selves be seen.
- Brené Brown

Authentic Servant Leadership relies on the explicit understanding that a leader is not primarily concerned with themselves but with others. An authentic, transformational leader creates trust through transparency; they communicate and share with others.[330] They display loyalty and recognize and reward their followers.[331] Through delegation and collaboration, they empower their followers while maintaining a positive relationship that allows for scaffolding[332] to occur; acting as coach and mentor.

Effective authentic practice can be measured. This is not something that is often talked about in literature. Measuring authenticity requires soliciting feedback. Who knows you? Not just who you talk to daily or who you go drinking with at the bars at night or who was your childhood best friend. Who intimately knows your character? Who knows what you behave like when the chips are down? On the flip side, who knows what you are at your best? Who knows what you are capable of when you put your mind to it? And this is very important: who has been around to see you over a span of time? Two easily avoidable leadership assessment mistakes that are all too common are 1. Attempting to judge the effectiveness of our authentic practice ourselves, without going through the

---

[330] Gottlieb & Sanzgiri, 1996.
[331] Huber, 2007.
[332] Scaffolding is the practice of building progressively challenging lessons for learners that is integral to the theoretical Zone of Proximal Development popularized by Soviet psychologist and social constructivist Lev Vygotsky (1896-1934).

discernment of critical reflection, or 2. Asking someone who we have not known over time.

> The purpose of life seems to be to acquaint a man with himself, and whatever science or art or course of action he engages in reacts upon and illuminates the recesses of his own mind. Thus, friends seem to be only mirrors to draw out and explain to us ourselves; and that which draws us nearer our fellow man, is, that the deep Heart in one, answers the deep Heart in another, -- that we find we have (a common Nature) -- one life which runs through all individuals, and which is indeed Divine. *Ralph Waldo Emerson*

Just like life itself, leadership is a journey. It is not a destination. You do not suddenly arrive at an understanding of yourself and start behaving like an authentic, servant leader from that point forward. You are improving or backsliding all the time.[333] No one ever promised that the journey toward leadership excellence would be easy. It does not matter that you followed a formulaic approach. It does not matter that you read this or any other book. There will be setbacks. It takes perseverance to succeed in your struggle. Since we are in a constant state of change, we need to have someone who can judge the way we were versus the way we are; a friend, a mentor, a trusted family member.

Organizations have started to figure out limited ways of taking a snapshot of the whole person. By instituting measures like 360° leadership assessment, organizations can ascertain some of the strengths and weaknesses that their employees have, based on guidance from subordinates, peers, and superiors. Though this

---

[333] Algera & Lips-Wiersma, 2012.

approach is a snapshot in time and relies on preformatted questions for each person to answer, it is an invaluable tool for the person receiving the feedback. Gaining an understanding of what people at any level think of you, comparing and contrasting their opinions, and incorporating that understanding into your leadership practice allows you to present a unified, authentic image of who you are.

It is easy to relapse into old patterns of behavior if a profound change has not been internalized. This phenomenon is called the "plastic paradox." Once our brains have been 'wired' to accept a behavior as normal, it becomes more difficult to change that behavior.[334] It is referred to as a paradox because when we typically think of neuroplasticity, we think of the phenomenal ability of the brain to form and re-form new structures that align with our behavior (i.e., if you consistently drink for pleasure, your brain wires the sensations and action of drinking to the pleasure centers of your brain). Breaking those connections requires intentional and consistent behavioral change.

Consequently, internal and external checking-in and following-up are necessary. Follow-up should be accomplished at regular intervals to ensure compliance with internal expectations. Talk to your friend, the person you have chosen to hold you accountable for the change you are trying to make. Ask them to check in with you on your authenticity practice progress. Then, thank them for their feedback; especially if it is difficult.

A leader should be both who they are *and* who they want to be at all times. They are not defined or limited by the positions they are in or the rank that they hold. Are you a front-line manager? Are you a director? Are you an executive? Does any of that matter in the way you behave? Do you think a certain job title will automatically make you

---

[334] Doidge, 2007, p. xx.

a better leader?

Your *decisions* define your leadership. As your choices define you, those choices that are visible to others define your leadership in their eyes. As you do the hard work to achieve congruence between your values and actions, you will be surprised how resilient, effective, and energized you can be![335]

> *Your words and deeds must match if you expect employees to trust in your leadership.*
> *- Kevin Kruse* [336]

Regardless of the situation, whether you are in a high-stress job, a combat situation, a teaching position, or a mid-to-high level civilian job, you should be who you always strive to be. Your actions should demonstrate that you care for your people first. If you change your behavior with your situation or with your position, you are inauthentic. Anyone who has known you through that transition will become suspicious of you as a leader and as a person (and rightly so!). Those who you lead will be able to recognize the change and as a result, will resent you for it and be suspicious of your motives.

> *Leadership is not about personality, possessions, or charisma,*
> *but all about who you are as a person.*
> *I used to believe that leadership was about style*
> *but now I know that leadership is about substance, namely, character.*
> *- James C. Hunter* [337]

What others see to be true is, in the final calculation, what is true to them. Our authentic practice

---
[335] Cashman, 2008.
[336] Founder & CEO at LEADx.org, bestselling author and entrepreneur.
[337] Internationally best-selling author on Servant Leadership.

must, therefore, be entirely visible to our followers. If the perceptions of others are such a large part of what makes or breaks our authentic leadership practice, it follows that understanding others in an empathetic way is a necessity. Once we can determine how we are perceived by others, we are better able to shape their perceptions based on a change in our behavior.

It is easy to slide into manipulative behavior using this method. Manipulation of others is *not* a desirable leadership attribute. *Leadership is influence*, according to John Maxwell. As leaders, it is our responsibility to ensure that manipulation does not wear the deceptive shroud of influence.

Authenticity *demands* integrity.

Rather than thinking of the conscious change in behavior on your part as manipulation of others, think of it as bringing into alignment their *perceptions* and your *intentions*. As long as your behavior imitates your internal intentions and is aligned with your dynamic lens of self-knowledge, you can rest assured that you are not falling into a pattern of hypocrisy. By acting in such a way that your behavior is perceived in the same way as you intended it to have been perceived, the image you project to others will be more effective and authentic.

> The honesty of authenticity, projecting your true self, and being vulnerable to the criticism and view of others requires that you reject the idea of shame for your actions. So often in business, we think that a very proper and stern way of conducting ourselves as 'know-it-alls' and macho men and women is the way to be. But I actually believe that business is built on relationships. Relationships are built on trust, and trust is built on vulnerability and transparency. *Marcus Lemonis*[338]

---

[338] Serial entrepreneur, investor, CEO of Camping World, and star of CNBC's

Chapter Recap

Authentic leaders are self-aware; their actions are aligned with a deep understanding of self. They embrace self-regulatory behaviors as part of their practice of authenticity.

- Leadership is a social process that involves genuine dialogue.
- Authenticity does not imply a life lived solely for the consumption of others. A leader reflects on their personally held beliefs and acts following them; their actions are not just for show.
- If you want to measure authenticity, ask a close friend or associate; someone who knows you well.
- Authentic practice requires time to develop. Authenticity is built on the decisions you make and the actions you take.
- An authentic leader does not manipulate their followers. Their actions must mirror their internal intentions and closely-held beliefs.

The Profit.

Control and Autonomy

You can't serve if you try to control the people you serve...
- Michael Gates Gill [339]

Seventh-floor storage was a mess. I had volunteered to lead the process improvement effort to implement a 6S program[340] to increase the functionality and efficiency of the clinical technology workspace at my hospital. I had no idea that 7th-floor storage even existed until my lead engineer, Craig, walked me up there one day with a knowing smirk on his face.

Like many things in a large organization with a lot of history, there are nooks and crannies just waiting to be discovered. Seventh-floor storage had existed in its state of miserable disarray for years. To give you an idea of the unusually large space, it was about 40 feet long and 15 feet wide, with 20-foot-high ceilings.

Initially, I was excited to learn that we had additional storage that I didn't know about. A recurring complaint from the biomedical engineers was that for our large projects we always had to use an inadequate space carved out of a drafty, crowded room where unused or in-need-of-repair hospital beds were stored. There were too few outlets for their instrumentation and tools and it was a dark and depressing space. Not like the 7th-floor storage that had large windows and ample electrical outlets... Once we got to the room, however, I learned the reason that my lead engineer was chuckling to himself.

I had established the reputation of being

---

[339] 2008, p. 176.
[340] 5S derives from the 5 Japanese words that make up the stages of 5S. Each word starts with the letter "S." 6S adds the additional "S" representing safety. For more information: https://www.epa.gov/sites/production/files/2015-06/documents/module_5_6s.pdf

enthusiastic, verbally espousing the tenets of servant leadership. This was my first real position out of the military, and I was excited and enthusiastic about doing the best I could. I worked closely with my subordinates and superiors and kept the lines of communication open to my dotted line on-site and my superiors at regional headquarters.

A man named Carlos was my first supervisor after the military. He was an Air Force veteran and had worked in the Biomed field for over 30 years. I had a great deal of respect for Carlos. He had often talked about the value that he placed on mentorship as a primary quality of his leadership practice.

Back to the 7th floor. Our storage was located on a patient care floor, dealing primarily with high-acuity telemetry patients. The other end of the floor had space for staging areas and additional storage. As Craig and I stood in front of the door, I remarked how strange it was that we had such a large space dedicated to our equipment, especially since our main shop space was so small. He just laughed at me and said, "Just wait 'til you see it, Chris."

He punched in the combination and opened the door...into pure chaos. The door only cracked open about six inches before it hit an obstruction. Craig pushed a little harder and was able to get it open just enough for us to slide into the room. It was packed floor-to-ceiling, back-to-front, side-to-side with medical equipment, refuse, and old supplies. I had never seen anything like it in my professional life. I remember opening the shipping containers in Iraq when we received updated equipment and how it was typically labeled and categorized. The contrast was stark.

I'm not ashamed to admit that it was an exciting discovery for me. I have a true bias toward action and I love to take on opportunities that will allow me to get my hands dirty. By the time I got back to my office, I had a plan in mind. I called Carlos and told him about the situation. I described the process of 6S and told him that I needed some managerial latitude to make decisions that might not be incredibly popular. He happily agreed, seeing an opportunity for one of his new hires to make a real difference.

Carlos gave me the autonomy I needed to gradually empty that room and make sure that all of the pieces of equipment were disposed of, put back in use, or properly organized. That is one of the most efficient and useful spaces in the region now with enough room to store anything needed for a major technology initiative. We saved thousands of dollars alone by putting equipment back in service! I can't imagine how difficult that process would have been, how demotivated I would have been, had I not had the support and autonomy granted by Carlos.

Employees who feel a natural, internal inclination to do what they are asked to do are more likely to perform well. This is a truism you do not have to search far to find proof of. This does not mean that, as the leader, you do not have the responsibility to direct work. That is absurd.

One of the key behaviors that determine your effectiveness as an inspirational leader is finding a way to motivate employees to do something that is meaningful to them and aligns with the organizational mission. Intrinsically motivated employees will continue to perform long after any external incentives have been exhausted. An intrinsically motivated follower is a highly desirable organizational asset because they embody the internal alignment of organizational goals.

Intrinsic motivation involves performing an action based on your desire to do so, rather than external pressure or incentive. In some career fields, it is easier to find a population of employees who are motivated to do their work based on a desire to make a difference. Look at first responders and hospital personnel as examples. Many of these brave and highly motivated personnel are admittedly underpaid and overworked, but they continue to strive for excellence at their day-to-day tasks, despite the lack of external rewards. Why? Because they perceive their work as meaningful.

Locus of causality[341] sounds intensely academic. It is not as complex or highbrow as it seems. Locus of causality simply refers to the perceived source of a behavior or attitude. For example, when an individual is offered a reward for performing to a specific standard, that individual will begin to perform the task to receive the reward, not because of any native interest. Behaviorists like Watson, Skinner, and Pavlov (just to name a few) have made a huge impact on popular perception of the utility of reward and punishment as external motivating factors. So much so that bureaucratic managers have been using behaviorism in one form or another in companies for decades and lauding their successes as backed by credible 'scientific' research.

On the other end of the control spectrum lies the internal locus. Having an internal locus of causality means that you are acting based on your desire to do so. You are predisposed to act because what you are doing is aligned with your goals or your passions. Intrinsically motivated action is longer-lasting and produces positive mental models about work.

This is crucial for leaders to understand. People motivated to do their jobs just for the money are typically not as content or loyal to the company as those who do something that they love. As the locus of the motivational orientation moves from internal to external on the continuum,[342] it is detrimental to a person's self-worth.[343] An intrinsically motivated person's loci of control is

---

[341] Figure 16.
[342] See Figure 16.
[343] Deci, Connell, & Ryan, 1989.

internal. That person will work harder because they want to, not because they are being controlled.[344][345][346][347]

Choice plays a crucial role in self-determination. When a person can choose and they are also highly intrinsically motivated, they will achieve great results![348] Would you be motivated to put forth your best effort if you did not have a choice but to do what you were told? What if you were forced to complete a task that you were not interested in doing in the first place? For most people, the answer is simple: they would be less intrinsically motivated to perform the task well. Even if people are offered extrinsic rewards, they are less likely to perform well if they do not have a choice in their task assignment.

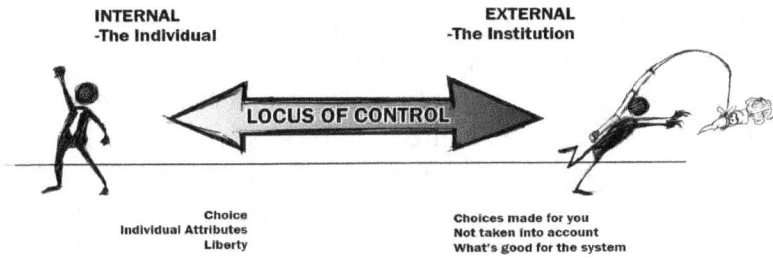

Figure 16. Locus of Control Continuum

For many leaders, it is almost instinctual to tighten control to increase efficiency. People are naturally inclined to micromanage or, if slightly more relaxed, but not too involved, manage by exception.[349] This is an anachronistic

---

[344] Burton, Lydon, D'Alessandro, & Koestner, 2006.
[345] Cameron, Pierce, Banko, & Gear, 2005.
[346] Cordova & Lepper, 1996.
[347] Deci & Ryan, 1985.
[348] Ewing, 2011.
[349] Management by exception (MBE) is a strategy that managers use when they

view of the all-encompassing bureaucratic organization. How many Dilbert[350] cartoons have been drawn about the pointy-haired boss attempting to control his subordinates? The counterintuitive truth is that investing authority in your followers, allowing them autonomy, will pay dividends in innovation and work ethic.[351] Once again, you must embrace vulnerability and cede some measure of control to lead effectively.

Leaders who control their followers, rather than trusting them by delegating, are ignoring the benefits of intrinsic motivation and high follower self-efficacy beliefs. Control decreases autonomy, which in turn, negatively affects intrinsic motivation.[352] Autonomous followers feel competent[353] because they are trusted by their leaders.

Competency beliefs are enhanced when a person believes that their behavior is self-directed or highly internal.[354] Pursuing a transformational leadership style that values the development of employees increases intrinsic motivation.[355] Individualized consideration[356] reaffirms their value, both as people and to the organization. As the individualized consideration[357] is applied, employees feel empowered to make a positive impact based on their performance,[358] shifting their locus of control in an internal direction.[359]

Transformational leadership is described as a process that motivates people by appealing to higher ideals

---

choose to deal only with outcomes or actions that fall outside of the norm.
[350] Comic strips by Scott Adams known for satirical office humor about a white-collar, micromanaged engineer, Dilbert.
[351] Amar, 2009, p. 22.
[352] Vadell & Ewing, 2011.
[353] de Charms, 1968.
[354] Ryan & Deci, 2000.
[355] Spears, 2010.
[356] Bass, 1998.
[357] See Table 2.
[358] Sendjaya & Sarros, 2002.
[359] Rotter, 1966.

and moral values, defining and articulating a vision of the future, and forming a base of credibility.[360] The transformational leader looks to the future, understands the need for change, and how to bring such understanding to followers.

As they envision the future, transformational leaders see opportunities and proactively pursue them. A positive orientation toward change is a common attribute of the transformational leader.[361] Two commonly agreed-upon characteristics of the transformational leader are (1) questioning assumptions and promoting non-traditional thinking, (2) developing their followers.[362][363]

In today's ever-changing VUCA environment, the transformational leader will be the one to bring it all together. They work to change from the inside out, focusing on the process, but not failing to remember the people involved. An organization seeking change needs transformational leaders to motivate and guide employees toward the organizational goal.[364]

Table 2. Qualities of transformational leadership styles

Idealized attributes / Influence *(transformational)*	Leaders are seen as respected, trusted role models, they can be counted on, and demonstrate high moral and ethical standards.
Inspirational motivation *(transformational)*	A leader's behavior motivates and inspires followers, team spirit is aroused, enthusiasm and optimism are displayed, and both leaders and followers create positive visions of the future.
Intellectual stimulation *(transformational)*	Leaders stimulate and encourage innovation, creativity, and questioning of old assumptions. New ideas are

---

[360] Tracey & Hinkin, 1998.
[361] Crant & Bateman, 2000.
[362] Tracey & Hinkin, 1998.
[363] Bass & Avolio, 1994.
[364] Tucker & Russell, 2004.

welcomed and there should be no fear of mistakes or going against the grain.

Idealized attributes, idealized behaviors, inspirational motivation, and intellectual stimulation constitute *Transformational Leadership*.	
Individualized consideration *(transformational)*	Special attention is paid to each individual's needs and differences. Effective listening, development of potential, and personalized interaction are all components of this leadership style.
Individualized consideration is the transformational half of a *Developmental Exchange*.	
Sources: Bass & Avolio, 1994, Bass, 1998, Avolio et al., 1999, Parry & Proctor-Thomson, 2002.	

In much the same way that prisoners become institutionalized, lowering the chance of success in their eventual transition to freedom, leaders who make their followers dependent are doing those followers a serious disservice. Any system that robs individuals of their liberty in exchange for convenience is guilty of perpetuating a cycle of dependence. It is a cycle that ultimately results in behavior that is characterized by an inability to function outside that system.

> Prudence, indeed, will dictate that Governments long established should not be changed for light and transient causes; and accordingly, all experience hath shewn, that mankind are more disposed to suffer, while evils are sufferable, than to right themselves by abolishing the forms to which they are accustomed.[365]

As employees act more like automatons, as opposed to autonomous individuals, they are less likely to produce

---

[365] Declaration of Independence, para 2, US 1776.

exceptional results. You have started treating them like machines. Like machines, employees who do not have autonomy will perform to standard – no more.

> *The most damaging phrase in the language is "We've always done it this way!"*
> *- Rear Admiral Grace Murray Hopper[366]*

It is not uncommon for a charismatic leader to fall into the same pattern as a narcissistic or controlling leader, micromanaging their followers. The trap here is more subtle, however. In the case of a charismatic leader, followers may choose emotional dependence voluntarily based on their feelings of attachment to the leader. An example of the charismatic leader from literature and history is King Henry V. The true history is a fascinating tale that is overshadowed by Shakespeare's triumphal St. Crispin's Day speech delivered by the title character, a speech still memorized and recited in schools today. That speech resulted in the English victory over the French, or so the poet would have you believe.[367] In fact, the English victory over the French at the Battle of Agincourt had more to do with the muddy battlefield being nearly impassable by French armored troops on horseback and the preponderance of longbow archers making up the remaining English force (those that weren't killed by dysentery along the march to Calais). The range of the longbow, coupled with the inability of the French to make use of their heavy mounted forces resulted in a one-sided win for the English against numerically superior French forces.

Emotional dependence is a direct result of a shift in the locus of causality from the individual to the system.

---

[366] In an interview in Information Week, March 9, 1987, p. 52.
[367] St. Crispin's Day speech can be found in William Shakespeare's play Henry V, Act IV, Scene iii.

Howell and Avolio conducted a study of 78 managers that indicated a correlation between transformational leadership behaviors and higher internal locus of control. It showed that transactional (read: behaviorist) actions resulted in poor business unit performance.[368] Transactional leaders focus on the stick and carrot approach to leading, using money or threats or other external levers to control their employees.

A leader, using emotionally abusive tactics, can cause emotional dependence, but they can just as easily do so by providing too much for subordinates. Followers will inevitably have lower self-efficacy beliefs if they do not have mastery experiences to influence their self-perception and feed their positive self-talk.[369] Mastery experiences need to be somewhat challenging; difficult to overcome, otherwise the person will feel infantilized and their experience will be cheapened. When subordinates do not feel that they are capable, they are less likely to take initiative when confronted with novel situations.

Micromanaging is a symptom of arrogance.[370]

Often, a leader will choose to focus on the process to the exclusion of the big picture. Micromanaging threatens a subordinate's perceived self by calling into question their ability to perform their job in an effective, self-directed manner. It irrevocably retards their progress toward becoming self-actualizing individual contributors. When employees feel controlled, they are demotivated.[371] When a follower is crushed under an oppressive manager, it removes their sense of agency; their locus of control is shifted away from themselves and toward the organization. Leaders who provide their employees with the autonomy to create value are encouraging the development of self-

---

[368] Howell & Avolio, 1993.
[369] Figure 3.
[370] Cockerell, 2008.
[371] Rockwell, 2013.

determination.[372]

> *We are called to live not as one without others, above or against others,
> but with and for others.*
> *- Pope Francis*

Behaviors are the physical manifestation of a person's beliefs and values.

While *Living your Leadership*, it is critical to consider stressing behaviors over goals in organizational personnel assessments. One of the fatal flaws encountered in most corporations that employ yearly evaluations and annual performance reviews is to place too much weight on the goals section of the document. There is often a disproportionately large weight given for the goals section. The goals section is quantifiable and objective-based. The behavioral section is composed of the soft skills that managers are required to display daily.

Goal setting and measurement is not inherently a bad thing. Individuals and organizations should have specific, measurable, actionable, and time-bound (SMART) goals against which to measure progress. The issue arises when those goals are pushed to the forefront at the expense of other competing concerns. The imbalance that is caused by focusing on business goals to the exclusion of more human concerns manifests itself in many ways.

The goals you find on yearly evaluations are obtained through a collective effort. Often, those goals are achieved through the efforts of hundreds, or even, thousands of people. Anyone taking responsibility for the work done on the front line is disingenuous at best.

You may have saved a few thousand dollars, but you alone certainly weren't responsible for hitting the

---

[372] Den Hartog & Belschak, 2012.

efficiency goal that was calculated in millions of dollars. In judging an individual on the goals achieved by the department during that year, there is an assumption that the individual was a necessary part of achieving each of those goals. This idea disregards at least one tenant of succession planning – no individual is crucial to any organization; anyone is replaceable.

What separates driven and charismatic individuals who have succeeded from those who have failed? It is embodied in the behavioral section of the annual interview. Key behaviors include: practicing humility, altruistic behavior, servant leadership, communication skills, accountability, and the list goes on and on.

Suppose you have an egotistical manager; one who routinely chooses to exert authoritarian control and micromanages their staff. Somehow, this manager still manages to achieve all of the department goals. Those goals are weighted at around 70%, while behaviors are only 30% weight on an annual review. Even if they score extremely low on all of the behavioral sections, the lowest *letter grade* they can get is *C-*.

Despite a keen focus on the attainment of goals, employee and customer satisfaction scores are often strikingly negative. What is the leader sacrificing to achieve those goals? If the weighting of the goal section and the behavioral section are skewed too far toward the goals, the score derived from that evaluation would indicate to anyone glancing at it that goals matter more than behavior. If that is the case, your climate assessment will reflect employee dissatisfaction.

You can whip a horse to a frenzy and beat all kinds of time records on the track, but the horse will suffer. Employees are not equine; though neither the horse nor the employee will benefit from literal or metaphorical whippings. They are human beings deserving of respect and dignity.

As leaders shift their focus to customers and quality, they realize that the old authoritarian leadership style does not work anymore. To achieve quality, service, and rapid response, leaders must utilize all available talent. They must find ways to inspire, involve, and empower employees. They must create a work environment that encourages commitment, innovation, and cooperation. Instead of evaluating, leaders now coach. Instead of doing, they delegate. Instead of telling, they facilitate. No one is expected to boss anyone. Everyone is expected to participate. *Dr. Suzanne Willis Zoglio*[373]

Dictatorial leaders represent themselves as invaluable to the organization. Why wouldn't they, after all? The desire to control others is evidence of their narcissism and an out-of-control ego. They revel in the measurable success that comes with attaining goals, regardless of the expense levied on the backs of their employees. Leaders such as these may have a venerable and charismatic public face. Traditional leadership models hail them as "heroic" leaders and they were often held up as the paradigm. In our fast-paced, technological world, with constant information overload, matrixed and complex organizations, and an increased focus on cultural adaptation in a global marketplace,[374] leaders need to be candid, flexible, proactive, humble, and empathetic. The need for commanding, ego-driven leaders has ended (and good riddance!).

The illustration of employee autonomy versus the exercise of management authority[375] indicates what happens to employees who are forced to serve under dictatorial leaders. Tyrannical leaders do not care about the

---

[373] *The Participative Leader*, p. 5.
[374] Van Zyl & Campbell, 2019
[375] Figure 14.

morale or humanity of their subordinates. They care only what their bosses think of them. They think to themselves: who is writing my paycheck? What do they care about? *Those people are below me for a reason. They exist solely to achieve the goals I am measured by.* The understanding of employees as beneath the leader is an example of *vertical* leadership and is the antithesis of a humble, servant leader. The Catechism teaches that "authority does not derive its moral legitimacy from itself. It must not behave in a despotic manner, but must act for the common good as a 'moral force based on freedom and a sense of responsibility.'"[376]

A Servant Leader realizes they and their employees are part of a team. Followers exist, for all intents and purposes, *horizontal* to the leader. Employees, front-line workers, are the most important people in the organization because they get the work done. The job of an authentic servant leader is to take care of their people. It is to clear the path for them and make sure they have the tools, time, and training necessary to get the job done efficiently and effectively.

All this talk about behaviors and goals may give the impression that behaviors are the end-all-be-all of an evaluative process. Organizational goals are not unimportant. That is an absurd idea. Measurable business success cannot be achieved without focusing on goals. The problem comes when the focus on goals overshadows attention that should be paid to the leadership behaviors. With autonomy supporting leadership, employees will want to work harder for intrinsic reasons. The result of that hard work will be the faster and superior achievement of goals.

Using emotional intelligence and sound moral reasoning, the transformational leader can motivate others to achieve beyond expectations. Moral decision-making

---

[376] CCC 1902.

involves using ethical tools to determine the moral character of a decision. In most solid ethical decision-making processes, the impact of a decision is also closely considered.

The relationship between transformational leadership and emotional intelligence is driven by the conceptual overlap between their respective characteristics. The leader's personal, emotional, and social skills[377] and the personal, social and emotional characteristics that make up EQ should be in alignment for a transformational leader to behave authentically.

Transformational-style leadership requires a certain level of political savvy. Political skill is the ability to leverage relationships to achieve organizational, team, and individual goals. Political skill is a capability that leaders must demonstrate daily.[378] There are four main practices for positive political skill:
1. social awareness,
2. interpersonal influences,
3. networking, and
4. sincerity.

Political skill, like any other leadership behavior, must be used ethically. The way a leader is perceived is mediated by the use of political skills. Conversely, political skills can be used to harm followers. It violates the respect a leader should have for their followers to influence them in an unethical way.

Misusing the influence that we have over others is the dark siren song[379] of charismatic, transformational

---

[377] Bass & Avolio, 1997.
[378] Ferris, et al., 2005.
[379] Sirens are creatures from Greek mythology that sang so beautifully that they enchanted sailors to their deaths. They famously appeared in Homer's Odyssey as they unsuccessfully attempted to lure Odysseus to his doom on his way back from the Trojan War.

leadership. It should be noted that charismatic leadership is not transformational leadership,[380] but is only part of the definition of transformational leadership as understood by the multifactor leadership questionnaire (MLQ) and other extant research.[381] Charisma is part of the *idealized influence* quality of transformational leadership.

> A fresh critical look is being taken at the issues of power and authority, and people are beginning to learn, however haltingly, to relate to one another in less coercive and more creatively supporting ways. A new moral principle is emerging, which holds that the only authority deserving one's allegiance is that which is freely and knowingly granted by the led, to the leader in response to, and in proportion to, the clearly evident servant stature of the leader. *Robert Greenleaf* [382]

---

[380] Bass, 1985.
[381] Bass & Steidlmeier, 1999.
[382] "Servant Leadership," p. 10.

Chapter Recap

Intrinsic motivation does not rely on outside consequences or contingent rewards to enhance or maintain performance. An intrinsically motivated person performs because of an innate desire to accomplish a task.

- Encouraging intrinsic motivation in employees means that they will be happier and more productive in the long term.
- Giving your followers choices is motivating since it cedes control from others to them.
- Controlling followers decreases autonomy; a crucial determinant in perceived self-direction.
- A further result of controlling employees over time, micromanaging, is that employees will become used to behaving with external control, thus determining their actions. This will preempt curiosity, initiative, and innovation.
- Behaviors are harder to measure, but they are what make up a person at work. Goals are typically a group effort and are less appropriate to weigh heavily in an annual evaluation.
- An emotionally intelligent leader considers the political and social ramifications of their words and deeds.

Leading Teams

A person who is worthy of being a leader wants power not for himself, but in order to be of service.
- Senator Sam J. Ervin, Jr.

No two teams are identical. Teams can be temporary or permanent. They can be virtual, geographically separated, small and close-knit, or giant and complex. All organizations have them and as a leader, you are responsible for the team; its dynamic, its efficacy, and its members as individuals.

That being said, focusing on the individual to the exclusion of the team constitutes a failure of vision. You are responsible for a high-performing *team*, not a group of individuals.[383] A team, working together, is greater than the sum of its parts. Leveraging team dynamics involves understanding the contributions of each individual to the group effort. Practicing transformational leadership behavior (e.g., servant leadership or mentoring) with individuals in your team adds value to the team and serves to encourage that individual in their journey toward becoming intrinsically motivated leaders themselves.

While interviewing for a director position, I was asked, "In your experience, what is the key to developing a good team?" After a moment of thought, I replied, "The most important element in developing a functional team is building it on a foundation of trust." Several weeks later, one of my 35-year union employees voiced during my first staff meeting that trust is something built through shared experience and it can be broken much more readily than it can be earned. She asked, "Why should we trust you?"

It was a valid question at the time since there had been

---

[383] Bennis, 2007.

a lot of internal bickering and management versus labor divisiveness in the past several years. Standing there, confident in my experience and my knowledge, but facing the inscrutable countenances of 40 staff members, I was struck by the frustration and pain that they had experienced. I could see it in their eyes, in the distrustful set of their shoulders as they sat, arms crossed, in their chairs around the conference table. I have made it a point to practice intentional reflection in my daily life, and that day was no exception. I reflected on the promises that had been given to me and broken in my professional life. I thought about the book that I was writing (the one you are reading now) and the practices that I had been outlining in it.

It is not in my nature to spew management jargon. In attempting to build trust in a team setting, very little turns people off as quickly as hearing slick and seemingly disingenuous phrases like *leveraging capabilities* or creating *labor/management synergy*. Trust is an emotional phenomenon[384] that should be viewed through a lens of empathy and nurtured through caring acts. How can you answer someone who asks why they should trust you, the leader when she has had her trust broken by leaders in the past?

She had asked the question during the hour that I had scheduled for the *round-robin*, a time for staff to question management about anything and everything in a non-attribution environment. This amount of time was purposefully excessive. With the level of distrust and dissatisfaction that the department had experienced in the recent past, it was important to me to air out the grievances so that we could identify and resolve them together. It was that context that gave me the answer I was looking for. I let her know that she should judge me by my actions.[385]

---

[384] Beatty & Brew, 2004.
[385] See Matthew 7:15-20.

I reminded the team that we were spending this time together to get to know each other, to talk candidly about issues, and to develop plans to deal with them *in community*. In effect, I was taking the first step in the trust narrative: I was committing to a course of action based on the team's concerns.

Regardless of the state of the organization you lead, there are fundamental leadership traits that are crucial to ensuring an enduring leadership legacy. It is easy to take from those words that I mean that your legacy of leadership within the department will live beyond your tenure. *That is not at all what I mean.* The leadership legacy can be carried on by any individual who embraces the *model* of leadership that you embodied during your tenure. A successful team requires a fundamental leadership strategy to endure.

Establishing trust among the team is a crucial step toward cohesion. There is an important distinction to be drawn between cohesiveness and conformity, however. Team cohesiveness involves allowing personal goals to be subsumed by a commitment to shared goals. Teams in danger of groupthink are typically led by charismatic leaders, those leaders who insist on conformity characterized by a suppression of individual, critical thinking.[386] Avoiding groupthink – avoiding conformity, involves leader humility and a culture of vulnerability in a team; a place where mistakes are learned from, rather than punished.

The stages of team development are forming, storming, norming, and performing.[387] In 1977, Bruce Tuckman and Mary Ann Jensen added adjourning to the model to indicate that groups complete tasks and come to a natural end.[388] Each stage of team development is necessary, and each will occur in any team, though not

---
[386] Janis, 2008.
[387] Tuckman, 1965.
[388] Tuckman & Jensen, 1977.

necessarily sequentially. The end state of the storming phase is trust amongst the members of the team. From there, establishing goals and vision, the more formulaic tasks can be attended to.

Figure 17. Tuckman's stages of group formation

Establishing trust is easier than people make it out to be. Reach out with your words and follow them with your actions. Do this consistently over time. **Trust is built on follow-through.** The onus is on the leader to demonstrate the value of their word. A promise fulfilled by action is worth more than any clever turn of phrase or clichéd leadership saying. Follow-through is most often demonstrated after difficult conversations.

Followers need direction and guidance. Sometimes, they need discipline or redirection. As a forward-thinking leader, you will have set expectations and communicated those expectations clearly using, as Kim Scott wrote: *Radical Candor*. As projects mature, as group dynamics shift, there will be hiccups. As a leader, you look out for those opportunities to gently, but firmly confront issues as they arise. As MLK suggested, a leader molds consensus. It is an active role that accepts constructive tension for the high-performing team to generate the best and most timely ideas.[389]

Human resources at your organization may have a specific way they would prefer the interaction to take place, but the basic format is typically the same. You take your employee aside and speak to them candidly about the issue you have observed. Start with an opening statement that reminds the employee of the expectation you had set. Address the issue by focusing on the action that was taken, being careful to never criticize the personhood of the employee. Lay out your continued behavioral expectations and establish a plan to follow up that is time-bound. Ask them if they have any questions or feedback for you.

From a continuous development and trust-building perspective, the most important action you can take is to follow up when you said you would. Make an appointment on your preferred work calendar. Jot a note in the calendar about the situation so that you are prepared for the conversation follow-up when it is time. Demonstrating that you care, that you are a person of integrity, will pay dividends in loyalty and personnel development down the road.

As you have read in the section on authenticity, the actions that you take as a leader should be transparent and perfectly aligned from your words to your actions. Transparency and integrity are key components of establishing trust in an organization because they are fundamental aspects of relationship building. Leadership revolves around relationships, and relationships are built on trust.

Establishing trust is the first step. There are so many

---

[389] Van Zyl, Campbell, & Lues, 2020

moving pieces in an organization that it is easy to neglect building relationships. Trying to focus on each step outlined in a theory, to mechanically follow the formula you read in that 10-steps-to-better-leadership blog is unhelpful. Even in most theories, leadership is not a linear process.

Real-life is messy and that is okay.

Start from a place where you authentically practice servant leadership. There are always problems in our messy workplaces. Express sincere concern for your followers. Be genuine. Offer to help. When there are issues requiring discipline, that is also your role as a leader. You must apply the rules regarding discipline in a fair and just manner, always remembering to feel keenly your great obligation to your employees as St. Augustine of Hippo indicated in his exhortation on the necessity of justice in leadership.[390]

Leaders who exhibit individual-focused behavior across a group, paying attention and trying to focus on the individual needs of each team member, are practicing differentiated leadership.[391] Differentiated leadership means that a leader is trying to use various leadership styles for each person. They are employing leadership practices as if they were a tool in a tool chest, pulling out a wrench for some employees and a screwdriver for another.

Some models of leadership, like Full Range Leadership Development (FRLD),[392] employ valid techniques that must be memorized and incorporated into your practice. One of the issues with leadership paradigms like these is that the models require constant, directed thought to maintain the analysis and recommended action cycle. A leader is expected to assess - either based on the

---

[390] Augustine of Hippo, 2013. Note: St. Augustine was the bishop of Hippo (in modern-day Algeria) from 396 to 430. He is recognized as a Saint, Church Father, and Doctor of the Church in Roman Catholicism.
[391] Wang & Howell, 2010, p. 1135.
[392] Stafford, 2010.

situation or the person being dealt with - what type of leadership behavior to adopt. If this is not performed with exquisite precision, it can easily be perceived as disingenuous behavior.

Caring for each member of the team is necessary, right, and just.

Never lose sight of the fact that the most important yardstick of your success will be how you treat other people.
- Barbara Bush

Treating group members differently negatively impacts collective efficacy and group identification, simultaneously making it difficult for team members to know their leader in any authentic way. Living *your* leadership implies an intuitive use of the tools that are authentically yours. A leader is on display; transparent. Their techniques may differ based on need, but they are all connected to the core beliefs and self-leadership model built in the first half of this text.

Team members are people deserving of respect regardless of their differences. The way to influence people and make that influence stick is through relationship building. High-quality relationships with your team members, collectively[393] make it more likely that they will perceive your leadership as fair. Treating your employees as uniquely deserving of respect and human dignity will enhance performance.[394]

As an ethical leader's influence impacts individual and team attitudes and values, team behaviors start to improve[395] and culture starts to morph. Leaders who are

---

[393] Wu, Tsui, & Kinicki, 2010.
[394] Graen & Uhl-Bien, 1995.
[395] Donohue & Wong, 1994.

negative spread their negativity to their team[396] in a downward spiral. If ignored by their leader, followers may not only deliver poor individual performance but may also undermine the performance of the team as a whole.[397]

To paraphrase Pope St. John XXIII, those things that unite us are more profound than those which divide us.[398]

The generation gap is not as large or insurmountable as some people describe it to be. The Center for Creative Leadership has conducted an ongoing survey since March of 2008[399] providing information on trends and issues related to generational cohorts. It has been discovered the three generations - the Boomers, Gen Xers, and Millennials - have more in common when it comes to the type of leadership that is most effective than is often speculated. All three generational cohorts agree on several characteristics of effective leaders: they participate, are team-oriented, charismatic, and human-oriented. Other relevant core attributes of an effective leader are: having consideration for others, being able to inspire, having respect for those around them, and being able to excite others to do their very best.[400]

In a story told by Simon Sinek in his book *Start with Why* he speaks about the American auto executives who visited a plant in Japan to learn more about their engineering process. The Americans had employed individuals whose job was to tap car doors with a rubber mallet to make sure that they fit straight off the assembly line. There did not seem to be such a person employed in that activity in Japan. When the Japanese engineer tour

---

[396] Barsade, 2002.
[397] Wang & Howell, 2010, p. 1140.
[398] A quote from Pope St. John-Paul II's 1995 encyclical, *Ut Unum Sint* attributed to Pope St. John XXIII.
[399] Deal, Stawiski, Gentry, & Cullen, 2013.
[400] Deal, Stawiski, Gentry, & Cullen, 2013.

guide was asked about this phenomenon, he replied that they designed the doors to fit during the engineering process and thus did not need to check it on the back end of the manufacturing process.

One of the truths that Mr. Sinek later mentions is that uniformly starting the thought process, starting with why, allows us to align our teams, our vision, and our processes short term. Reactive solutions are not necessary to correct anomalies in the process later, when you start with why. If, as a leader, you start with a solid understanding of where you are going and engineer the process carefully by putting the right people in the right places, starting with the kinds of people Jim Collins suggests (i.e. indomitable will, exceptionally humble), the need for motivation and inspiration will not be necessary.

One of the Air Force's mantras is *flexibility is the key to airpower*. If you start with solid people, build processes, and work to ensure those processes are measured, continued, and repeated in the same formal and foresighted manner as when you started, you can be relatively assured that issues will not appear down the line unless there is external change. The need for flexibility in the face of unanticipated change decreases to such an extent that questioning the reason why people need to be flexible in the first place seems ludicrous.

There are always things that are completely out of your control. The Air Force's motto about flexibility is not wrong. Hire the right people for the right jobs. Use foresighted strategical and tactical planning. Relying on the flexibility of your team is less efficient than designing an aligned process in the first place. Flexibility is almost always reactive. It is great in a pinch, but expecting to rely on the MacGyver-like skills[401] of your followers is

---

[401] An action-adventure TV series created by Lee David Zlotoff. MacGyver works for a clandestine organization and relies on his unconventional problem-solving skills in each episode to escape from harrowing situations and to save

shortsighted.

Figure 18. Yerkes-Dodson interpretation (replace *arousal* with *pressure*) [402]

You've read that, as a leader, you are always visible to your subordinates. Followers may form an opinion of you as a leader before you even take the formal role. They may have had expectations of anyone who holds the position you will be filling. Since that belief precedes your interaction with the team, it is necessary to consider how your first actions can garner trust and empower your team.

A self-aware leader realizes that the view of others in an organization directly impacts their leadership effectiveness. Initial actions set the tone for leadership tenure. Leaders should be sensitive to the reputational

---

lives.
[402] The Yerkes-Dodson Law describes an empirical relationship between arousal and performance. It was developed by psychologists Robert Yerkes and John Dodson in 1908.

consequences that all of their decisions have,[403] most especially their first interactions with the team. You have taken over a team, but you have made mistakes.

Those mistakes do not have to define your tenure in the position or your leadership legacy. As an educated self-leader, you know that everyone makes mistakes. Working to overcome those missteps involves admitting fault, owning the consequences, and moving on.

Your best is all that can ever be reasonably asked or expected of you.

Empowering subordinates holds consequences for the way that others perceive your leadership. Suppose, for instance, that a leader delegates many important tasks to subordinates. Is the organizational culture such that their action would be viewed as weak? Would the typical employee or group of employees understand their delegation as a form of personal incompetence or would they see it as employee empowerment?

Surround yourself with the best people you can find, delegate authority, and don't interfere as long as the policy you've decided upon is being carried out.
- Ronald Reagan

The organizational setting is extremely important in examining the contextual effects of employee empowerment. The organizational setting can affect the way that subordinates perceive leadership attributes. It informs expectations of a leader and the level of empowerment that is appropriate. When a leader empowers their employees, it does not detract from the perceived stature of those leaders.[404] Rather, leaders who empower their employees are perceived to have higher-order

---

[403] Campbell & Campbell, 2011.
[404] Campbell & Campbell, 2011.

leadership abilities than those who do not empower their employees.

Employee empowerment does not divest the leader of her accountability. A leader is ultimately accountable. The buck stops at the leader.

Remember the chapter that focused on humility? That is a topic worthy of revisiting when we think about group behavior. It is not uncommon, especially in high-stress scenarios, to go along with a group norm or decision to fit in or to avoid criticism. If the unexpressed but obvious goal of the group is to avoid criticism, the relationships in the organization have failed and there is a toxic atmosphere penetrating the group dynamic.

Social conformity is a powerful social-psychological pressure. It takes guts to stand up to what we often call peer pressure. We know this from case studies in United States history with the Challenger disaster. On January 28, 1986, the Space Shuttle Challenger broke apart just over a minute into its flight, killing all aboard. The RCA (root cause analysis) determined that there were many opportunities to correct cascading errors, but a lack of communication abetted by the social phenomenon of groupthink (the need for consensus over offering alternatives or delivering a critique), led to inexcusable errors that ultimately led to the loss of life and catastrophic failure of the mission. Developing relationships; fostering a culture in your team that encourages dissenting opinions and respectful dialogue will help avoid groupthink.

During change management, if a change is directed at the organizational level, you are accountable for the execution of the actions necessary for that change. You represent the organization and have the obligation to align your team's execution of policy change with the greater organization. When an employee asks, "Who directed this change?" as a prelude to questioning the wisdom of the effort, you should know what to say. As a leader who takes personal responsibility, you do not blame the situation on those who have authority over you.

> *A leader is one who knows the way, goes the way, and shows the way.*
> *- John Maxwell*

You own the change. That is not to say you do not have the obligation to challenge directives if they are unethical, immoral, or unlawful, however. With an understanding that the change is none of those things, you should exercise your responsibility and enthusiastically own the process.

There may be times that as a leader, you agree with your subordinates regarding the unpopularity of a particular policy or directive from those above you. When I had to tell my flight that we were going to be participating in 72-hour alerts, you can imagine that I was no happier than my subordinates that I'd be spending that much time away from my family with no real return on that sacrifice...especially with the knowledge that this had already been tried unsuccessfully in the past! There are two avenues to approach negative change that will contribute to your leadership legacy: 1. Authentically empathizing with your followers; listening to their concerns with the intent to listen and appreciate their point of view and 2. Soliciting ideas for improvements to the plan.

While you can always attempt to change your boss's mind, complaining to those you lead is never the answer.

As a leader, you are ultimately accountable.

As we move from the topic of team leadership to servant leadership, keep in mind that it is not one or the other, but that *Living your Leadership* is a unitary paradigm that encourages development from the inside out. The topics discussed in previous sections should be incorporated into the practices outlined in later sections so that the holistic nature of the paradigm can be realized. A leader is not judged as often by how they lead, but by how they serve; value is achieved through service.[405]

---

[405] Cashman, 2008.

Chapter Recap

Leaders must lead themselves, focus on individuals, but realize that leadership endeavors involve a community of followers. Leading a team requires strategy and forethought, as well as carefully developed skills.
- Team development progresses in stages. The stages are not sequential but are all necessary.
- Trust is foundational to effective teams.
- Trust is established by follow-through and consistent feedback and guidance.
- Each member of a team should be treated with justice, fairness, and consistency. Care for others should guide your decisions.
- Start with why: design your processes for the end state.
- Leaders are always on display. They own their decisions, empower their followers and embrace change.
- Ultimate accountability rests with a leader.

Servant Leadership

The servant-leader is servant first… Becoming a servant-leader begins with the natural feeling that one wants to serve, to serve first. Then conscious choice brings one to aspire to lead. That person is sharply different from one who is leader first… The difference manifests itself in the care taken by the servant first to make sure that other people's highest priority needs are being served. The best test, and the most difficult to administer, is this: Do those served grow as persons? Do they, while being served, become healthier, wiser, freer, more autonomous, more likely themselves to become servants?
- Robert Greenleaf

    I got fired. It wasn't a proud day for me. I was finishing my dissertation and working 60-hour weeks in a high-level position at what was to be my last Air Force base. My boss was a rabid micromanager and extremely uncommunicative. The man didn't take the time to give feedback on the work that I did. If he didn't like a detail of the speech I had spent hours writing, he would take the piece of paper it was written on and tear it halfway through and leave it on my desk for me to find in the morning.

    To be fair, I should have realized what I was getting myself into. He prominently displayed Machiavelli's *The Prince*[406] on his bookshelf and insisted he be called by his callsign (he wasn't a pilot and had never been to a combat zone, but had "earned" his nickname in a school setting).

---

[406] Among the gems you can find in Machiavelli's work, these quotes stand in stark contrast to *Living your Leadership*: "If an injury has to be done to a man, it should be so severe that his vengeance need not be feared." "Never attempt to win by force what can be won by deception." "Since love and fear can hardly exist together, if we must choose between them, it is far safer to be feared than loved" and "He who wishes to be obeyed must know how to command."

On a day just like any other, I came into the office and learned that I had been reassigned.

Rather than being allowed to return to my previous position, I was forced into an operational job in a squadron run by one of the sycophants of the man who had fired me.

I decided to separate from active military service that day.

It was a bittersweet choice. The Air Force was my life. I had dedicated myself to the service and had excelled in every assignment, save for the last one. There was a lot of planning involved in choosing a civilian life. I had to find a job, figure out how to make the transition successful for my wife and two little boys, and move my family to a new location. In addition to the practical aspects of the transition, I had to deal with the emotional upheaval that my perceived failure had generated. Ultimately, I embraced the struggle.

Based on my solid performance as a junior officer, I was accepted by a firm that acts as a headhunter for companies nationwide, looking for talented, experienced military leaders to serve in corporate America. During the hiring event, I was interviewed and chosen by Kaiser Permanente for a healthcare management position in Northern California.

Healthcare administration was the perfect crucible[407] for putting some of the tenants of self-sacrificial and servant leadership into practice.

> *Do nothing from selfish ambition or conceit, but in humility, count others more significant than yourselves. Let each of you look not only to his own interests, but also to the interests of others. Philippians 2:3-4 (ESV)*

Servant leadership (SL) is a large topic, and the

---

[407] De Pree, 1989.

characteristics of servant leaders are well defined.[408] It is a field of study that organizations like The Greenleaf Center[409] and the School of Business at Regent University[410] specialize in. This chapter is not meant to add to the scholarly research on the subject or to present a comprehensive review of the theory. Rather, it provides a practical overview of SL and how it applies in the *Living your Leadership* practice.

The highest of distinctions is service to others.
- King George VI

Servant Leadership derives from *agapao*, or sacrificial love.[411] *Agapao* is an Ancient Greek term that describes charity as an unreciprocated loving action. Not to be confused with transformational leadership, in which the leader's focus is on organizational goals and relies on charisma for power and influence, SL orients itself primarily on followers. Servant Leaders show genuine interest in the lives of their followers.

A Servant Leader unabashedly cares.[412]

Though it may sound touchy-feely, loving your followers is a necessary part of leadership; it is an active investment in those you lead.[413] Many influential thought leaders have implied that a servant leader's motivation stems from their principles, values, and beliefs,[414] or their humility and spiritual insights.[415] These very personal factors enable servant leaders to engage themselves in self-

---

[408] Read about the 10 characteristics of a servant leader from Spears, 2010 at: https://www.regent.edu/acad/global/publications/jvl/vol1_iss1/Spears_Final.pdf
[409] https://www.greenleaf.org/
[410] http://www.regent.edu/sbl/
[411] Patterson, 2003.
[412] Crom, 1998.
[413] Lorenz, 2012.
[414] Farling, M.L., Stone, AG., & Winston, B.E., 1999.
[415] Graham, W., 1991.

sacrificial,[416] altruistic behaviors.[417]

A servant leader is a steward. A steward holds responsibility for an organization and followers in trust for future leaders. A good steward uses their time, talent, and treasure[418] to provide for their followers in meaningful ways. The idea that one *serves* first, rather than *leads* first is a fundamental presupposition of Servant Leadership that distinguishes it from other models.[419]

I'd like you to consider this excerpt from a homily from my local parish priest, Fr. Jesús Hernández:

> There is a story told about a group of pilgrims who were visiting the Holy Land with the assistance of a native tour guide. The guide was telling them about the work of shepherds in the area, and to note the particular aspect of how shepherds would never walk behind the sheep but rather in front of them, leading them. The sheep would hear the shepherd's voice and they would follow even if there were other shepherds and sheep together... But as the guide finished the explanation, the group laughed when they saw a man walking behind a flock of sheep, trying to drive them along with a stick. "I thought you said that the shepherds here always lead the sheep in front of them," someone said. "What is wrong with that shepherd?" But the tour guide answered, "Sir, that's not a shepherd. That's a butcher."
>
> That's not a shepherd. That's a butcher. What a radical difference, isn't it? The two seemed to be doing the same thing. But the end for the sheep is so

---

[416] Choi, Y. & Mai-Dalton, R.R., 1998.
[417] Sendjaya & Sarros, 2002.
[418] See Matthew 6:21.
[419] Sendjaya & Sarros, 2002, p. 61.

different. I have never been to Holy Land, but I grew up on a farm, and ever since I can remember, I was taught that shepherding and "sheep herding" are not the same thing. A herder, like a cowboy, drives or pushes sheep wherever he wants, normally by causing some fear or pain to the sheep. A shepherd, on the other hand, draws them to himself. The sheep come to him when they hear the shepherd's voice after they learn that it's ok, that they are safe, that he will protect them from any danger.[420]

A servant leader will attend to the needs of their followers. Their needs will preempt the needs of the organization.[421] This is a bifurcated process: (1) serving the needs of the followers and helping to reach their full potential (2) inspiring them and maturing them to be leaders.[422] The servant style is designed to prepare followers for their leadership journey. Mutual trust and empowerment are crucial for the servant-style leader to be successful.[423] Servant leaders empower their followers. They help followers grow and develop according to their needs and not at the whim of the organization. Power is ethically used, and teams work collaboratively and in an atmosphere of mutual respect and trust under an SL.[424]

---

[420] Father Jesús Hernández at Holy Trinity Parish in El Dorado Hills on the Fourth Sunday of Easter, May 3, 2020.
[421] Howatson-Jones, 2004.
[422] Greenleaf, 1998.
[423] Spencer, 2007.
[424] Greenleaf, 1998.

*Ye call me Master and Lord: and ye say well; for so I am.
If I then, your Lord and Master, have washed your feet;
ye also ought to wash one another's feet.
For I have given you an example,
that ye should do as I have done to you.
- John 13:13-15 (KJV)*

*Christ Washing the Disciples' Feet
By Giotto (c.1305)*

As Robert Greenleaf famously said, the best test of SL success is whether "those served grow as persons; do they, while being served, become healthier, wiser, freer, more autonomous, more likely themselves to become servants?" One of the biggest problems with that particular statement is that employee growth toward a servant orientation is difficult to measure. It is not difficult to measure because tools do not exist to measure the phenomenon; it is difficult to measure because it requires an incubation period. That being said, investing time in people is an integral part of Servant Leadership.

Prioritize people over tasks.
- Cathy Engelbert [425]

It can sometimes take years before Servant Leadership takes full effect in those served. Robert Greenleaf understood this. As the head of the Servant Leader Institute (SLI) pointed out in his essay, servant leadership is a long-term transformational approach[426] and one that is holistic, affecting both life and work.

There are practical and specific strategies for the implementation of servant leadership that move past the purely theoretical. Showing employees that you care about each of them as people can take many forms. Here are a few to try on for size:

Learn the names of all of your people. This may seem basic, but it is important to recognize and use first names whenever possible because everyone matters.[427] If you are at all like me, it is extremely difficult for you to

---

[425] An American business executive and the first Commissioner of the Women's National Basketball Association (WNBA). Before joining the WNBA, she had been with Deloitte for 33 years, including as its first female CEO from 2015–2019/
[426] Spears, 2005.
[427] Treasurer, 2014.

match faces with names. Something that I have done is to have pictures taken of all of my people and put their names underneath to memorize them on my own time. Try out some other tactics: when you are introduced, look at the person carefully and repeat their name in conversation several times. This tends to cause a link in your mind between the face and name.

Another tactic to show care for the individual is to ensure that you know something about each of your employees. What is important to them? Do they have a young family? Is one of the children about to graduate from college or high school? Are they foster parents? Do they compete in any sports or activities? Mention their details and endeavor to follow up on important events.

Ensuring that you work with all of your people in the most respectful and personable manner means that they will be able to perceive that you care. They will know that you care about more than just getting the job done but about the things that matter to them. An additional benefit is that you will be able to determine the kind of leadership direction your followers are most ready to accept. By this, I do not mean that you should change yourself to accommodate any single employee, but that you should use a more or less authoritative style when dealing with certain individuals.

Here's a question to ask yourself: are you the most important person in the room? The answer to that question for any servant leader will *always* be no. Any and every person in that room is not only deserving of your respect, but their needs should be placed ahead of yours. This manifests itself in many ways. Perhaps you have been working on several initiatives that will affect your work unit. This has cost you an enormous amount of time and effort, but there were other people involved in the project that report to you. How you handle the success or failure of any of those initiatives shows those employees something about you as a leader.

The proponents of SL set their practice in stark contrast to the traditional, autocratic, and hierarchical leadership styles. They emphasize that servant leadership involves cooperative decision-making, ethical behavior, and the growth of the frontline worker. Many of the thinkers that you have been reading about in this book are proponents of either servant leadership, facilitative leadership, or some other form of leadership that does not tend to view workers as cogs in the industrial machine; thinkers like Robert Greenleaf, Stephen Covey, Max DePree, Ken Blanchard, and Jim Collins.[428]

Over the last fifteen or more years, SL has been expanding. The concept began with a person who wanted to serve, emerging into a leader. The servant-leader style has spread across the world. The two words *servant* and *leader*, having very opposite meanings, when joined describe an emerging paradox. Having a leader that serves her employees, helping to expand their knowledge and skills is a radical concept. Thankfully, many organizations are moving toward this type of leadership style.

> *I slept and dreamt that life was joy,*
> *I awoke and saw that life was service,*
> *I acted and behold, service was joy.*
> *- Tagore* [429]

The servant-leader puts the needs of others before themselves. Greenleaf[430] described servant leadership as, "[beginning] with the natural feeling that one wants to serve. Then conscious choice brings one to aspire to lead. The difference manifests itself in the care taken by the

---

[428] Spears, 2005.
[429] Rabindranath Tagore (1861-1941) was the Nobel Prize winner in Literature in 1913.
[430] 1977.

servant first to make sure that others' highest priority needs are being served." The characteristics of an SL are based on carrying the needs of those they serve forward, giving their followers the ability to progress and develop.[431]

> Here again, he hints that strife and party-spirit, love of rule and presumptuousness, had been the causes of their error, for the desire of rule is the mother of heresies. By saying, "Be servants one to another," he shows that the evil had arisen from this presumptuous and arrogant spirit, and therefore, he applies a corresponding remedy. As your divisions arose from your desire to domineer over each other, "serve one another;" thus will ye be reconciled again. *Saint John Chrysostom*[432]

Servant leadership, in the context of transformational leadership behaviors, encourages personal initiative and task performance.[433] Among the other powerful benefits of Servant Leadership on the follower is that it reduces instances of burnout,[434] [435] a serious psychological issue in the workplace characterized by emotional and physical fatigue,[436] by mitigating negative emotional interactions and reducing the external factors that lead to burnout that are in the leader's scope of control.[437]

Those in authority have a moral obligation to those they serve.[438]

Servant leaders empower their followers. There is

---

[431] Spears, 2005.
[432] Commentary on the Epistle to the Galatians 5:13.
[433] Judge & Piccolo, 2004.
[434] Figure 18.
[435] Rude, 2003.
[436] Shirom, 2003.
[437] Maslach, Schaufeli, & Leiter, 2001.
[438] CCC 2235.

no valid reason not to allow your subordinates to make decisions and to follow through on those decisions. Empowerment will allow them to become wiser by learning from their mistakes and successes. Decentralizing the day-to-day operations of your work unit will allow for more agile operations while giving younger or less experienced individuals the opportunity to stretch their wings.

Servanthood is inextricably linked to the appreciation of human dignity. Equality of persons regardless of their immutable characteristics[439] is a given for those practicing the *Living your Leadership* paradigm.

Father Peter Claver[440] served the African slaves coming to the New World. He would go to the ships as they docked at Cartagena, Colombia, and to the warehouses, bringing with him medicine, clothes, food, and water. He served in that capacity for 27 years until his death. Servanthood does not only apply to our own, handpicked followers. We are called to be servants to all, especially those in most need.

We must speak to them with our hands, before we try to speak to them with our lips.
- St. Peter Claver, SJ

Stories about how a leader's self-sacrifice has had a profound positive effect on followers are common throughout history. Self-Sacrificial Leadership behaviors communicate an unambiguous message that the leader has an orientation that is pro-organization and, more to the point, follower-centric.[441] A servant leader *always* puts the needs of the followers before her own.

---

[439] Among these are race, color, national origin, religion, or sex.
[440] For more about his life and mission, visit http://catholicism.org/slave-of-slaves.html
[441] De Cremer, van Knippenberg, van Dijke, & Bos, 2006.

Service before self is that virtue within us all which elevates the human spirit, compels us to reach beyond our meager selves to attach our spirit to something bigger than we are.
- General John P. Jumper, 17th Chief of Staff of the Air Force

Depending on the job being performed, a servant leader may well put the mission above themselves, as well. A servant leader is not interested in promoting themselves. They do not care to preserve their power, but to use their power (read: influence) to better the lives of their followers and accomplish the mission. It is likely that the surrender of power, counterintuitively, results in greater power in the person of the leader as they are more likely to have gained influence through their self-sacrificial and altruistic actions.

The more one forgets himself
- by giving himself to a cause to serve or another person to love -
the more human he is and the more he actualizes himself.
- Viktor Frankl [442]

My time in Iraq was a humbling and eye-opening experience for me. My experiences in North America had in no way prepared me for the transition to the Middle East. The concrete barriers, oppressive dust that was so fine it turned into a paste when wet, and camel spiders the size of dinner plates were just some of the new and exciting experiences the country had to offer. Here is an excerpt from a letter to my wife describing the journey to my FOB:

> It gets dark early in the winter in the desert. This place has already left an indelible impression on me with its awkward concrete structures rimmed with

---

[442] 1963, p. 133.

barbed wire, the late afternoon sky set ablaze by the setting sun, and the dust. Dust is everywhere. I should explain more about the sky. It is beautiful but would seem strange to you. Imagine driving down HWY 50 into Sacramento. In the heart of the city, it is smoggier than you have ever seen it, but the smog is not caused solely by emissions. Rather, the filth in the sky is composed of the ever-present dust and the detritus of civilization. It forms an impenetrable, translucent layer that positively shimmers in the heat. *Tuesday, October 7, 2008.*

I mentioned that a piece of my soul would go with the soldiers when they exited the FOB for convoy operations. Sometimes, they didn't come back, sometimes they didn't come back whole. My job was Electronic Warfare Officer and Instructor. This means that I was responsible for the vehicle jamming systems that were employed against radio-controlled improvised explosive devices (RCIEDs). I also trained soldiers on the proper operation and troubleshooting of those devices.

In the theater of operations, bravery seemed almost routine. These young men and women would put themselves in harm's way to shield their fellow service members. They traveled all over the city and beyond, protecting the local populace from terror threats. The stoicism of the company commanders remains a model for me to attempt to emulate; their calm exterior shielding their almost obsessive planning and care for their troops.

Just as those company commanders were authentically committed to their troops, willing to face any danger for them, your authenticity must be seamlessly woven throughout your leadership practice. You may never lead a team into combat, but you will stand in the front of your team and lead with your words and actions. Make them real, make them count.

Leader self-sacrifice should not be tied to any specific context. You should never have to think to yourself, "because I'm in this situation with these particular people, I would choose to act self-sacrificially." That negates the authenticity of the act. Any person who sees that you are uninterested in treating all people with the same dignity will disbelieve your commitment to self-sacrifice. You must be willing to subordinate your ego, engage your humble self, and act as a servant to all. In the same way that a leader makes a conscious decision to be a servant, the choice should be made to make sacrifices, though that is often not the case.[443]

A leader is not manipulative.

If a leader publicizes their self-sacrificial behavior, it is a sure bet that they do not authentically espouse the value of self-sacrifice. If they make a big deal out of their self-sacrificial behavior, then they are likely attempting to manipulatively earn a reciprocal response from their followers.[444] Altruistic leader behavior stems from a genuine caring feeling for their subordinates. A leader can be jovial or quiet; humorous or reserved, but ultimately, their caring nature shows through. Take a famous example from literature, screen, and state: in Charles Dickens' *A Christmas Carol*, Scrooge says of Fezziwig, "He has the power to render us happy or unhappy; to make our service light or burdensome; a pleasure or a toil. Say that his power lies in words and looks; in things so slight and insignificant that it is impossible to add and count them up: what then? The happiness he gives is quite as great as if it cost a fortune."[445]

Leaders create atmosphere and atmosphere influences culture. As a caring human being, someone who

---

[443] Matteson & Irving, 2006.
[444] Choi & Mai-Dalton, 1998.
[445] Dickens, Charles, 1812-1870. (1995). *A Christmas carol and other stories.* New York: Modern Library.

works for their people, a servant leader's workplace should feel palpably positive. This is a somewhat ephemeral quality to talk about, but it exists, nonetheless. You know what it feels like to enter a workplace where people are unhappy. Their expressions were downcast, mumbling to each other about the work and management and generally wishing to be somewhere else. You also know what it feels like to enter a workplace where people feel motivated to work; it can be noisy or quiet, but the workplace is wholesome. People speak of the difference they are making, they look for improvement possibilities, and they share a mutual respect for each other and the organization.

If you encounter a leader that worries first about the WIIFM (What's in it for me?) question, then you have found someone who is selfish, not selfless. The first concern of a leader is for their people, not for their own selfish goals.[446] A servant leader never encourages reciprocity for self-sacrificial behavior[447] and does not first concern themselves with their image, ego, or benefit. **Caring for followers should supersede *any* tangible or intangible reciprocal benefit.**

Nobody cares how much you know, until they know how much you care.
- Theodore Roosevelt

Taking meals after your employees has a long tradition, from Biblical King David[448] to George Washington in the snows of Valley Forge, but is this behavior in a time of plenty anything more than false humility? Its history is well-known, which makes the traditional act seem like an attempt to draw on the legitimacy of past great leaders. Self-sacrificial behaviors

---

[446] Matthew 20:26.
[447] Matteson & Irving, 2006.
[448] The Holy Bible, 1984, 2 Samuel 23.

should be meaningful and linked to the needs of followers[449] and the setting, rather than an empty gesture. If there is plenty of food, but not plenty of time (a more typical modern occurrence), which would more likely show your followers that you care about them, spending the plentiful commodity or the scarce one?

Leaders show up early, they work hard on their tasks, and they go home late. Burnout among high-performing leaders (and employees) is a real danger, even in an exciting and engaging work environment. Do not work late for the sake of working late. That is inefficient. More importantly, do not work late so that your followers can see you doing it. That is manipulative behavior. Take the time required to do the job right.[450]

Self-sacrifice should hurt a bit.

When performed authentically, self-sacrificial behaviors engender trust and are powerful examples that followers will talk about. They will try their best to emulate those behaviors. As a side effect, those followers will begin to develop a mindset that involves humility, a recognition of the equality of persons, and their place as servants.

Delegation of authority, giving opportunities to excel to your followers is leading from behind. When there are useful tasks back on the base, tasks that will allow your troops to grow and experience praise for a job well done, that is not the time to do the work for them. Like a good parent, mastery experiences are encouraged in their children, while dangerous situations require intervention. That is demanded of any good mentor and leader, but it is not the whole equation.

When a company commander is the first through a door in a combat situation, his soldiers are more likely to *want* to follow his example. That leader is self-sacrificially

---

[449] Philippians 2:4.
[450] Cockerell, 2008.

taking the brunt of the initial danger. Especially in command-and-control situations, like the military, you can simply order someone to perform a task. Your example will always be far more impactful. Authentic and meaningful self-sacrifice is inspirational. [451]

It is better to lead from behind and to put others in front, especially when you celebrate victory when nice things occur.
You take the front line when there is danger.
Then people will appreciate your leadership.
- Nelson Mandela

Altruism views leadership through the lens of benefit to the follower and self-sacrifice demands some specific loss to the leader.[452] One of the links between others and self during the development of leadership attributes is the image that you project. Not only should it be authentic since your actions reflect your true characteristics, but that what you project is what is perceived by others. Practicing leader self-sacrifice by giving up power or privilege will be interpreted by your followers as an act of selflessness inspired by humility. It will serve to reduce the social distance between leader and followers.[453]

Perception is reality.

Self-sacrifice, or any other attribute, is ultimately only as useful as the perceptions of others. This sentence can be a painful revelation. What you do matters, even if it is not seen, but unless it is recognized by others, in some ways it is as if it did not happen. Does that mean that you abandon your integrity and only work during times when it is visible to others? Naturally not. You are worthwhile,

---

[451] Choi & Mai-Dalton, 1998, p. 475.
[452] Choi & Mai-Dalton, 1998.
[453] Choi & Mai-Dalton, 1998.

your contributions make a difference, and your time has value. As a leader, however, the utility of your actions is most often determined by the perception of others.

Oftentimes, our ego, informed by an inflated sense of self, can lead us to believe that because we feel that our actions match our intentions, that *others* see what we are doing in the same way *we* see what we are doing. You must take the time to determine whether what you are doing, whether your team's actions reflect an obvious alignment with your mission.

Similarly, you know that you are proud of your people, but how do they know that you are proud of them? You have to show it through your words and actions. Be deliberate, but not too effusive. There is no shame in making sure that those under you know that you care, but, unless you are a naturally effusive person, pushing it can easily tip over into disingenuity.

Placing the greater need of the group above their desires is the mark of a leader employing self-sacrificial behaviors.

> Leaders we admire do not place themselves at the center; they place others there. They do not seek the attention of people; they give it to others. They do not focus on satisfying their own aims and desires; they look for ways to respond to the needs and interests of their constituents. They are not self-centered; they concentrate on the constituent... Leaders serve a purpose and the people who have made it possible for them to lead... In serving a purpose, leaders strengthen credibility by demonstrating that they are not in it for themselves; instead, they have the interests of the institution, department or team and its constituents at heart. Being a servant may not be what many leaders had in mind when they choose to take responsibility for

the vision and direction of their organization or team, but serving others is the most glorious and rewarding of all leadership tasks. *James Kouzes and Barry Posner*[454]

It is a time-honored adage that a leader accepts none of the credit and takes all of the blame. These sayings stick around; it is because they have a grain of truth to them. A high-performing team trusts its leadership. Build the faith in your team that things will be taken care of by their managers by following through. Use the word *we,* to describe success and *I,* to describe blame. That is not to say that your employees can do nothing wrong. The progressive disciplinary process exists for a reason.

No man will make a great leader who wants to do it all himself,
or to get all the credit for doing it.
- Andrew Carnegie

When the leader can take a blow to their ego by accepting blame when something does not go right, they act as a shield between their employees and the criticism of outsiders. It is a sign of immaturity when a person is unable to accept blame for something that happened because of their actions. Conversely, acting selflessly and sharing the credit for achievements will pay untold benefits in team esprit de corps and loyalty.[455] Though you recognize that you are not responsible for the thing you take the blame for, ultimately, as a leader you are accountable.

Accountability implies acknowledgment of your role in a situation, good or bad. A solid sense of self, developed through self-reflection, means that you will have

---

[454] Kouzes & Posner, 1993, p. 185.
[455] Hayward, 2007.

the ability to take a step outside of your ego. By subordinating your ego, you can accept responsibility for something that may or may not have been directly attributable to you, as the leader. The subordination of ego applies here in the same manner that it does when you are humble.

A humble leader accepts blame and distributes credit.

It may seem to some that I am encouraging self-flagellating servanthood; that I am painting a rather bleak picture of a humble whipping boy. But that is not at all the case. A true servant leader exudes enthusiasm; they are grateful to serve. Reading through Jim Collins's masterwork *Good to Great*, you see several examples of CEOs that led with great humility but were still prosperous and well-respected in their industry.

> *Everybody can be great...because anybody can serve. You don't have to have a college degree to serve. You don't have to make your subject and verb agree to serve. You only need a heart full of grace. A soul generated by love.*
> *- Martin Luther King, Jr.*

As someone *Living your Leadership*, you can walk into any leadership scenario and succeed. The foundation of self-knowledge is a steady platform to exercise the flexibility that is built into the model. A servant leader is not concerned by how uncomfortable a leadership scenario is. They are sure of themselves and their mission to serve first.

Chapter Recap

Servant leadership begins and ends with caring.
- Servant leaders consciously build their followers into servant leaders in their turn.
- Move beyond the theoretical by practicing servant behaviors.
- The servant-leader is humble and willing to listen. They lead through influence and cooperation.
- Self-sacrificial behaviors are normal for servant leaders.
- Servant leaders do not manipulate their followers, ethics define the center of the practice.
- Accountability means taking the blame. A servant leader empowers their followers, freely giving credit while accepting more than their fair share of any blame.

Denouement

*The challenge of leadership is to
be strong, but not rude;
be kind, but not weak;
be bold, but not bully;
be thoughtful, but not lazy;
be humble, but not timid;
be proud, but not arrogant;
have humor, but without folly.
- Jim Rohn*

Pitfalls

> ...*before it is an honor, leadership is trust;*
> *Before it is a call to glory,*
> *Leadership is a call to service;*
> *...before all else, forever and always,*
> *leadership is a willingness to serve.*
> *- Father Edson Wood, OSA, Cadet Catholic Chaplain*[456]

You cannot offer the best of your authentic self without exposing your failures and vulnerabilities. This is the reason that *Leading Yourself* is the first half of the book. A leader has to develop themselves, internally reconcile their failings, and own their internal narrative before authenticity can be achieved. The power of vulnerability and the important role of shame is described nowhere better than by Brené Brown.[457] I've tried to demonstrate that embracing vulnerability, despite the challenge that presents and the courage it takes, will pay dividends in your leadership journey.

Egotism

We already mentioned the difficulty that our disconnected society fosters when it comes to a lack of empathy, but egotism also runs rampant and is fed by our fiendish desire to be recognized as unique, as well. The two go hand-in-glove. Ego is fed by elevating yourself and empathy is killed though focus on self at the expense of the

---

[456] Invocation at Assumption of Command, U.S. Military Academy, August 11, 2004.
[457] Brown, 2012. Brené Brown is a qualitative researcher who has, for more than a decade, studied the effects of shame in our culture and our individual lives.

other.

Now more than ever, our culture fans the flames of ego. It's never been easier to talk, to puff ourselves up. We can brag about our goals to millions of our fans and followers—things only rock stars and cult leaders used to have. We can follow and interact with our idols on Twitter, we can read books and sites and watch TED Talks, drink from a fire hose of inspiration and validation like never before (there's an app for that). We can name ourselves CEO of our exists-only-on-paper company. We can announce big news on social media and let the congratulations roll in. We can publish articles about ourselves in outlets that used to be sources of objective journalism.[458]

A self-assured leader is either 1. false or 2. someone who has accepted her past and grown from it. The odds in favor of the latter are not great, but as Indra Nooyi indicated, "Whatever anybody says or does, assume positive intent."[459] Self-assurance should buoy a leader, putting a damper on self-doubt. In many cases, self-assured leaders are simply loud and cocky. They lead without having done the hard self-development work. When someone is leading without having bothered to develop themselves, their ego will guarantee wildly unpredictable and probably unhealthy leadership behaviors.

Being open with your insecurities paradoxically makes you more confident and charismatic around others. The pain of honest confrontation is what generates the greatest trust and respect in your relationships. Suffering through your fears and anxieties is what allows you to build courage and

---

[458] Holiday, 2016, p. 4-5
[459] Chairman and CEO of PepsiCo, Indra Nooyi was asked about the best leadership advice she had received and gave this answer.

perseverance. *Mark Manson*[460]

Fear

It would be foolish to say that successful leaders do not experience fear. Everyone experiences fear in one way or another. Perhaps you are suffering from imposter syndrome; the idea that you are not a leader, just someone inadequately filling the role.[461] Perhaps you are unused to speaking in front of people; afraid of the judgment of others and your ability to inspire either through body language or other forms of communication. A successful leader will take that experience of fear, analyze and determine its antecedents, and positively use that negative emotion.

There are ways to get started in defeating imposter syndrome that are highly effective. Starting on the inside, remind yourself of your past successes. Our inner voice speaks to us much more often than outside ones, and it is a good place to start. We have already discussed the cumulative power of positive self-talk and this is a good opportunity to practice. Another internal tactic is to imagine the worst-case scenario if you are a 'faker' in your given situation. Realizing that the consequences are not dire will free up your mind to take external steps to mitigate your fear.

Still concerned that you are not the leader you think you should be? Ask for feedback and be prepared for it to be critical. Too often, when we ask for feedback, it is a rote action; something we know we should do, but we do not want to hear that we are doing anything wrong or that we are not up to the task. Take critical or glowing feedback with humility befitting you as a person and learn from it.

Fear should be transmuted into inspirational

---

[460] Manson, 2016.
[461] The point labeled "mount stupid" in the Dunning-Kruger Effect figure in the chapter "Temet Nosce."

courage.

I know that is an aspirational statement that doesn't necessarily communicate the struggle inherent in the activity it suggests. The transmutation of fear into anything else is a process. It requires a similar process that has been described in this book as the leadership journey (i.e. self-examination leading to self-awareness and ultimately, self-management). If you have gone through the process of self-improvement, you know it is not an easy process. That's why books on self-improvement are still so popular; we want a guide, a rulebook, a set of instructions.

Improvement is tough. Working on yourself can be emotionally and physically draining. Facing your fear is a decision that many people simply refuse to make. The fact that you are sitting here, reading this, means that you are at least entertaining the idea of self-improvement and you should feel proud of that choice! Time is our most precious commodity, and spending it on overcoming fear and growing as leaders is crucial.

All we have to decide is what to do with the time that is given us.
J.R.R. Tolkien (through the character of Gandalf the Gray)
– The Fellowship of The Ring

Narcissism

Transformational leadership has an inherent risk of narcissism and undue influence. The use of idealized influence by a charismatic individual is potent. As a charismatic leader, your strength of personality impacts the level of influence you have on followers. Using your personality to influence others isn't bad in and of itself. There are several reasons to avoid leading solely by dint of personality, however.

If the strength of your personality is all that people

choose to follow, they will be bereft if you leave the organization. If you do not have a tight grip on your ego, using appropriate self-regulatory behaviors, you may start to believe that you are owed something (loyalty, respect, submission) based on your merit. That narcissism can lead to manipulative behaviors and corruption, especially if it is coupled with a lack of self-reflection.[462] Transformational leadership is not alone in the pitfall arena. Servant Leadership and Self-Leadership, despite their power, flexibility, and depth, are also subject to failings in execution.

Reciprocity

Servant leadership can also be fraught with unanticipated consequences and dangers. One of these dangers is the idea of servant-leader reciprocity. A servant leader serves their followers. Due to rendering that service, there is an inherent psychological obligation to the leader from the follower.[463] From the individual served to the leader who has served them, there exists the feeling of a debt that should be paid. This feeling of obligation is transactional and is probably an explanation for why transactional leadership *feels* natural to many people. The problem with that reciprocal relationship is that a servant leader's job is not to create indebtedness in his followers but to encourage his followers to become servants themselves.

Lies

Dishonesty seems like something that should be simple to avoid. In practice, dishonesty is all too common.

---

[462] Giampetro, et al., 1998.
[463] Cialdini, 2001.

Little white lies and omissions corrupt an organization's transparency. They damage the trust and loyalty that followers have in a leader. Building and encouraging an atmosphere of open and honest feedback will make backstabbing and political, passive-aggressive behavior much rarer.[464] When candor is employed, there are few secrets to leverage for political gain. Few lies survive courageous conversations.

Disrespect

Disrespect is commonly used by the insecure and the weak. As a leader, you should never tolerate disrespect amongst your followers or to yourself. Showing a lack of respect for another person in your organization is enormously damaging to the morale of the unit. Disrespect comes in many forms. Some of the more common instances to look out for are gossip, condescension, or the formation of exclusive cliques. In an organization where respect is practiced, an atmosphere of cooperation and trust will endure. Disrespect eats away at the esprit de corps of an organization.

Ingratitude

Ingratitude is one of the cardinal sins of leadership. Any self-aware leader should understand that they did not get to where they are solely by chance or their hard work. Humble leaders understand that they have been propped up by those they have led and by the mentors, friends, and professional connections that they have made along the way. A leader who displays ingratitude often focuses on themselves, which is another reason to subdue the ego and develop a solid inner humility. That leader will not reward

---

[464] Scott, 2017.

followers for their effort if it undermines their perceived self-worth. Ingratitude directly leads to egotism.

Favoritism

If you want to destroy trust in your leadership, employ favoritism. Favoritism takes many shapes including cronyism and nepotism. If you have a team of 10 individuals, do not spend 90% of your time with three or four of them. Do not take one or two of them to lunch and ignore the rest on a routine basis. Spend time talking with each of them.

Make sure that the time that you do spend, especially with those that you may not like as much, is visible to the entire team. You have to be genuine in your care and concern for those individuals. If you are not able to be genuine, then you will have to do some self-reflection concerning the inherent value of human dignity.

Any leader who thinks that the team does not see the amount of time that they spend with one or another of their peers is delusional. Your followers know the amount of time, effort, and care that you bestow on each of them. Team members are much more likely to give you the benefit of the doubt if you have taken steps to ensure that you are not showing favoritism.

Poor Communication

You have likely heard it before: communication is key. Communication allows you to keep everyone informed about your vision, goals, objectives, and plans of action. Confusion about roles and responsibilities or tasks and expectations are most often due to a lack of communication.

Something to consider: a lack of communication may not be as detrimental to your leadership as poor communication. You can be brief, but precise to convey your meaning. Being professional and forthright in communication with your followers and with your superiors is necessary. Confusion can be avoided, and clarity can be achieved as long as you are brief and at the same time, complete, in the way that you email, speak, write, and otherwise communicate.

Brevity breeds clarity.

Concerning forms of *remote* communication: they are not as effective or meaningful as meeting face-to-face interactions.

You will never get the whole picture from a report, e-mail, or phone conversation. Looking at men and women in the eye will give you a good sense of your team and how they are performing.
- Donald J. Freeman, Command Sergeant Major, United States Army

Just because you send an email does *not* mean that you have effectively led. Mechanical sending and receiving of messages is not communication.[465] An email is a useful tool, but it is not the end-all-be-all of workplace communication. The overuse of email can make a leader seem disingenuous and detached. Email communication is useful up to a point, but we all have seen inboxes get crowded with dozens or hundreds of emails every day which can lead to a marked decrease in productivity.[466]

A majority of human communication occurs in the form of nonverbal cues and body language. When you interact solely via email, the communication contains less information for a recipient to make a clear decision about. If you are not a very careful wordsmith, you will

---

[465] De Pree, 1989.
[466] LugoSantiago, 2014.

inadvertently cause misunderstanding. Now, instead of having easily communicated something, you have created workplace conflict which detracts from the level of trust and cooperation in your environment.

Rigidity

Earlier in the book, you read about flexibility as a trait to be sharpened and exercised by leaders. The flip side of flexibility is rigidity. You should not be flexible concerning your vision and your ethical values. However, you must be flexible and adaptable in your methods. Followers who notice that leaders are rigid and inflexible often feel - with good reason - that their leaders are no better than faceless managers.

That is to say that a machine could very likely do the *leader's* work. If you are practicing management by exception or leading from a spreadsheet, then you are demonstrably rigid. Flexible leaders know the value of foresight and use various innovative methods to get the job done.

Wrap-up: *Living your Leadership*

The True Gentleman is the man whose conduct proceeds from good will and an acute sense of propriety, and whose self-control is equal to all emergencies; who does not make the poor man conscious of his poverty, the obscure man of his obscurity, or any man of his inferiority or deformity; who is himself humbled if necessity compels him to humble another; who does not flatter wealth, cringe before power, or boast of his own possessions or achievements; who speaks with frankness but always with sincerity and sympathy; whose deed follows his word; who thinks of the rights and feelings of others rather than his own; and who appears well in any company; a man with whom honor is sacred and virtue safe.
- John Walter Wayland, 1899

Concurrent with my military and civilian service, I achieved the rank of associate professor. I have taught and developed undergraduate and graduate curriculum at multiple universities. I've had the opportunity to observe thousands of students as they proceed through their academic journeys. I was privileged to direct the Masters in Human Resource Management program at Touro University Worldwide. As an academician, entrepreneur, corporate leader, and combat veteran, the *Living your Leadership* model for management consulting is firmly cemented in my practice.

My unique experience as an Officer, Manager, Director, Professor, and Consultant has demonstrated to me that we all start in different places and come from different backgrounds. A single, unifying theory for personal growth and leadership has to start with what we all have in common – ourselves. Moving from the development of self, it is natural and logical to proceed with a more general approach to leadership practice; one that is holistic and practicable, but also general enough to apply to a variety of individuals.

These generalizations provide the opportunity to incorporate tools that are applicable regardless of your current level of self-improvement or understanding of specific principles of leadership. Experience is the best teacher, but just making it through things does not guarantee that you will be able to fully connect theory to practice. An experienced leader can still be a terrible leader. That is why reading and studying leadership texts from the world's past and present leadership experts and historians are extremely crucial so that you can continue to learn and grow in your knowledge.

Leadership and learning are indispensable to each other.
- John F. Kennedy

It takes curiosity to learn. It takes courage to unlearn.
Learning requires the humility to admit what you don't know today. Unlearning requires the integrity to admit you were wrong yesterday.
Learning is how you evolve.
Unlearning is how you keep up as the world evolves.
- Adam Grant[467]

Self-knowledge, together with perfecting the precepts and practices of self-leadership, enables personal growth. That foundational understanding and critical reflection will allow for the practice of transformational and servant leadership. A word of caution: just reading a book like this one does not mean that you will improve. As Lao-tzu wrote, "A Sage will practice the Tao. A fool will

---

[467] Adam Grant is an organizational psychologist at Wharton, bestselling author, and host of the TED podcast WorkLife

only admire it."⁴⁶⁸

> *One's philosophy is not best expressed in words;*
> *it is expressed in the choices one makes.*
> *In the long run, we shape our lives and we shape ourselves.*
> *The process never ends until we die.*
> *And the choices we make are ultimately our own responsibility.*
> *- Eleanor Roosevelt*

    As business continues to move upward and onward with expanding global interconnectedness, the leaders in every organization should be equipped and ready to handle day-to-day challenges. Diversity in the global workforce means that a more inclusive understanding of leadership is needed. Leadership has changed greatly over the last few decades. The charismatic, dictatorial leader is no longer viewed as the best choice for the global organizations of tomorrow in a VUCA environment.

> *You must realize that authority is not to*
> *be wielded absolutely but charitably.*
> *- Saint Louise de Marillac*⁴⁶⁹

    Leadership is trending toward the transformational and servant styles. The need to have someone with integrity, empathy, self-awareness and the understanding of others moves organizations in a direction that keeps employees motivated and committed. Motivating employees to achieve organizational goals through delegation and empowerment aids in employee satisfaction and retention. Maintaining employees in the workforce saves the cost of training, lawsuits, recruitment efforts, and

---

⁴⁶⁸ 1996.
⁴⁶⁹ Also known as Louise Le Gras, she was the co-founder, with Saint Vincent de Paul, of the Daughters of Charity.

extrinsic incentives.

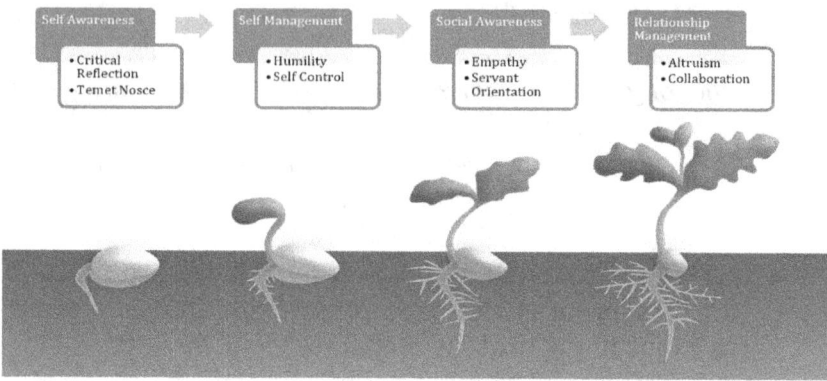

Figure 19. Progress during *Living your Leadership*

Leadership can be learned and improved upon.
Mastery of the skills outlined in this text will enhance your ability to lead. Leading with humility and openness will engender loyalty and trust in leadership. Without dedicated followers, leaders will not be able to accomplish up to expectations. *Leadership is alchemy.* When organizational chaos or oppressive hierarchy comes into contact with servanthood, a change in the substance of the organization occurs. It is a precursor to positive culture change.

A transformational leader exerts influence by broadening and elevating followers' goals and providing them with confidence to perform beyond the expectations specified in the implicit or explicit agreement.[470] The transformational leader exhibits charismatic behaviors, arouses inspirational motivation, provides intellectual stimulation, and treats followers with individualized

---

[470] Bass & Avolio, 1994.

consideration. Transformational leaders are also able to imbue work with meaning while communicating an inspirational vision for the organization.[471] The transformational leader can help followers reach their full potential, generating the highest levels of performance.[472]

> *Project authenticity and vulnerability, be present, be accepting, and see your role as being useful, as being the servant.*
> *- James A. Autry*[473]

The servant-leader is defined by Greenleaf as *first* being a servant. The characteristics that are attributed to a servant leader and central to their development are listening, empathy, healing, awareness, persuasion, conceptualization, foresight, stewardship, commitment to the growth of people, and building community.[474] The practice of *Living your Leadership* hinges on the conscious choices that you choose to make each day.

> Man constantly makes his choice concerning the mass of present potentialities; which of these will be condemned to nonbeing, and which will be actualized? Which choice will be made an actuality once and forever, an immortal "footprint in the sands of time"? At any moment, man must decide, for better or for worse, what will be the monument of his existence. *Viktor Frankl*[475]

Both transformational and servant styles focus on followers and how leaders can help them to develop and

---

[471] Bass, 1985.
[472] Dvir, Eden, Avolio, & Shamir, 2002.
[473] From *Practicing Servant Leadership.*
[474] Greenleaf, 2002.
[475] 1963, p. 143.

reach their full potential. Each shares similar attributes, but transformational leadership tends to place a greater emphasis on organizational goals. The servant-leader is more often associated with public service industries, while the transformational leader is seen more often in business settings.

The content of most textbooks is perishable,
but the tools of self-directedness serve one well over time.
- Albert Bandura

Living *your* Leadership journey does not end when you put down this volume. I hope that you incorporate the practices you have read in these pages into your daily practice; that you explore the suggested readings, and that you seek to serve in all you do.
The first responsibility of a leader is to define reality.
The last is to say thank you.
In between, the leader is a servant.
- Max De Pree

Thank you!

Chris

Acknowledgments

Like any human endeavor, this book didn't simply spring from the mind and fingertips of the author. It has been an iterative process and I would be remiss, not to acknowledge some of the main contributors to the project.

Dr. Jamiel Vadell, whose enthusiasm and optimism fueled this journey. Jamiel has been my friend and mentor since the day he took me on my first nuclear alerts to the Alternate Command Post while we were stationed together in Minot AFB, North Dakota. Jamiel has been my boss and has seen me at my best and my worst. He is my brother in the truest sense of the word.

Lieutenant Colonel Christopher "Braden" Stutheit, USAF, and Lieutenant Colonel Linn VanWoerkom, USAFR for their consultation and contribution to this work related to nuclear operations. These gentlemen legitimately care about their role as leaders.

Colonel Charley 'Chuck' Morris who initiated my thoughts on leadership in ROTC all those years ago. Having had no tangible example in my personal life, Chuck was the first *leader* that I worked with. His continued success as a pilot and commander in the USAF is a testament to his adherence to the principles which he taught us cadets so many years ago.

Michelle Reinstatler, PhD. My friend and English language and literature savant. Because of Michelle, I wasn't the only cadet to have chosen an English major in AFROTC.

Colonel Marné Deranger, USAF (Retired), for her mentorship and support. I've already talked about her contributions to my theories and experience in the text, so I won't belabor it here.

Robert J. Gore, executive consultant and editor par excellence. This book would not have assumed its final state without the invaluable guidance he provided from his distinguished career.

Colonel Jed Davis, USAF, (Retired) for his leadership during difficult times. I learned more from your example than you will ever know.

Thank you seems inadequate for my wife, Missy. She has spent years listening to my ideas, my complaints, editing my work, and talking over the idea of becoming an author. Her editing of this second edition of my work has vastly improved its quality and faith-related content.

Gloria Patri, et Filio, et Spiritui Sancto. Sicut erat in principio, et nunc, et semper, et in saecula saeculorum. Amen.

About the Author

Chris Ewing is an experienced management consultant and educator working in leadership consulting and higher education.

Chris is a former Active Duty Air Force Officer with a specialty in Space and Missile Operations. He is the COO of Paradigm Leaders, LLC, a Florida-based SDVOSB that designs and delivers leadership development and management curriculum He teaches graduate courses in leadership at various universities and is an editor for a peer-reviewed management journal.

His academic background includes a BA in English from Saint Louis University, MA in Adult Education from Central Michigan in Education, a PhD from Capella University in Educational Psychology, a Certificate from Cornell University in Executive Leadership for Healthcare Professionals, and a Lean Six Sigma Black Belt Certification from Juran Global.

Chris lives in Central Florida with his wife and four children. He is a tenor in the St. James Cathedral Choir and is an active member of the Knights of Columbus.

Abbreviations

AFB - Air Force Base
AFM - Air Force Manual
AOM - Academy of Management
AOR - Area of responsibility
APA - American Psychological Association
ASV - American Standard Version
DV - Distinguished visitors
EBITDA - Earnings Before Interest, Taxes, Depreciation, and Amortization
EQ - Emotional intelligence
FOB - Forward Operating Base
FRLD - Full Range Leadership Development
ICBM - Intercontinental Ballistic Missile
ICE - Integrity, courage, empathy
KJV - King James Version
LCC - Launch control center
LMS - Learning Management System
MBE - Management by exception
MBWA - Management by walking around
MLQ - Multi-factor leadership questionnaire
NIV - New International Version
QLRC - Quality of Life Research Center
RCA - root cause analysis
RCIED - Radio-controlled improvised explosive devices
ROTC - Reserve Officer Training Corps
SJ - Society of Jesus
SL - Servant leadership
SLI - Servant Leader Institute
SMART - Specific, measurable, actionable, and time-bound
SME - Subject matter expert
TWA - Trans World Airlines
VUCA - volatile, uncertain, complex, and ambiguous

WSSR - Weapon System Safety Rules
USAF - United States Air Force
ZPD - Zone of Proximal Development

References

Air Force Instruction (AFI) 91-114, Safety Rules for the Intercontinental Ballistic Missile System, 30 June 2015. Retrieved from: www.e-publishing.af.mil

Albion, M.S. (2006). *True to Yourself: Leading a values-based business.* San Francisco, CA: Berrett-Koehler.

Algera, P.M. & Lips-Wiersma, M. (2012). Radical authentic leadership: Co-creating the conditions under which all members of the organization can be authentic. *Leadership Quarterly, 23*: 118–131.

Amar, A. (2009). To Be a Better Leader, Give Up Authority. *Harvard Business Review, 87*(12), 22-24.

August, V. (2001). *Know thyself, show thyself: A guide to becoming the person you've always dreamed of being.* San Jose: Writers Club Press.

Ausonius, D.M. & Evelyn-White, Hugh G. (1919). *Ausonius.* London (England): New York (New York): W. Heinemann; Putnam.

Baltes, P.B. & Reese, H.W. (1984). *The life-span perspective in developmental psychology.* In M. H. Bornstein & M. E. Lamb (Eds.), *Developmental psychology: An advanced textbook* (p. 493-531). Hillsdale, NJ: Erlbaum.

Bandura, A. (1978). The self-system in reciprocal determinism, *American Psychologist, 33*, 344-358.

Bandura, A. (1986). *Social foundations of thought and action: A social cognitive theory.* Englewood Cliffs, NJ: Prentice-Hall.

Bandura, A. (1989). *Social cognitive theory.* In R. Vasta (Ed.), *Annals of child development. Vol. 6. Six theories of child development* (p. 1-60). Greenwich, CT: JAI Press.

Baron, L., Rouleau, V., Grégoire, S. and Baron, C. (2018).

Mindfulness and leadership flexibility. *Journal of Management Development, 37*(2), 165-177.

Barsade, S.G. (Dec. 2002). The Ripple Effect: Emotional Contagion and Its Influence on Group Behavior. *Administrative Science Quarterly, 47*(4), 644-675.

Bartlett, F. (1932). *Remembering.* Cambridge: Cambridge University Press.

Bass, B.M. (1998). *Transformational Leadership; Industry, Military, and Educational Impact.* Lawrence Erlbaum Associates, Mahwah, NJ.

Bass, B.M. & Steidlmeier, P. (1999). Ethics, Character, and Authentic Transformational Leadership Behavior', *Leadership Quarterly 10*(2), 181-217.

Beatty, B.R., & Brew, C.R. (2004). Trusting relationships and emotional epistemologies: a foundational leadership issue. *School Leadership & Management, 24*(3), 329-356. doi:10.1080/1363243042000266954

Bell, G.B. & Hall Jr., H.E. (1954). The relationship between leadership and empathy. *The Journal of Abnormal and Social Psychology, 49*(1), 156-157. doi: 10.1037/h0053927

Bennis, W.G. (2007). The challenge of leadership in the modern world. *American Psychologist Association, 62*(1), 2-5.

Bennis, W.G., & Thomas, R.J. (2002a). Crucibles of leadership. *Harvard Business Review, 80*(9), 39-45.

Bennis, W.G., & Thomas, R.J. (2002b). Leadership crucibles. *Executive Excellence, 19*(11), 3-4.

Berkovich, I. (2014). Between person and person: Dialogical pedagogy in authentic leadership development. *Academy of Management Learning & Education, 13*(2), 245-264.

Bodie, G.D. (2011). The Active-Empathic Listening Scale (AELS): Conceptualization and Evidence of

Validity Within the Interpersonal Domain. *Communication Quarterly, 59*(3), 277-295.

Brown, M.E., & Treviño, L.K. 2006. Ethical leadership: A review and future directions. *Leadership Quarterly, 17*, 595-616.

Brown, R. (2012). The Power of Vulnerability: Teachings on Authenticity, Connection, & Courage. [Audio Download]. Sounds True.

Burton, K.D., Lydon, J.E., D'Alessandro, D.U., & Koestner, R. (2006). The differential effects of intrinsic and identified motivation on well-being and performance: Prospective, experimental, and implicit approaches to self-determination theory. *Journal of Personality and Social Psychology, 91*(4), 750-762.

Cameron, J., Pierce, D.W., Banko, K.M., & Gear, A. (2005). Achievement-based rewards and intrinsic motivation: A test of cognitive mediators. *Journal of Educational Psychology, 97*(4), 641-655.

Campbell, D., & Campbell, K. (2011). Impact of decision-making empowerment on attributions of leadership. *Military Psychology, 23*(2), 154-179. doi: 10.1080/08995605.2011.550231

Canadian College of Health Leaders. (2010). *Lead self: The root of the matter*. Ottawa, Canada: Canadian Health Leadership Network.

Catholic Church. (1963). Peace on earth: Encyclical letter of Pope John XXIII, 'Pacem in terris', 1963. London: Catholic Truth Society.

Catholic Church. (1995). Catechism of the Catholic Church. New York: Doubleday.

Caza A., Jackson B. 2011. Authentic leadership. In Bryman D., Collinson K., Grint B., Jackson B., Uhl-Bien M. (Eds.), Sage handbook of leadership: 350-362. Thousand Oaks, CA: Sage.

Center for Creative Leadership. (2008). *The Role of Power*

in Effective Leadership. [White Paper]. Retrieved from http://www.ccl.org/leadership/pdf/research/roleOfPower.pdf

Center for Creative Leadership. (2012). *The Care and Feeding of the Leader's Brain*. [White Paper]. Retrieved from http://www.ccl.org/leadership/pdf/research/CareFeedingLeadersBrain.pdf

Chan, D.W. (2007). Leadership and Intelligence. *Roeper Review, 29*(3), 183-189.

Chandler, C.L., & Connell, J.P. (1987). Children's intrinsic, extrinsic and internalized motivation: A developmental study of children's reasons for liked and disliked behaviours. *British Journal of Developmental Psychology, 5*, 357–365.

Chemers, M.M., Watson, C.B., & May, S.T. (2000). Dispositional affect and leadership effectiveness: A comparison of self-esteem, optimism, and efficacy. *Personality & Social Psychology Bulletin, 26*, 267-277.

Chen, W. & Jacobs, R. (1997). *Competence Study*. Boston, MA: Hay/McBer.

Cialdini, R.B. (2001). *Influence: Science and practice*. Needham Heights, MA: Allyn & Bacon.

Challoner, R., & Tweedale, M. (2008). *The Holy Bible: Douay-Rheims version: the Old Testament first published by the English College at Douay, A.D. 1609, and the New Testament first published by the English College at Rheims, A.D. 1582*. London: Baronius Press.

Choi, Y. & Mai-Dalton, R.R. (1998). On the leadership function of self-sacrifice. *Leadership Quarterly, 9*(4), 475-501.

Cockerell, L. (2008). *Creating magic: 10 common sense leadership strategies from a life at Disney*. New

York: Currency Doubleday.
Collins, J. (2001b). Level 5 leadership: The triumph of humility and fierce resolve. *Harvard Business Review, 79*(1), 67-76.
Cordova, D.I., & Lepper, M. (1996). Intrinsic motivation and the process of learning: Beneficial effects of contextualization, personalization, and choice. *Journal of Educational Psychology, 88*(4), 715-730.
Crant, J.M. & Bateman, T.S. (2000), Charismatic leadership viewed from above: the impact of proactive personality. *Journal of Organizational Behavior, 21*, 63–75.
Crom, M. (1998, July). The leader as servant. *Training, 35*(7), 6-10.
Csikszentmihalyi, M. (1990). *Flow: The psychology of optimal experience.* New York: Harper & Row.
Deal, J.J., Stawiski, S., Gentry, W., Cullen, K.L. (October, 2013). What makes a leader effective? *Center for Creative Leadership.* Retrieved from: http://www.ccl.org/leadership/pdf/research.pdf
Dempsey, M.E. (August 25, 2017). Leadership Instincts: Listen, Amplify, Include. [LinkedIn Pulse article]. Retrieved from: https://www.linkedin.com/pulse/leadership-instincts-listen-amplify-include-general-martin-e-dempsey
Descartes, R. (1979). *Meditations on first philosophy.* (D. A. Cress, Trans.). Indianapolis, IN: Hackett Publishing. (Originally published in 1641.)
Deci, E.L. (1971). Effects of externally mediated rewards on intrinsic motivation. *Journal of Personality and Social Psychology, 18*(1), 105-115.
Deci, E.L., Connell, J. P., & Ryan, R. M. (1989). Self-determination in a work organization. *Journal of Applied Psychology, 74*, 580-590.

Deci, E.L., & Ryan, R.M. (1985). The general causality orientations scale: Self-determination in personality. *Journal of Research in Personality, 19,* 109-134.

De Charms, R. (1968). *Personal causation: The internal affective determinants of behavior.* New York: Academic Press.

De Cremer, D., van Knippenberg, D., van Dijke, M., and Bos, A.E.R. (2006). Self-sacrificial leadership and follower self-esteem: When collective identification matters. *Group Dynamics: Theory, Research, and Practice, 10*(3), 233-245.

Den Hartog, D., & Belschak, F. (2012). When does transformational leadership enhance employee proactive behavior? The role of autonomy and role breadth self-efficacy. *The Journal of Applied Psychology, 97*(1), 194-202.

Dhiman, S. (2009). Mindfulness in Life and Leadership an Exploratory Survey. Interbeing, 3(1), 55-80.

Doidge, N. (2007). *The brain that changes itself: Stories of personal triumph from the frontiers of brain science.* Penguin.

Donohue, K.S. & Wong, L. (1994). Understanding and Applying Transformational Leadership. *Military Review, 74*(8).

Dvir, T., Eden, D., Avolio, B.J., & Shamir, B. (2002). Impact of transformational leadership on follower development and performance: A field experiment. *Academy of Management Journal, 45,* 735–744.

Efron, L. (2015, May 11). The Three Fundamental Leadership Traits That Support Enduring Organizations. Retrieved from https://www.forbes.com/sites/louisefron/2015/05/11/the-three-fundamental-leadership-traits-that-support-enduring-organizations/#46ad59fc4b7c

Escriva de Balaguer, Jose Maria. (2002). The way -- Furrow -- the Forge. Seven Hills, NSW: Little Hills

Press.
Ewing, C. (2011). Does causality orientation moderate the relationship between assignment choice and academic achievement in Air Force officers performing the nuclear mission? Boca Raton, FL: Dissertation.com.
Farling, M.L., Stone, AG., & Winston, B.E. (1999). Servant leadership: Setting the stage for empirical research. *The Journal of Leadership Studies, 6*(1/2), 49-72.
Ferris, G.R., et al. (2005). Development and validation of the political skill inventory. *Journal of Management 31*, 126–152.
Firth-Cozens, J., & Mowbray, D. (2001). Leadership and the quality of care. *Quality in Health Care, 10*: 3–7.
Galanis, E., Hatzigeorgiadis, A., Zourbanos, N., & Theodorakis, Y. (2016). *Why self-talk is effective? Perspectives on self-talk mechanisms in sport.* In M. Raab, P. Wylleman, R. Seiler, A.-M. Elbe, & A. Hatzigeorgiadis (Eds.), *Sport and exercise psychology research: From theory to practice,* p. 181–200. Elsevier Academic Press.
Gardner, W.L., Avolio, B.J., & Walumbwa, F.O. (2005). Authentic leadership development: Emergent themes and future directions. In W. L. Gardner, B. J. Avolio & F. O. Walumbwa (Eds.), *Authentic leadership theory and practice: Origins, effects and development*: 387– 406. London: Elsevier.
Gardner, W.L. & Cole, C.L. (1988). Self-monitoring procedures. In E.S. Shapiro & E.R. Kratochwoll (Eds.), *Behavioral assessment in schools*: 206-246. New York: Guilford Press.
Giampetro, M.A., T. Brown, M.N. Browne and N. Kubasek. (1998). Do We Really Need More Leaders in Business? *Journal of Business Ethics, 17*(15), 1727–1736.

Gill, M. (2008). *How Starbucks saved my life: A son of privilege learns to live like everyone else.* London: Gotham Books.

Givens, R.J. (2008). Transformational leadership: The impact on organizational and personal outcomes. *Emerging Leadership Journeys, 1*(1), 4-24.

Goldfein, D.L., & Air University (U.S.). (1999). Sharing success--owning failure: Preparing to command in the twenty-first century Air Force. Maxwell Air Force Base, Ala: Air University Press.

Goleman, D. (2004). What Makes a Leader? *Harvard Business Review, 82*(1), 82-91.

Gottlieb, J.Z. & Sanzgiri, J. (1996). Towards an Ethical Dimension of Decision Making in Organizations. *Journal of Business Ethics 15*(12), 1275-1285.

Graen, G.B., & Uhl-Bien, M. (1995). Relationship-based approach to leadership: Development of leader-member exchange (LMX) theory of leadership over 25 years: Applying a multi-level multi-domain perspective. *Leadership Quarterly, 6,* 219–247.

Graham, W. (1991). Servant-leadership in organizations: Inspirational and moral. *Leadership Quarterly, 2*(2), 105-119.

Hayward, M. (2007). *Ego check: Why executive hubris is wrecking companies and careers and how to avoid the trap.* Chicago: Kaplan Pub.

Headquarters, Department of the Army. (2006). Army Leadership (FM 6-22). Washington, D.C.: Government Printing Office.

Herodotus. (2007). *The Landmark Herodotus: The histories.* New York: Pantheon Books.

Howatson-Jones, I. (2004). The servant leader. *Nursing Management (Harrow, London, England: 1994), 11*(3), 20-24.

Howell, J.M., & Avolio, B.J. (1993). Transformational

leadership, transactional leadership, locus of control, and support for innovation: Key predictors of consolidated-business-unit performance. *Journal of Applied Psychology, 78*(6), 891-902. doi:10.1037/0021-9010.78.6.891

Huber, R. (2007). *What Makes a Leader.* America Star Books, United States.

Hume, D. (2000). Inquiry Concerning Human Understanding, in Readings in Modern Philosophy Vol. II: Locke, Berkeley, Hume, and Associated Texts, ed. Roger Ariew and Eric Watkins, Indianapolis, IN: Hackett Publishing Company, 328-394.

Irving, J.A. (2005). Servant leadership and the effectiveness of teams. Published dissertation. Regent University, School of Leadership Studies.

Janis, I. (2008). Groupthink: Actions. *IEEE Engineering Management Review, 36*(1), 36–44.

Johnson, R.D. (2003). USAWC Strategy Research Project: Leadership. US Army War College, Carlisle Barracks, PA.

Judge, T.A., & Piccolo, R.F. (2004). Transformational and transactional leadership: A meta-analytic test of their relative validity. *Journal of Applied Psychology, 89*, 755–768.

Katzenbach, J.R. (1997). *Teams at the Top: Unleashing the Potential of both Teams and Individual Leaders.* Boston, Harvard Business School Press.

Kellett, J.B., Humphrey, R.H., & Sleeth, R.G. (2006). Empathy and the emergence of task and relations leaders. *The Leadership Quarterly, 17*(2), 146-162.

Kernis, M. & Goldman, B. (2006). A multicomponent conceptualization of authenticity: Theory and research. *Advances in Experimental Social Psychology, 38*, 283-357.

Kiel, L., & Watson, D.J. (2009). Affective Leadership and Emotional Labor: A View from the Local Level. *Public Administration Review, 69*(1), pg. 22. doi: 10.1111/j.1540-6210.2008.01936.x

Kolenda, C.D. (2001). *Leadership: The Warrior's Art.* United States: Army War College Foundation Press.

Kotter, J. P. (1990). What Leaders really do. *Harvard Business Review, 68*(3), 3–11.

Kouzes, J.M. & Posner, B.Z. (1989). *Leadership is in the Eye of the Follower.* Developing Human Resources, J. William Pfeiffer, Editor, San Diego, California: University Associates.

Kriger, M. & Seng, Y. (2005). Leadership with inner meaning: A contingency theory of leadership based on the worldviews of five religions. *The Leadership Quarterly, 16,* 771-806.

Kroon, B., van Woerkom, M. and Menting, C. (2017). Mindfulness as substitute for transformational leadership. *Journal of Managerial Psychology, 32*(4), 284-297.

Kruger, J.M. & Dunning, D. (1999). Unskilled and unaware of it: How difficulties in recognizing one's own incompetence lead to inflated self-assessments. *Journal of Personality and Social Psychology, 77,* 1121-1134

Kruse, K. (2013, May 12). What is authentic leadership?. Forbes.com LLC, Retrieved from http://www.forbes.com/sites/kevinkruse/2013/05/12/what-is-authentic-leadership/

Lad, L.J. and Luechauer, D. (1998). *On the Path to Servant-Leadership.* In L. Spears *Insights on Leadership: Service, Spirit, and Servant Leadership.* New York, NY: John Wiley.

Lee, H. (1960). *To Kill a Mockingbird.* Philadelphia: Lippincott.

LeDoux, J. (1998). *The emotional brain: The mysterious underpinnings of emotional life.* Simon and Schuster.

Leonard, N.H., Beauvais, L.L., & Scholl, R. W. (1995). A self-concept based model of work motivation. *Academy Of Management Best Papers Proceedings,* 322-326. doi:10.5465/AMBPP.1995.17536607

Lindebaum, D., & Cartwright, S. (2011). Leadership effectiveness: The costs and benefits of being emotionally intelligent. *Leadership & Organizational Development Journal, 32*(3), 281-290.

Lorenz, S.R. (2012). *Lorenz on Leadership: Lessons on Effectively Leading People, Teams, and Organizations.* Air University Press, Air Force Research Institute: Maxwell AFB United States.

LugoSantiago, J.A. (2014). *On the Leadership Journey: 30 Conversations about Leading Yourself and Others.* Air University, Air Force Research Institute: Maxwell AFB United States.

Machiavelli, N., & Mansfield, H.C. (1998). *The prince.* Chicago, Ill: University of Chicago Press.

Maister, D.H. (2014). *Practice what you preach: What managers must do to create a high achievement culture.* New York: Free Press.

Manz, C.C. and Sims, H. 2001. *The new super leadership: Leading others to lead themselves.* San Francisco: Berrett-Koehler Publishers.

Martinez, M.E. (2006). What is metacognition?. *Phi Delta Kappan, 87*(9), 696-699.

Maslach, M., Schaufeli, W.B., & Leiter, M.P. (2001). Job Burnout. *Annual Review Psychology. 52,*397-422.

Maslow, A.H. (1943). A theory of human motivation. *Psychological Review, 50,* 370-396.

Matteson, J. & Irving, J. (2006). Servant versus self-sacrificial leadership: A behavioral comparison of two follower-oriented leadership theories. *International Journal of Leadership Studies, 2*(1), 36-51.

May, R. (1975). *The courage to create.* New York: Norton.

Mehrabian, A., & Epstein, N. (1972). A measure of emotional empathy. *Journal of Personality, 40*: 525–543.

Merton, T. (1972). *New seeds of contemplation.* New York, NY: New Directions.

Miyamoto, M., & Harris, V. (1974). *A book of five rings.* New York: Overlook Press.

Montgomery III, W.H. (2007). Beyond Words: Leader Self-awareness and Interpersonal Skills, USAWC Strategy Research Project, Defense Technical Information Center, Army War College. Carlisle Barracks, PA.

Nixon, M.M. (2005). The servant leadership: Followership continuum from a social psychology cognitive perspective. *Proceedings of the Servant Leadership Research Roundtable.* Retrieved from http://www.regent.edu/acad/global/publications/sl_proceedings/

Noddings, N. (1998). Care and moral education. In H. S. Shapiro & D. E. Purpel (Eds.), Critical social issues in American education: Transformation in a postmodern world, p. 309–320. Mahwah, NJ: Lawrence Erlbaum Associates.

Owens, B.P. and Hekman, D.R. (30 Apr 2015). How Does Leader Humility Influence Team Performance? Exploring the Mechanisms of Contagion and Collective Promotion Focus. *Academy of Management Journal, 59*(3).

Page, D., & Wong, T.P. (2000). A conceptual framework for measuring servant leadership. In S. Abjibolosoo (Ed.), *The human factor in shaping the course of history and development.* Lanham, MD: University

Press of America.

Parry, K.W. & Proctor-Thomson, S.B. (2002). Perceived integrity of transformational leaders in organisational settings. *Journal of Business Ethics, 35*(2), 75-96.

Patterson, K.A. (2003). Servant leadership: a theoretical model. Servant Leadership Roundtable, Regent University, Virginia Beach. October, 2003).

Peters, T.J., & Waterman, R.H. (1982). *In search of excellence: Lessons from America's best-run companies.* New York, N.Y.: Harper & Row.

Peterson, C., & Seligman, M.E.P. (2004). Character strengths and virtues: A handbook and classification. New York: Oxford University Press and Washington, DC: American Psychological Association. www.viacharacter.org

Pfeffer, J., & Sutton, R.I. (2000). *The knowing-doing gap: How smart companies turn knowledge into action.* Boston, Mass: Harvard Business School Press.

Phillips, D. (1993). Lincoln on Leadership: Executive Strategies for Tough Times. New York: New York: Business Plus.

Poon, R. (2006). A model for servant leadership, self-efficacy and mentorship. In Proceedings of the 2006 Servant Leadership Research Roundtable.

Poore, J. (2012, October). The STAR leader's role in creating exceptional experiences. Speech presented at Kaiser Permanente STAR Leader Forum, San Jose, CA.

Pope St. John Paul II. (1981). *Laborem Exercens [Encyclical on human work].* Vatican, VA: Libreria Editrice Vaticana.

Pope Leo XIII. (1891). *Rerum Novarum [Encyclical on capital and labor].* Vatican, VA: Libreria Editrice Vaticana.

Posner, M.I., & Boies, S.J. (1971). Components of

attention. *Psychological Review, 78*(5), 391-408. http://dx.doi.org/10.1037/h0031333

Ringma, C. & Alexander, I. (2015). *Of Martyrs, Monks, and Mystics: A Yearly Meditational Reader of Ancient Spiritual Wisdom*. Wipf and Stock Publishers; Eugene, OR.

Rockwell, D. (2012, November 8). [Web log message]. Retrieved from http://leadershipfreak.wordpress.com/2012/11/08/facing-the-3-pressing-challenges-of-leadership/

Rockwell, D. (2013, February 1). [Web log message]. Retrieved from http://leadershipfreak.wordpress.com/2013/02/01/how-to-motivate-the-unmotivated/

Rosenberg, M. (1979). *Conceiving the self*. New York: Basic Books.

Rosenberg, M.B. (2015). *Nonviolent Communication: A language of life*. PuddleDancer Press: Encinitas, CA.

Rotter, J.B. (1966). Generalized expectancies for internal versus external locus of control of reinforcement. Psychological Monographs: General and Applied, SO (Whole No. 609).

Rude, W. (2003). Paradoxical leadership: The impact of servant-leadership on burnout of staff. *Proceedings of the Servant Leadership Research Roundtable*. Retrieved from http://www.regent.edu/acad/global/publications/sl_proceedings/

Ryan, R.M. (1995). Psychological needs and the facilitation of integrative processes. *Journal of Personality, 63*, 397–427.

Ryan, R.M. & Deci, E.L. (2000). Intrinsic and extrinsic motivations: Classic definitions and new directions. *Contemporary Educational Psychology, 25*, 54–67.

Ryan, R.M., Kuhl, J., & Deci, E.L. (1997). Nature and autonomy: Organizational view of social and neurobiological aspects of self-regulation in behavior and development. *Development and Psychopathology, 9*, 701–728.

Sandage, S.J., & Wiens, T.W. (2001). Contextualizing models of humility and forgiveness: A reply to Gassin. *Journal of Psychology and Theology, 29*, 201.

Sauer S., Kohls N. (2011) *Mindfulness in Leadership: Does Being Mindful Enhance Leaders' Business Success?*. In: Han S., Pöppel E. (eds) *Culture and Neural Frames of Cognition and Communication. On Thinking.* Springer, Berlin, Heidelberg.

Schein, E.H. (2013). *Humble inquiry: the gentle art of asking instead of telling.* San Francisco: Berrett-Koehler Publishers.

Sendjaya, S. & Sarros, J. (2002). Servant leadership: Its origins, development, and application in organizations. *The Journal of Leadership Studies, 9*(2), 61.

Shakespeare, W. (1992). *The Tragedy of Hamlet, Prince of Denmark.* New Folger's ed. New York: Washington Square Press/Pocket Books.

Shapiro, S., & Carlson, L. (2009). *The Art and Science of Mindfulness: Integrating Mindfulness into Psychology and the Helping Professions.* NE, Washington, DC: American Psychological Association (APA).

Shirom, A. (2003). Job-related burnout. In J.C. Quick & L.E. Tetrick (Eds.) Handbook of occupational health and psychology. Washington, DC: American Psychological Association.

Sivanathan, N., & Fekken, C.G. (2002). Emotional intelligence, moral reasoning and transformational leadership. *Leadership and Organization*

Development Journal, 23(4), 198-204.
Spears, L.C. (2005). The understanding and practice of servant leadership. *Proceedings of the Servant Leadership Research Roundtable*. Retrieved from http://www.regent.edu/acad/global/publications/sl_proceedings/
Spears, L.C. (2010). Character and servant leadership: Ten characteristics of effective, caring leaders. *The Journal of Virtues & Leadership, 1*(1), 25-30.
Spencer, L.J. (2007). The new frontier of servant leadership. *Proceedings of the Servant Leadership Research Roundtable*. Retrieved from http://www.regent.edu/acad/global/publications/sl_proceedings/
Stafford, M.C. (2010). The Full Range Leadership Model: A Brief Primer. Air University.
Stefano, S.F. & Wasylyshyn, K.M. (2005) Integrity, courage, empathy (ICE): three leadership essentials. *Human Resource Planning, 28*(4), 5-7.
Stone, G.A., Russell, R.F., & Patterson, K. (2004). Transformational versus servant leadership: A difference in leader focus. *Leadership & Organization Development Journal, 25*(4), 349-361.
Sutton, R.I. (2007). *The no asshole rule: Building a civilized workplace and surviving one that isn't.* New York: Warner Business Books.
Tan, C. (2010, November). Everyday compassion at Google. Retrieved from https://www.ted.com/talks/chade_meng_tan_everyday_compassion_at_google
The Holy Bible (New international version). (1984). Grand Rapids, MI: Zondervan Publishing House.
Thompson, B.L. (1995). The Manager's Handbook, Chapter Six, Influencing Skills, Richard D. Irwin, Inc.
Thoreau, H. & Levin, J. (2005). *Walden; and, Civil*

disobedience. New York: Barnes & Noble Classics.
Tracey, B.J. and Hinkin, T.R. (Sep 1998). Transformational leadership or effective managerial practices? *Group Organization Management, 23*(3) 220-236.
Treasurer, B. (Sep 9, 2014). Getting Real about Leadership. [Blog]. University of California, San Diego. Retrieved from: http://rady.ucsd.edu/blog/posts/getting-real-about-leadership.html
Tucker, B.A. and Russell, R.F. (Spring 2004). The influence of the transformational leader. *Journal of Leadership & Organizational Studies 10*(4), 103-111.
Tuckman, B.W. (1965). Developmental sequence in small groups. *Psychological Bulletin, 63*, 384-399.
Tuckman, B.W. & Jensen, M.A.C. (1977). Stages of small group development revisited. *Group and Organizational Studies, 2*, 419- 427.
Tzu, L. (1996). *Tao Te Ching of Lao Tzu.* New York: St. Martin's Press.
Tzu, S. (1971). *The Art of War, translated by Samuel B. Griffith.* New York N.Y: Oxford University Press.
Ury, W. (1991). *Getting past no: Negotiating with difficult people.* New York: Bantam Books.
Vadell, J. & Ewing, C. (2011). Intrinsic Motivation and servant leadership: A case for autonomy supporting work environments in the military. *International Journal of Humanities and Social Science, 1*(19), 249-251.
Vanderkam, L. (2012). *What the most successful people do before breakfast: A short guide to making over your mornings-- and life.* Rego Park: Gildan Media Corp.
van Knippenberg, B., & van Knippenberg, D. (2005). Leader Self-Sacrifice and Leadership Effectiveness: The Moderating Role of Leader Prototypicality.

Journal of Applied Psychology, 90(1), 25-37. doi:10.1037/0021-9010.90.1.25

Van Zyl, E. & Campbell, A. (2019). *Peace leadership: Self-transformation to peace.* Johannesburg, South Africa: KR Publishing.

Van Zyl, E., Campbell, A., & Lues, L. (2020). *Chaos Is a Gift? Leading Oneself in Uncertain and Complex Environments.* Johannesburg, South Africa: KR Publishing.

Veldsman, T.H. & Johnson, A.J. (2016). *Leadership in context: Perspectives from the frontline.* Johannesburg: KR Publishers.

Vergote, A. (1988). A psychological approach to humility in the rule of St. Benedict. *American Benedictine Review, 39*(4), 404-429.

Vitz, P.C., Nordling, W.J., and Craig, S.T. (2020). *A Catholic Christian Meta-Model of the Person for Psychology and Mental Health Practice.* Institute for the Psychological Sciences Inc., Hopewell.

Vygotsky, L.S. (1978). *Mind in society.* Harvard University Press, Cambridge.

Wachowski, A. & Wachowski, L. (1999). The Matrix. Burbank, CA: Warner Bros. Pictures, DVD.

Wang, X., & Howell, J.M. (2010). Exploring the dual-level effects of transformational leadership on followers. *Journal of Applied Psychology, 95*(6), 1134-1144. doi:10.1037/a0020754

Ward, D., LtCol. (2011, September). Don't come to the dark side. *Defense AT&L, Better Buying Power, (Special Issue)*, 67-70.

Winston, B.E. (2003). Extending Patterson's servant leadership model: Explaining how leaders and followers interact in a circular model. Servant Leadership Roundtable, Regent University, Virginia Beach. October, 2003.

Wood, D., Bruner, J., and Ross, G. (1976). The role of tutoring in problem solving. *Journal of Child Psychology and Psychiatry, 17*, 89–100.

Wu, J.B., Tsui, A.S., & Kinicki, A.J. (2010). Consequences of differentiated leadership in groups. *Academy of Management Journal, 53*, 90-106.

Yerkes, R.M. & Dodson, J.D. (1908). The relation of strength of stimulus to rapidity of habit-formation. *Journal of Comparative Neurological Psychology, 18*, 459-482.

Yukl, G. (1999). An evaluation of conceptual weaknesses in transformational and charismatic leadership theories. *Leadership Quarterly, 10*, 285–305.

Zaccaro, S. J., Rittman, A. L., & Marks, M. A. (2001). Team leadership. *Leadership Quarterly, 12*, 451–483.

Zachary, L.J. (2005). Raising the bar in a mentoring culture. *Training and Development, 59*(6).

Zak, P.J. (2018). The neuroscience of High-trust Organizations. *Consulting Psychology Journal: Practice and Research, 70*(1), 45–58. http://dx.doi.org/10.1037/cpb0000076

Zaleznik, A. (1992). Managers and leaders: Are they different? *Harvard Business Review, 70*, 126-135.

Zoglio, S.W. (1994). *The participative leader.* Burr Ridge (Ill.): Irwin.

Additional References
& Recommended Reading

> *Not all readers are leaders, but all leaders are readers.*
> *- Harry Truman*

Atkins, P.W.B., & Reb, J. (Eds.). (2015). *Mindfulness in organizations: Foundations, research, and applications.* Cambridge, UK: Cambridge University Press.

Augustine of Hippo & Bettenson, H. (Ed.). (2003). *City of God.* Strand, London, England: The Penguin Group. (Original work composed 427).

Augustine of Hippo. (2006). *Confessions.* Translated by F.J. Sheed. Second edition. Indianapolis and Cambridge: Hackett.

Bass, B.M. (1985). *Leadership and performance beyond expectations.* New York: Free Press.

Bass, B.M. & Avolio, B.J. (1994). *Improving organizational effectiveness through transformational leadership.* Sage Publications: Los Angeles.

Blanchard, K. & Johnson, S. (1982). *The one minute manager.* New York, NY: The Berkley Publishing Group.

Bryant, A., & Kazan, A.L. (2013). *Self-leadership: How to become a more successful, efficient, and effective leader from the inside out.* New York: McGraw-Hill.

Bstan-'dzin-rgya-mtsho, Dalai Lama XIV, 1935-. (2011). *Beyond religion: Ethics for a whole world.* Boston: Houghton Mifflin Harcourt.

Burkeman, O. (2012). *The antidote: Happiness for people who can't stand positive thinking.* Melbourne, Vic.:

Text.

Burns, J.M. (1978). *Leadership*. New York: Harper & Row, Publishers.

Cain, S. (2012). *Quiet: The power of introverts in a world that can't stop talking*. New York: Crown Publishers.

Carnegie, D. (1998). *How to win friends and influence people*. USA: Gallery.

Carroll, M. (2007). *The Mindful Leader: Ten Principles for Bringing Out the Best in Ourselves and Others*. New York: Trumpeter

Cashman, K. (2008). *Leadership from the Inside Out: Becoming a Leader for Life, 2nd Edition, Revised and Expanded*. Berrett-Koehler Publishers: San Francisco.

Collins, J. (2001a). *Good to great: Why some companies make the leap and others don't*. New York: HarperBusiness.

Covey, S.R. (1989). *The seven habits of highly effective people: Restoring the character ethic*. New York: Simon and Schuster.

De Pree, M. (1989). *Leadership is an art*. New York: Doubleday.

Frankl, V.E. (1963). *Man's search for meaning: An introduction to logotherapy*. New York, N.Y: Pocket Books.

George, B. (2003). *Authentic leadership: Rediscovering the secrets to creating lasting value*. San Francisco, CA: Jossey-Bass.

George, B. (2015). *Discover your true north*. Hoboken, New Jersey: Wiley.

Goleman, D. (2005) *Emotional intelligence: Why it can matter more than IQ*. New York: Bantam Books.

Goleman, D. (1998). What makes a leader? *Harvard Business Review, 76*(6), 93–102.

Goleman, D. (2006). *Social Intelligence: The New Science*

of Human Relationships. Bantam Books.
Greenleaf, R.K. (1977). *Servant Leadership.* Mahwah, NJ: Paulist Press.
Holiday, R. (2016). *Ego is the enemy.* New York, New York: Portfolio, Penguin.
Kerpen, D. (2017). *The art of people 11 simple people skills that will get you everything you want.* London: Portfolio Penguin.
Kouzes, J.M. & Posner, B.Z. (1993). *Credibility: How Leaders Gain and Lose It, Why People Demand It.* San Francisco: Jossey-Bass.
Lipman-Blumen, J. (1996). *Connective leadership. Managing in a changing world.* Oxford: Oxford University Press
Manson, M. (2016). *The subtle art of not giving a f*ck: A counterintuitive approach to living a good life.* HarperOne: New York, NY
Maxwell, J. (2014). *15 invaluable laws of growth: Live them and reach your potential.* New York: Center Street.
Northouse, P. (2004). *Leadership: Theory and practice.* Thousand Oaks, Calif: Sage.
Peterson, J. B. (2021). *Beyond order: 12 more rules for life.* [New York, New York]: Penguin/Portfolio.
Peterson, J. B., Doidge, N., & Van Sciver, E. (2018). *12 rules for life: an antidote to chaos.* Toronto: Random House Canada.
Sarah, R.C. (2018). *The Power of Silence: Against the Dictatorship of Noise.* Unabridged Blackstone Publishing.
Scott, K. M. (2017). *Radical candor: How to be a kickass boss without losing your humanity (First edition.).* New York: St. Martin's Press.
Sinek, S. (2011). *Start with Why: How great leaders inspire everyone to take action.* Portfolio/Penguin.
Taylor, L. (2013). Tame your terrible office tyrant: How to

manage childish boss behavior and thrive in your job. Hoboken, N.J: Wiley.

Welch, A., & Welch, S. (2005). *Winning*. HarperCollins.

Zaki, J. (2019). *The war for kindness: Building empathy in a fractured world*. New York: Crown.

www.ingramcontent.com/pod-product-compliance
Lightning Source LLC
Chambersburg PA
CBHW071446220526
45472CB00003B/691